LITERATURE AND M
NINETEENTH-CENT

Although we have come to regard "clinical" and "Romantic" as oppositional terms, Romantic literature and clinical medicine were fed by the same cultural configurations. In the pre-Darwinian nineteenth century, writers and doctors developed an interpretive method that negotiated between literary and scientific knowledge of the natural world. Literary writers produced potent myths that juxtaposed the natural and the supernatural, often disturbing the conventional dualist hierarchy of spirit over flesh. Clinicians developed the two-part history and physical examination, weighing the patient's narrative against the evidence of the body. Examining fiction by Mary Shelley, Carlyle, the Brontës, and George Eliot, alongside biomedical lectures, textbooks, and articles, Janis McLarren Caldwell demonstrates the similar ways of reading employed by nineteenth-century doctors and imaginative writers and reveals the complexities and creative exchanges of the relationship between literature and medicine.

JANIS McLARREN CALDWELL practiced emergency medicine for five years before pursuing a Ph.D. in English Literature. She now teaches literature and science at Wake Forest University, where she is an Assistant Professor of English. An expert in nineteenth-century literature and medicine, she has received grants for research at Cambridge University and at Harvard University's Radcliffe Institute for Advanced Study. Her published work focuses on medical history and ethics in Romantic and Victorian literature.

Nineteenth-century British literature and culture have been rich fields for inter-disciplinary studies. Since the turn of the twentieth century, scholars and critics have tracked the intersections and tensions between Victorian literature and the visual arts, polities, social organization, economic life, technical innovations, scientific thought – in short, culture in its broadest sense. In recent years, theoretical challenges and historiographical shifts have unsettled the assumptions of previous scholarly synthesis and called into question the terms of older debates. Whereas the tendency in much past literary critical interpretation was to use the metaphor of culture as 'background', feminist, Foucauldian, and other analyses have employed more dynamic models that raise questions of power and of circulation. Such developments have reanimated the field.

This series aims to accommodate and promote the most interesting work being undertaken on the frontiers of the field of nineteenth-century literary studies: work which intersects fruitfully with other fields of study such as history, or literary theory, or the history of science. Comparative as well as interdisciplinary approaches are welcomed.

A complete list of titles published will be found at the end of the book.

LITERATURE AND MEDICINE IN NINETEENTH-CENTURY BRITAIN

From Mary Shelley to George Eliot

JANIS McLARREN CALDWELL

CAMBRIDGE
UNIVERSITY PRESS

CAMBRIDGE UNIVERSITY PRESS
Cambridge, New York, Melbourne, Madrid, Cape Town, Singapore, São Paulo

Cambridge University Press
The Edinburgh Building, Cambridge CB2 8RU, UK

Published in the United States of America by Cambridge University Press, New York

www.cambridge.org
Information on this title: www.cambridge.org/9780521843348

First published 2004
Third printing 2006
This digitally printed version 2008

A catalogue record for this publication is available from the British Library

Library of Congress Cataloguing in Publication data
Caldwell, Janis McLarren.
Literature and medicine in nineteenth-century Britain: from Mary Shelley to
George Eliot / Janis McLarren Caldwell.
p.   cm. – (Cambridge studies in nineteenth-century literature and culture)
Includes bibliographical references and index.
ISBN 0 521 84334 0
1. English literature – 19th century – History and criticism.   2. Medicine in literature.
3. Literature and medicine – Great Britain – History – 19th century.   4. Women and
literature – Great Britain – History – 19th century.   5. English fiction – Women
authors – History and criticism.   I. Title.   II. Series.
PR868.M42C35   2004
820.9´3561 – dc22   2004052122

ISBN 978-0-521-84334-8 hardback
ISBN 978-0-521-06667-9 paperback

In Memoriam
George L. McLarren, M.D.

Contents

Acknowledgments

I am greatly indebted to Gary Handwerk who guided my transition from medical doctor to academic, and who continues to offer, in his inimitable way, a combination of warm encouragement and acute critique. Gillian Beer, who graciously provided scholarly direction during a year's research at Cambridge University, continues to inspire my thinking about literature and science. I am grateful to Kathleen Blake for her important influence on the early development of this book. Scott Klein contributed insightful suggestions for the manuscript and Gillian Overing encouraged me through the publication process.

The Radcliffe Institute for Advanced Study at Harvard University granted me fellowship for 2000–2001, in which most of this book was written. I am grateful especially to my fellow Radcliffe fellows for a year of stimulating interdisciplinary conversation. Wake Forest University's Archie Foundation provided travel grants that gave me the opportunity to conduct my research in London and Cambridge. Librarians of Cambridge University Library, the Wellcome Library for the History and Understanding of Medicine, the Brontë Parsonage Museum Library, and the Countway Medical Library of Harvard University gave immeasurable assistance in providing access to their collections. Versions of chapters two and five have appeared in, respectively, *The Ethics in Literature*, ed. Andrew Hadfield, Dominic Rainsford, and Tim Woods (Basingstoke: Macmillan, 1998), and *Victorian Literature and Culture* 31.2 (2003). I am grateful to the editors and publishers of these works for granting permission to present revised versions here.

I owe a special debt of gratitude to friends still giving their lives to the practice of medicine – Drs. Lauri Costello, Dave Nowels, and Chris Schramm – for conversations about the present-day culture of medicine.

I have been exceptionally fortunate in knowing congenial fellow Victorianists who have enlarged my thought as well as my life. Suzy Anger has been both mentor and friend, and I am indebted particularly to her scholarship on hermeneutics. I have treasured long conversations with Caroline Levine in which we hashed out exciting new ideas about how to live and work; her notion of pleasurable suspense may yet transform my dour Presbyterian severity. Lisa Sternlieb's inventive critical style and political activism are a daily inspiration, as necessary to me as her endless fund of sympathy. I have learned so much from Jan Schramm's intellectual fascination with everything from details of Victorian history to world travel; her deep understanding and enduring friendship have sustained me from start to finish.

Finally, I owe my greatest thanks to my husband, Rick Caldwell, in all of his guises: tireless reader, trusted editor, soul mate, and best friend.

CHAPTER I

Introduction: Romantic materialism

This book is about a remarkable episode in the history of literature and of medicine, in which several influential literary and medical writers were allied in one project, that of negotiating between two distinctly different ways of knowing – between, that is, personal experience and scientific knowledge of the natural world. Although we have come to regard "clinical" and "Romantic" as oppositional terms, clinical medicine emerged from the same culture that nourished Romantic literature. In the first half of the nineteenth century, a number of leading doctors and writers cultivated a form of double vision which I will call "Romantic materialism": Romantic because they were concerned with consciousness and self-expression, and materialist because they placed a particularly high value on what natural philosophy was telling them about the material world.

My argument, in short, is that Romantic materialists, as inheritors of the conceptual structure of natural theology, read the world through "two books": the Book of Nature and the Book of Scripture. But, unlike traditional natural theologians, Romantic materialists accepted disjunctions between the two ways of knowing and called for an interpretive method which tacked back and forth between physical evidence and inner, imaginative understanding. This dialectical hermeneutic yielded innovations in both medical diagnostics and literary representation. Clinical practitioners developed the two-part history and physical exam, tolerating the tensions between the patient's narrative and the evidence of the body. Literary writers produced potent myths like *Frankenstein*, *Sartor Resartus*, and *Wuthering Heights*, featuring startling and incongruous juxtapositions of the natural and the spiritual, and often disturbing the conventional dualist hierarchy of spirit over flesh. Examining works of imaginative literature by Mary Shelley, Thomas Carlyle, and Emily and Charlotte Brontë, alongside medical lectures, textbooks, and journal articles, I propose that these writers constitute, if not formally or self-consciously a movement, at least a striking cultural formation – certainly more substantial than a fleeting transitional phase between literary or historical periods.

Romantic materialism is a phrase that Gillian Beer applied to Charles Darwin when she explored his linguistic development in *Darwin's Plots*. Beer traces Darwin's dual interest in imagination and the material world and argues that the resultant "romantic materialism" drives him "to substantiate metaphor, to convert analogy into real affinity."[1] George Levine in *Darwin and the Novelists* echoes Beer's phrase, explaining the seemingly paradoxical conjunction as a confluence of traditions. "Darwin," writes Levine, "though an inheritor of eighteenth-century materialist thought, had nevertheless absorbed the organicist assumptions of the romantic poets."[2] I think both Beer and Levine are right about Darwin's dialectical heritage, and will argue moreover in chapter six that this dialectic was crucial to the generation of his theory of natural selection. But both Darwin and later Darwinists, though intellectually indebted to a two-text epistemology, offered the possibility of strictly materialist readings of nature, shedding the "Romantic" side of the dialectic and effectively putting an end to the primacy of natural theology. I am proposing, then, that the term "Romantic materialism" is particularly apt for pre-Darwinian science and literature, for Darwin's heritage rather than his legacy.

The very category of "pre-Darwinian" literature, by which I mean literature from 1800 to 1859, before the publication of *The Origin of Species*, wreaks havoc with traditional literary periodization. Why import a landmark in the history of science into a consideration of literature? Not, certainly, to grant science primacy over literature, but rather to cross-fertilize the disciplines for a new perspective. The imaginative literature of this period that most completely addresses the medical body is interestingly the very literature which has most successfully evaded categorization as Romantic. The first three pre-Darwinian literary texts I discuss, *Frankenstein*, *Sartor Resartus*, and *Wuthering Heights,* have never sat very comfortably in their designated literary periods. *Frankenstein* (1818), although safely within a Romantic chronology, is often regarded as atypically Romantic, or even anti-Romantic, with Gothic trappings surrounding elements of incipient science fiction. George Levine, for instance, advances *Frankenstein* as a proto-realist novel because of its explorations of an empiricist epistemology.[3] *Sartor Resartus* (1834), though typically considered Victorian since it so strongly influenced the age, is a thinly veiled redaction of German Romanticism for the British public. And *Wuthering Heights* – is it Gothic romance, early social realism, or, as Nancy Armstrong concludes, an incoherent mixture of the two?[4] There is a family resemblance in these texts that situates them somewhere between the Romantic and the Victorian. Their supernatural obsessions signal some debt to the romance or the Gothic, and their insistent return to the physical world signals perhaps a nascent realism, or interest in the natural and medical sciences. When these texts are compared to pre-Darwinian medical literature, this resemblance comes into focus as a cross-disciplinary (or to some extent pre-disciplinary) cultural formation of Romantic materialism.

I also use "Romantic materialism" to characterize one strain of the several "Romanticisms" posited by recent critics. Identifying this particular strain is significant, in that it constitutes a formative period in science and contributes major texts to Romantic narrative. The first three narratives I consider share many formal properties. All have been considered "mythic" for their time; I refer here not to the use of classical themes, but to the property of serving an explanatory function, of being a story that bridges, in fictional terms, the supernatural and the natural worlds. All had a powerful resonance for their century, with themes and fragments being repeated almost obsessively in other literary works and in more popular forms. All were initially branded as crude, primitive, messy, or wild, with overt attention not just to nature, but also to embodied experience. All tend toward fragmentation, or are not overly concerned with realistic connections and plausibility. All are first-person narratives. Formally, they employ a frame or set of frames, and use multiple first-person narratives couched within one another. These common formal properties suggest at least a subgeneric grouping, neither neo-Gothic nor proto-realist, not simply transitional, but a coherent mythic patterning with resonance for a whole culture.

One problem with the use of the term "Romantic materialism" is that it risks sounding like a synonym for "natural supernaturalism" – and in one sense it is, although a synonym for Thomas Carlyle's coinage in *Sartor Resartus* rather than for M. H. Abrams's interpretation in his book by that title.[5] The difference is that Abrams has taken "natural supernaturalism" to indicate a secularization, the supernatural recast in natural media, whereas Carlyle emphasizes a duality, an ongoing conversation between the sacred and the secular that is sustained in Britain until Darwin's revolution. The reception of Darwin's theory marks a widespread secularization, but the pre-Darwinian environment was decidedly dualistic. Although ideas of evolution were "in the air" before Darwin, ideas of materialism, or a one-text world, were dangerously foreign and much feared.

The logic of Romantic materialism runs counter to many prior explanations of Romanticism. A long tradition holds that British Romanticism was fostered by disillusioned radicals, who, appalled at the physical ravages

of the French Revolution, forsook the political arena to take their revolution inward, into the recesses of the mind and imagination. By this
account, the radical energy of Romanticism was disabled from its incep-
tion by its removal from the material world. Whereas Romanticism has
been associated with internalization, whether of a failed political project
or of a Bloomian romance quest, Romantic materialism emphasizes exteri-
orization, incarnation, or, as Carlyle puts it, "bodying forth."[6] Preserving
the paradox implicit in "natural supernaturalism," Romantic materialism
reinvigorates religious mystery by refiguring it anew in explicitly material terms.[7] Although this dialectic bears a strong resemblance to previous
definitions of Romantic irony, in that its two sides resist resolution or uni-
fication, Romantic materialism differs in preserving its interest in patterns
rather than chaos, in creativity rather than deconstruction, in net developmental change rather than endless flux. It tolerates disjunctions due to the
desire to explain provisionally in the face of incomplete knowledge, not in
celebration of irresolution.

  This brand, or relative, of Romantic irony resembles Clyde Ryals's
"enabling fiction in a world of possibilities" more than Anne Mellor's endless
becoming in an infinitely abundant chaos.[8] It differs from Ryals's conception, however, in its ethical concern. Anne Mellor identifies "the ethical
problem implicit in the stance of the romantic ironist" according to her
or Ryals's usage – that is, "the impossibility of making an enduring commitment to a particular political or moral program that might over time
produce greater social or legal justice."[9] Both Mellor and Ryals derive their
definitions of Romantic irony from Schlegel's early work, and fail to recognize the "ethical irony" that Gary Handwerk, by contrast, has argued is
present in Schlegel's later development.[10] Furthermore, Mellor and Ryals
identify German theory too closely with British literature, missing the
Romantic materialism that brings British and German influences into conversation with one another. In the texts I consider, the influence of German
Romantic irony is tempered by native empiricism, resulting in a hermeneutic ethics concerned with both transcendence and embodiment. Because
Romantic materialism does not neglect the body, and because it argues for
the possibility of a provisional or working knowledge of the world, it can
espouse an ethics and address questions of material justice.

ROMANTIC MEDICINE

In 1993, G. S. Rousseau complained that "there has been no sustained
effort or synthetic attempt to link 'Romanticism' (disparate as any historical

movement called 'romanticism' may have been) to the development of 'real science.'"[11] Rousseau acknowledged the value of single-author studies such as Hermione de Almeida's *Romantic Medicine and John Keats*, but called for a more holistic approach that would take into account "the ingrained, unverbalised, preformative 'medical gaze' of . . . 'Romantic' culture."[12] Andrew Cunningham and Nicholas Jardine crack the door to such a project with their edited collection *Romanticism and the Sciences* (1990). Their introductory essay entitled "The Age of Reflexion" suggests a general trend in science and literature to turn inward to examine the self. The essays which follow, however, give brief introductions to a number of specialized topics instead of supporting an overarching thesis about Romantic literary and scientific culture.[13]

The "medical gaze" to which Rousseau refers derives, of course, from the theory of Michel Foucault. In *The Birth of the Clinic,* Foucault argues that, as the "clinic" or French teaching hospital developed the new diagnostic tool of morbid anatomy, the medical profession acquired far-reaching disciplinary power. In the post-mortem examination, the interior pathological processes of the body were brought to the surface, exposed to the "brightness" of the medical gaze.[14] Suddenly disease, once thought of in terms of taxonomic categories, was localized in the body itself. Foucault quotes Xavier Bichat, the French founder of "tissue theory," or early pathology:

For twenty years, from morning to night, you have taken notes at patients' bedsides on affections of the heart, the lungs, and the gastric viscera, and all is confusion for you in the symptoms which, refusing to yield up their meaning, offer you a succession of incoherent phenomena. Open up a few corpses: you will dissipate at once the darkness that observation alone could not dissipate.[15]

Foucault emphasizes the insidious disciplinary control exercised by medicine, masked particularly by the trope of bringing things to light. Death permits the pathological anatomist to read the disease process backward in time, granting him the power of seeing and knowing the previously invisible and inviolable.

In the final pages of *The Birth of the Clinic*, Foucault gestures toward the paradox apparent in the twin births of Romantic literature and clinical medicine:

In what at first sight might seem a very strange way, the movement that sustained lyricism in the nineteenth century was one and the same as that by which man obtained positive knowledge of himself; but is it surprising that the figures of knowledge and those of language should obey the same profound law, and that the irruption of finitude should dominate, in the same way, this relation of man to death, which, in the first case, authorizes a scientific discourse in a rational form, and in the second, opens up the source of a language that unfolds endlessly in the void left by the absence of the gods?[16]

Foucault sweeps aside his paradox by explaining that Romantic writers and doctors both responded to a confrontation with death, with clinicians dissecting cadavers to gain positive knowledge, and Romantic poets writing into the "void" left by the death of "the gods." But British medicine, which was sustaining the long pre-Darwinian twilight of natural theology, had yet to experience to any great degree Foucault's "death of the gods." British medical reformers, if not overtly religious themselves, often found themselves in league with religious thinkers, from Evangelicals to High-Church natural theologians. This book, then, poses Foucault's paradox as a starting place for an in-depth inquiry into British pre-Darwinian medical culture, but finds a Foucauldian explanation insufficient for British history.

In order to avoid the Foucauldian associations attached to "clinical," then, I will refer to the medicine of my Romantic materialists as "Romantic medicine." Within this category, I mean to include "reform medicine," the term used by medical historians to emphasize the licensing of apothecaries, surgeons, and general practitioners early in the century. But because my emphasis is less on the politics of medicine than its epistemology, I think "Romantic medicine" a more apt term for the argument presented here. It should be clear at this point that by "Romantic" doctors, I do not mean to conjure strict idealists or thoroughgoing vitalists, who, within the medical community, were few and far between (as I discuss in chapter two). Rather, I mean to indicate the vitalistic materialism typical of the medicine actually practiced in the pre-Darwinian period.

Most of the work to date on nineteenth-century literature and medicine has attempted to map Foucault's reading of French history onto the British scene.[17] Lawrence Rothfield, in *Vital Signs*, reaches for a comprehensive definition of the "medical gaze."[18] Rothfield argues that realist authors modeled themselves after doctors, borrowing cultural authority from the distanced, all-seeing gaze of the clinician. Like medicine, realism aspired to mimesis through exactitude in recording ordinary, unlovely facts and details. According to Rothfield, realist narrators, like doctors, cultivated clinical distance as well as precision of observation. This argument, however, creates a distorted trajectory of the rise and fall of the medical profession. Rothfield depicts medical prestige reaching its zenith in the first half of the nineteenth century and plummeting by late century, when naturalism and the detective story, in Rothfield's assessment, overtake realism.

Most medical historians, however, track a much later and steadier climb, culminating in the twentieth century with the age of antibiotics, when therapeutic success finally catches up with the increasing skill in diagnostics. They see a decline beginning only in the late twentieth century, related more to patients' dissatisfaction with doctor/patient relationships than to epistemological doubt about scientific methodology.

Rothfield works with French as well as British texts, and extends his study to later in the nineteenth century, which might explain why he sees medicine as a powerful profession that generated literary emulation.[19] But this Foucauldian argument for the disciplinary power of medicine cannot account particularly well for the interactions between literature and medicine early in nineteenth-century Britain. Responding to the cataclysmic changes in France, Britain kept its distance, sending medical students there for training, but retaining much of the national preference for British practice over French philosophy. While Britain sought to establish its own version of the clinic, or teaching hospital, British hospitals were less centralized, corpses for dissection were difficult to obtain, autopsies not widely practiced; thus, clinical-pathological correlations were drawn less frequently. Medical historians Roger French and Andrew Wear characterize the British medicine of the period in this way:

The hospitals were comparatively small and the doctor could not make wide-ranging comparisons. The physician, calling on his well-to-do client at home, still negotiated with him about his disease and its treatment. In this case as well as lower down the profession, the medical man based his treatment on what the patient told him about his illness, rather than on signs he could make the patient's body give.[20]

British medical reform focused on the licensing of the general practitioner, who competed with surgeons and physicians by blending the physical and intellectual approaches of both. The new general practitioners introduced French examination techniques of percussion and auscultation, but continued to negotiate treatment with the patient rather than relying primarily on physical signs. In part, this was an economic necessity. Unlike the state-appointed French physicians, British physicians had to be solicitous of their wealthy patrons, who were often of higher class status and who might easily consult another physician if unhappy with their diagnosis or care. For less remunerative cases, a glut of general practitioners competed with local surgeons and apothecaries. The literature of the period is full of accounts of the doctor struggling to make ends meet, his economic situation inducing him to maintain a high respect for his patients' desires and opinions.

So, while Foucault makes the birth of hospital medicine in France the most important medical event of the nineteenth century, I will argue in chapter seven that the most important development of nineteenth-century British medicine was the "history and physical" format for diagnosing illness. Still in use today, the "history and physical" title for consultations between doctor and patients demonstrates its bipartite deep structure, which evolved over the course of the nineteenth century. Before 1800, British doctors relied heavily on the patient's narrative alone, without an examination of the body, prescribing sometimes by correspondence.[21] Early in the century, case reports show an intermixture of patient's and doctor's language, and by mid-century the patient's subjective narration is often entitled "history," with the doctor's objective evidence separated out and listed later under "physical examination." In the twentieth century, the rise of respect for scientific evidence had so elevated the reliance on the physical exam (and, especially in the late twentieth century, reliance on the physical evidence of the laboratory or imaging technology) over the patient's account of his or her experience that, if the two were in conflict, physical evidence superseded the patient's story.[22] Thus, although the "history and physical" is still in use, the hermeneutic potential of one side of the dialectic, the patient's story, has been seriously degraded. Romantic medicine was remarkable, then, for its efforts to balance the patient's story and the body's evidence, and this balancing act was a breakthrough for medical diagnostics.

TWO BOOKS: NATURAL THEOLOGY IN LITERATURE
AND MEDICINE

The balanced dialectic of the history and physical coincided, crucially, with a number of other efforts to read two disparate texts in parallel. Natural theology, yoking science and religion in an effort to find them mutually reinforcing, supplied an overarching structure for these widespread interpretive practices. The structuring power of natural theology has been overlooked by many of the recent cultural histories of the period for a variety of reasons. First, natural theology looks, and probably is, epistemologically inconsistent, and is often therefore dismissed as a misguided ideology antagonistic to evolutionism. Second, natural theology has been mistakenly associated primarily with the elite "gentleman scientist" and less often with the urban, middle-class doctor struggling to attain professional status. Because of its prominent religious component, natural theology has too often been cast as politically conservative, when in fact it drew supporters from across political ranks. Finally, as witnessed throughout the history of the "two cultures" debate, it is much neater to think of the sciences and the humanities in perpetual combat than to imagine a "both-and" culture that is also aware of some of the problems that mutual tolerance would entail.

But of course, for much of the history of science, "both-and" has been the name of the game: both science and religion, in particular. Steven Shapin reminds us that, throughout the scientific revolution, natural knowledge was viewed as "*supporting* and *extending* broadly religious aims":[23]

It was widely said that God had written two books by which his existence, attributes, and intentions might be known. The one was Holy Scripture, but the other was increasingly referred to in the early modern period as the Book of Nature.[24]

The metaphor of God's "two books" can be detected in early Christian writings and especially in the late fourth-century works of Saint Augustine, but came into heavy usage during the early modern period.[25] In *The Advancement of Learning* (1605), Bacon writes:

Our saviour saith, "You err, not knowing the scriptures, nor the power of God"; laying before us two books or volumes to study, if we will be secured from error; first the scriptures, revealing the will of God, and then the creatures expressing his power; whereof the latter is a key unto the former: not only opening our understanding to conceive the true sense of the scriptures, by the general notions of reason and rules of speech; but chiefly opening our belief, in drawing us into a due meditation of the omnipotency of God, which is chiefly signed and engraven upon his works.[26]

According to Bacon, the second book, the "power" of God manifest in Nature, operated as a "key" to Scripture in order to increase both reason and faith, albeit indirectly. But Bacon warned that the two books should remain separate: one should not "unwisely mingle or confound these learnings together."

By the nineteenth century the two-books doctrine was the stuff of popular literature and conventional piety. Patrick Brontë quizzed his young children on the two books, and in their personal copy of Edward Young's *Night Thoughts* they would have imbibed the following:

> Read Nature; Nature is a friend to truth;
> Nature is Christian; preaches to mankind;
> And bids dead matter aid us in our creed[27]

Much of this literature seems to focus on making the study of Nature seem less daunting to the young and/or untrained. Nature is an open book, accessible to all readers; what's more, it's friendly and familiarly

Christian: "dead matter" is enlivened, anthropomorphized, and sacralized
into eloquent preacher. Similarly, John Keble's best-selling *Christian Year*
makes the study of natural history into a devotional activity:

> There is a book, who runs may read,
> Which heavenly truth imparts,
> And all the lore its scholars need,
> Pure eyes and Christian hearts,
> The works of God above, below,
> Within us and around,
> Are pages in that book, to show
> How God himself is found.[28]

In this light-hearted, simple verse, the only tools one needs for an accurate
reading of Nature are "pure eyes and Christian hearts." For a lay audience,
as Susan Cannon writes, natural science "served to baptize fresh-air fun.
One could roam the mountains or the moors, protected from the pressure
of Evangelical duty, if one brought back beetles or bits of rock, for the
study of nature was the study of one of God's two great books."[29] At least
in popular culture, the two-books doctrine widened the opportunities for
Christian endeavor to include natural history, and in turn gave natural
history a moral purpose.

But, as John Hedley Brooke notes, natural theology was characterized by
an "ambivalence": it could be used either to defend or to attack traditional
religious interests. Not only could theologians claim the findings of natural
philosophy as proof of God's wisdom, but students of nature could also use
the doctrine to mask revolutionary ideas in the clothing of orthodox piety.[30]
James Moore goes further in attributing this ambivalence to a conscious and
expedient political arrangement: Bacon's two-book doctrine is "a political
compromise offering illustrations of the divine omnipotence . . . in exchange
for the freedom of students of nature from harassment by interpreters
of biblical texts."[31] Whereas Moore treats Bacon's doctrine as "a piece of
ideology . . . from the start," my approach posits that the dual structure
of natural theology can be seen as an interpretive strategy emerging from
an ethical stance. Reading nineteenth-century literature for its treatment
of alterity, one finds, rather than easy compromise, the development of a
dialogue between naturalism and theology that sharpens and sustains both
in a mutually productive engagement.

The two-books doctrine appears frequently throughout the history of
poetry and fiction, even when no clear compromise is being forged between

religious and scientific authority. Of course the "two books" metaphor appealed to the literary writer because it elevated authorship to God-like status, and made interpretive skills crucial to the understanding of God's work, which became in this trope as textual as his word. But the metaphor also had ambivalent implications for literary interpreters of the "Book of Nature." First, the Book of Nature was accessible to the individual reader, in good Protestant fashion, without the mediation of either a religious or a scientific priesthood. But second, it was infinitely complicated, requiring interpretive activity, and forever eluding full human comprehension. In *Paradise Lost*, Milton uses the "two books" doctrine to legitimate Adam's curiosity about the stars. The archangel Raphael teaches Adam:

> To ask or search I blame thee not, for Heav'n
> Is the Book of God before thee set,
> Wherein to read his wond'rous works.[32]

Milton echoes Bacon in considering the natural world of God's "wond'rous works" a text to be had for the reading. Although Raphael later points Adam toward more answerable questions, he by no means suppresses Adam's interest in natural knowledge, entertaining at length several possible explanations for Adam's observations. Milton presents natural science as both permissible and inevitably exceeding human capacity, a perpetually renewable pursuit full of open questions.

John Donne also employs the two-books metaphor freely, and, despite his Christian spirit/matter dualism, passionately advocates the claims of the material world. In "The Ecstacy," Donne presents two lovers reclining on a bank, hands and gazes intertwined until they seem to grow into one pure soul. But by the end of the poem he recalls the lovers to their material bodies:

> Loves mysteries in soules doe grow
> But yet the body is his booke

For Donne, the body is the book through which the mystery of love may be read, just as Nature and Scripture are the Books demonstrating the mystery of God. Citing this text, Elaine Scarry has called Donne a "volitional materialist," meaning that he views the affirmation of embodiment as a choice, an imitation of the "willful materialism" of the Christian God who chose to become incarnate in the person of Jesus. Explicating Donne's Easter Sermon, 1625, Scarry writes:

What inflames Donne's imagination, what takes hold of his mind, is not the fact of God's materialism per se (however miraculous that is; and it is, of course, the Easter miracle of the resurrected body that provides the materialist premise of the whole sermon). It is instead the fact that that materialism is wholly willed: it is volitional and freely chosen. How easily might God have dissociated Himself from the body; yet how consistently he chose to be associated. How at liberty to disavow: hence how breathtaking the refusal to disavow.[33]

This volitional materialism is of course not unique to Donne, but implicit in much of Christianity – in the doctrine of the incarnation, in the "resurrection of the body" claimed in the Apostles' Creed not only for Christ but for all believers, and in the Roman and orthodox eucharist, in which the bread is translated into the substance of Christ's body, to be consumed by and incorporated into the bodies of the communicants. In Western and particularly Protestant Christianity, this materialism has been overshadowed by Pauline denigration of the flesh, giving rise to just criticism of Christian dualism. But Scarry's reading of Donne brings us bracingly into contact with a materialist strand of Christianity, a type of dualism that chooses to value the body.

Donne's volitional materialism persists in the tradition of natural theology, since, at least in theory, natural theology heeds Bacon's caution against the "unwise mingling" of the two books (maintaining dualism) at the same time as it specifically promotes the Book of Nature as worthy of study (thus valuing matter). As scientific knowledge gained authority, the two books were sometimes conflated, with natural theologians using science to "prove" God's existence, or using theology to deduce their science. This is the natural theologian of popular caricature, who, as was said of Philip Gosse, reconciled his literalist religion with his science by concluding that God created, in seven days, a universe full of fossils in order to test our faith.[34] But natural theologians of varying stripes posited varying degrees of commensurability (or incommensurability) between the two books, everything from a literal correspondence to a great divide. Many of the central proponents emphasized division, heeding Bacon's warning not to confound the two books. In the eighteenth century, Bishop Butler designated the relationship between the books an "analogy," as the title of his natural theological treatise, *Analogy of Religion*, indicates. George Levine points out that Butler's analogy is self-consciously dualistic and comparative rather than logical, since strict logic would imply the dependence of the spiritual world on the natural. Butler was therefore "careful to argue that the evidence of the natural merely helped confirm what had already been revealed spiritually."[35]

In 1802, William Paley in his *Natural Theology* proclaimed his faith in the ultimate comprehensibility of nature, but found meaning in the gaps between the two books. Mark Francis, countering the tendency to read Paley as a naïvely teleological thinker, reminds us of the split Paley preserves between divine and material explanations: "Though backed by Divine Will, Paley's discussion of animal and human life was a rigorously materialist one."[36] And, although Paley has been represented as a proponent of "perfect adaptation,"[37] his first and most influential proposition, of nature's "contrivances," emphasized the awkwardness of such adaptation: "Contrivance, by its very definition and nature, is the refuge of imperfection. To have recourse to expedients, implies difficulty, impediment, restraint, defect of power."[38] Furthermore, Paley's second proposition was that creatures enjoyed a happiness in excess of any useful purpose. Certainly, he emphasized the artful design of nature, but it is little recognized how curiously inexplicable Paley found much of it. God's plan exceeded what Paley knew of it; science revealed unexpected curiosities and oddities. Paley's was a natural theology that emphasized the roughness of the analogy between the two books, with wonder arising from an excess of happiness, an imperfection of contrivances, and current ignorance of God's plan.

The *sine qua non* of natural theology is often said to be its "argument from design" – that is, that patterns of fitness in nature imply an intelligent Designer. Furthermore, the standard line goes, this argument from design springs from teleological reasoning: natural processes occur because the Designer intends an intelligible final result. But, especially by some nineteenth-century natural theologians, my "Romantic materialists," teleological reasoning was considered theologically arrogant and scientifically unsound. In his Bridgewater Treatise, written to promote natural theology, William Whewell wrote that "final causes are to be excluded from *physical inquiry*; that is, we are not to assume that we know the objects of the Creator's design, and put this assumed purpose in the place of a physical cause."[39] For Whewell, faith in an ultimate design did not permit teleology to direct scientific investigation. Speculation as to the divine plan should be deferred until physical data were fully confirmed. Nor was Whewell an exception for his time. According to John Durant, many natural theologians eschewed teleology, joining Whewell in the widespread belief that God did not participate in the world via episodic interventions, but rather through the establishment of general laws.[40]

If we attend to the "two books" doctrine rather than the "argument from design," we see that natural theology may have had a part in shaping the theoretical medicine of the period. The bitextual habit may have allowed the parallel introduction of different national influences, for instance. British doctors, often seeking foreign education, imported French science but tempered it with German philosophy, giving a peculiar mix of materialism and transcendentalism to domestic anatomy. The resultant "higher anatomy" or "transcendental anatomy" attempted to describe the "morphological laws of animal development,"[41] organizing a set of common structural patterns – an Ideal Plan – that animal bodies demonstrated as they progressed from embryos to adult forms. From the 1820s to 1859, in the sustained pause before Darwin's revolution, transcendental anatomy persisted as the medical expression of natural philosophy. In its widespread cultural appeal, the vogue of transcendental anatomy crossed political lines: pioneered by political radicals, it fascinated gentlemen scientists as well. Philip Rehbock attributes the persistence and plasticity of British transcendental anatomy to a dialectic of French and German national traditions:

In his classic exposition of anatomical traditions, *Form and Function* (1916), E. S. Russell said of transcendental anatomy that "The philosophy seems to have come chiefly from Germany, the science from France." To that terse assessment we might add that its variety and longevity seem most manifest in Britain.[42]

And one might further add to Rehbock's assessment that Britain was particularly receptive to a dialectical conversation between French materialism and German transcendentalism because of its long tradition of a dually structured natural theology.

Adrian Desmond, in *The Politics of Evolution: Morphology, Medicine, and Reform in Radical London*, has pointed out that medicine played a large part in shaping this pre-Darwinian natural philosophy, a fact which Darwin scholars have too often ignored.[43] Desmond focuses on radical medical dissidents rather than on natural theologians. He valorizes the secular importers of transcendental anatomy Robert Knox and Robert Grant, whose careers were plagued by various forms of censorship of their ideas, and regrets the ceding of transcendental anatomy to the moderates, like Richard Owen and Peter Mark Roget, who could make it palatable to the medical establishment. But Desmond's appealing metanarrative – of the tragic silencing of radicals and the unfortunate domestication of their ideas – does not do justice to the multifaceted appeal of transcendental anatomy in the first place. Because it examined relationships between species, it could be marshalled to support early evolutionary theory. But the idealist component could be nicely adapted by those natural theologians who were willing to read God's design in terms of form rather than of function.

Another Bridgewaterist, Peter Mark Roget, M. D. (incidentally, the Roget of thesaurus fame), was as reluctant as Whewell had been to fix the means of God's work, expecting to find God's design in general laws rather than in "insulated interpositions." Roget's position on the two-books doctrine was anti-reductionist: the Book of Nature was too complex, and the workings of God too subtle, to meet in anything other than physiological laws. God's "'distant purposes' worked through an 'immense chain of causes and effects.'"[44] The remarkable, "transcendental" patterns of morphology were certainly enough to signal God's design – but in form, rather than in function.

Richard Owen, founder of the natural history department of the British Museum, was one of the chief disseminators of transcendental anatomy in Britain. He compared vertebrate skeletons in an effort to construe an "archetype" or ideal plan underpinning the various actual skeletons of different species. Owen was for a time (i.e., prior to the publication of *The Origin of Species*) Britain's foremost naturalist, in part because he translated continental anatomy into terms intelligible to British culture. Under the aegis of Christian natural theology, Owen grafted idealist philosophy onto keen scientific observation of the natural world. Although Owen was in the end an antagonist of Darwin's, his archetypes nonetheless demonstrated the "homologies" (similarities of anatomical form between species) that Darwin later attributed to common evolutionary descent rather than divine plan.

From Bacon's two books to Butler's analogy, Paley's imperfect contrivances, Whewell's distant general laws, and Owen's transcendental form, we can see that the central figures of natural theology steered clear of Biblical literalism on the one hand, and scientific reductionism on the other. What characterizes natural theology in this view is less "the argument from design" than its both-and, bitextual structure. While preserving faith in a common author of the two texts, these natural theologians tentatively proposed, and often suspended judgment about, other kinds of links. The plasticity of definition of this speculative link (moving from contrivances, to functional laws, to formal morphology) has suggested to many historians a bad-faith, last-ditch effort to plug the breaking dam of unbelief, with religion in retreat from the encroachments of science. Certainly there is some validity to this picture of an ideological scramble, but it would be perverse to ignore the earnest professions of faith and genuine attempts at tolerance that would also explain such a picture. Given the fundamental premise of natural theologians – that God is the author of two ways of knowing – and a tendency toward skepticism about the capacity of human reason, one would expect to find natural theologians both in search of analogies between matter and spirit, and flexible about defining the precise nature of those analogies.

Charles Darwin's *The Origin of Species* is arguably, to quote John Durant, "[t]he last great work of natural theology."[45] Many have noted Darwin's debt to natural theology, citing his tribute to Paley in a letter of 1859, "I do not think I hardly ever admired a book more than Paley's 'Natural Theology.' I could almost formerly have said it by heart."[46] Dov Ospovat notes a continuity between Paley's contrivances and adaptation and Darwin's early belief in "perfect adaptation." More important, as I will argue in chapter six, is the bitextual structure of natural theology that Darwin puts to dialectical use in generating his theory of natural selection. Significantly, Darwin inserts quotations from two natural theologians, Bacon and Whewell, in the frontispiece to the 1859 edition:

> "But with regard to the material world, we can at least go so far as this – we can perceive that events are brought about not by insulated interpositions of Divine power, exerted in each particular case, but by the establishment of general laws."
> W. Whewell: *Bridgewater Treatise*

> "To conclude, therefore, let no man out of a weak conceit of sobriety, or an ill-applied moderation, think or maintain, that a man can search too far or be too well studied in the book of God's word, or in the book of God's works; divinity or philosophy; but rather let men endeavour an endless progress or proficience in both."
> Bacon: *Advancement of Learning*

Although this was undoubtedly a diplomatic gesture, an effort to appease believers, it also reveals how integral the two-books doctrine was to Darwin's thinking. Bacon urges advancement in the study of both "the book of God's word [and] the book of God's works"; Whewell seeks the connection between the two in the operation of general law.

HERMENEUTICS

Historians Lorraine Daston and Peter Galison have developed the notion of a "moralized" nineteenth-century objectivity.[47] I think that hermeneutics, rather than the implied pre-existing objectivity with a superimposed morality, is a better model to understand how Romantic materialists employed bitextual reading practices to arrive at provisional knowledge. Overviews of Victorian doubt often gesture to the parallel between scientific naturalism and German higher criticism as twin causes of erosion of faith. I hope to complicate this picture by calling attention to the native British typological hermeneutics of the pre-Darwinian period, as well as to the influence of German Romantic hermeneutics which were less naturalistic than the "higher" criticism of Strauss and Feuerbach, as translated by George Eliot.

Typology has a long history, but by the nineteenth century it had become a popular protestant tradition of reading all of the Bible with a double reference – both to human history and to divine plan. Most often, this took the form of interpreting events of the Hebrew Scriptures as both historical and prophetic of Christ's life, death, and resurrection, but typology could also take the form of interpreting later events, even in the reader's life, as shadows of the Christian story. George Landow, who finds typology underpinning even secular Victorian culture, notices in both procedures "a simultaneous emphasis upon two poles of meaning, or two levels of existence . . . [such as] fact and imagination, materialism and idealism."[48] Herbert Sussman also emphasizes the simultaneity of the typologist's vision:

The highest power of the imagination, then, lies neither in the accurate perception of the phenomenal nor in the unmediated vision of the transcendent, but in the integrated sensibility that can see with the greatest acuity the phenomenal fact while simultaneously reading the fact as sign of a higher reality.[49]

Typology then has a built-in dualism which refuses to diminish the importance of the material world. The human story is never discarded as a husk from which the spiritual kernel has been extracted.

Sussman also argues for a relationship between typology and natural theology, in which "the facts and the laws of the natural world are presented in the most minute detail, but . . . are so organized as to be seen as signs of transcendental truth."[50] The dualism of both is undoubtedly related to the two-books doctrine. If there are two books, Scripture and nature, then all events have a heavenly meaning and an earthly meaning. We would expect, then, to see some scientists performing typological hermeneutics on the Book of Nature. Historian of science Susan Cannon finds a strain of type-thinking in some of the foremost scientists of the early nineteenth century:

Ruskin's "language of Types," derived from Evangelical sources as it may have been in his case, was similar in kind to Richard Owen's "archetypes" in anatomy or Edward Forbes's "genera-ideas" in paleontology; and theories of types had a considerable vogue among French chemists. The successful attempt to find a real relation between artistic activity, general moral laws, and the language of stones was being conducted in private by Charles Darwin. Until he published, however, type-thinking was one of the interesting new ways to tackle scientific problems.[51]

Cannon goes on to assert that, if indeed this "type-thinking" amongst scientists came from methods of Biblical interpretation, it might lead "to an
interesting new idea in the history of science." In chapter three I demonstrate that, at least in Richard Owen's anatomy, this was very probably
the case, and in chapter six I explore Darwin's debt to Owen's typological
thought.

In addition to the typologists, many leaders of scientific societies
embraced early versions of German Biblical criticism in an attempt to work
out the complex and difficult relationship between the Book of Scripture
and the Book of Nature. Martin Rudwick, writing about the geological
scene in the early nineteenth century, observes,

[M]any of the most prominent scientific geologists were men of acknowledged
personal piety, and some held ecclesiastical positions, the duties of which they
fulfilled conscientiously (e.g., Buckland, Conybeare, Sedgwick). But such men
were theological liberals who were well aware of the critical hermeneutics being
developed by German biblical scholars at this period. They had not hitched their
religious beliefs onto literalistic modes of biblical exegesis; indeed, they were among
the most vehement critics of the scriptural geologists. In their view, the literalism
of the scriptural geologists was just as outdated and unscientific (in the broad
Continental sense of the word "science") as the deviant "geology" that those writers
proposed.[52]

Emphasizing the analogous relationship between science and religion, these
latter-day natural theologians welcomed hermeneutic theory, which was
then articulating a way both to attend to the material, historical reality and
to respect a religious sense – but without a literalist reading practice.

Rudwick's claim may seem confusing to literary scholars who know
that George Eliot had not translated Strauss's *Das Leben Jesu* into English
until 1846; how would early nineteenth-century British scientists have been
exposed to German Biblical criticism? Of course, Charles Hennell had
approached the Bible as a set of secular historical documents and inde-
pendently arrived at some of Strauss's conclusions by 1838, demonstrating
that such ideas were also being explored in Britain.[53] Note, however, that
Rudwick refers not to the "higher criticism" but to earlier German theology, and gestures toward Cambridge dons as the disseminators. Julius
Hare had spent much time in Germany, had met the leading philosophers,
had translated Schleiermacher, and was a powerful, enthusiastic teacher.
Cannon identifies an influential community of scholars at Cambridge in
the 1820s, with Hare teaching at Trinity College under Whewell as tutor:

At Trinity College in the 1820's the undergraduates met a harmonious and sociable set of Fellows who were spreading a heady combination of historical scholarship, German Idealism, and Romantic poetry, along with the best of modern science, and all this in a Christian context.[54]

The Cambridge Apostles grew out of this nexus, but Trinity in the 1820s was more than a secret society. Cannon cites a number of intellectual leaders who emerged from this community, influentially spreading British Romanticism and modern science, while connecting them via German hermeneutics – that is, the Romantic hermeneutics largely of Schleiermacher rather than later, "higher" criticism.

Friedrich Schleiermacher developed two different ways of reading to interpret not only the Bible, but all kinds of written and spoken texts. Schleiermacher called his two classes of reading the "grammatical" and the "psychological." The grammatical approach, somewhat unhelpfully named, attended not only to the rules of syntax, but also to the historical context and the communal linguistic usage, what we would now call the culture of the original author or authors. The psychological approach, which Wilhelm Dilthey, in his recovery of Schleiermacher's hermeneutics, disproportionately emphasized, included the attempt to "divine," intuit, empathize with, or reconstruct the author's intent, to "know the author better than he does himself." Hermeneutics was the reading practice of moving back and forth between these two different approaches, holding them in dialectical conversation, until they modified and approximated agreement with one another, at which point one would have a satisfactory interpretation. In practice, Schleiermacher acknowledged, such a process could come to rest only at a provisionally acceptable interpretation, and continue whenever demand for further interpretation arose.

Schleiermacher's approach is perhaps best captured in the figure of the "hermeneutic circle," a concept which he developed from Friedrich Ast's basic formulation:

The basic principle of all understanding and knowledge is to find in the particular the spirit of the whole, and to comprehend the particular through the whole; the former is the analytical, the latter, the synthetic method of cognition. However, both are posited only with and through each other. Just as the whole cannot be thought of apart from the particular as its member, so the particular cannot be viewed apart from the whole as the sphere in which it lives. Thus neither precedes the other because both condition each other reciprocally, and constitute a harmonious life.[55]

Schleiermacher objected to the vagueness of Ast's "spirit" but recognized the usefulness of the hermeneutic circle. Although the hermeneutic circle commonly refers to a movement back and forth between part and whole, the general structure of shuttling back and forth between contrasting ways of reading in search of a provisional interpretation is more important for my purposes than the terms "part" and "whole." That is, Schleiermacher often changes his terms, yet one can trace the structure of the circle throughout his writings. For instance, he relates grammatical and psychological interpretation as follows:

> In order to complete the grammatical side of interpretation it would be necessary to have a complete knowledge of the language. In order to complete the psychological side it would be necessary to have a complete knowledge of the person. Since in both cases this is impossible, it is necessary to move back and forth between the grammatical and psychological sides, and no rules can stipulate exactly how to do this.[56]

For Schleiermacher, the grammatical includes not only linguistic rules but also cultural context, and the psychological includes a gestalt understanding or divination of the author as well as a comparative analysis of his writing. Schleiermacher's terms here look more like psyche and surroundings, or inside and outside, rather than whole and part. Furthermore, hermeneutic circles between various terms may intersect, as when Schleiermacher makes a distinction between the grammatical/psychological axis and the subjective/objective axis. In part, this complication looks like a growing recognition that one must also take into account a circling interaction between reader and writer – and between the reader's psyche and culture and the writer's. Rather than defining terms of the hermeneutic circle, or fixing it as a complete method, it is important to recognize in the circle the impulse to consider two sides, neither in complete harmony nor in warfare, but in productive conversation. This circling is both a potentially endless process that resists facile synthesis, and an endeavor which aims for, and believes in the possibility of, fuller understanding.

METHODOLOGY

Far from having been altogether erased or supplanted by Darwinist materialism, this hermeneutic shuttling between two ways of reading leaves its trace on contemporary thought. Modern philosophical hermeneutics, pioneered by Gadamer, Habermas, and Ricoeur, and developed out of Schleiermacher's theory via the philosophy of Dilthey and Heidegger, offers one of the most viable options for a constructive approach to reading difficulties. Increasingly, over the course of development of philosophical hermeneutics, there has arisen an acknowledgment that discrepancies between ways of reading often persist, and that an important part of the dialectic is to resist collapsing these differences, to defer closure of hermeneutic questions, and sometimes to accept the stereoscopic benefits of holding different perspectives in tension. The terms of Schleiermacher's dialectic have been variously reinterpreted.[57] Paul Ricoeur, dealing particularly with the reader's contribution to interpretation, seeks an interchange between "appropriation" and "distanciation." The reader appropriates the text, or makes it his or her "own" by finding his or her common ground with it. Then distanciation intervenes as the text asserts its otherness. Otherness may to some degree be appropriated – and Ricoeur does not mean compromised or colonized, but rather partially understood – but otherness will always persist in some degree inasmuch as one is never identical to the text, even if one has authored it. Innovative meaning, for Ricoeur, inheres in the tension between appropriation and distanciation, and meaning fails if this tension is not sustained. Full appropriation would dissolve meaning into sameness, whereas complete distanciation would render the text into incomprehensible noise.

Following Ricoeur, I adopt a hermeneutic stance in my own discussion of these Romantic medical and literary texts in order to reveal the legacy of Romantic hermeneutics for literary study in our own time. My influences have been undeniably eclectic, and my reader will find my technique ranging from close reading and formalist analysis to historical and cultural criticism. I hope to circle between these admittedly contrasting literary techniques, finding interpretations that the text's formal properties and cultural embeddedness seem to converge upon. At times, I find it useful to approach the text without suspicion, assuming that it is the site of meaning, and at times I seek to lay bare the text's cultural assumptions. Both are important. There is a danger in attempting understanding without critique, lest we lightly accept the text's cultural assumptions at the same time that we enjoy the pleasure of the text. But there is also a danger in performing critique without understanding, in that we too often assume a position of cultural superiority that fails to critique itself, and in so doing lose the pleasure that brought us to the study of literature in the first place.

My goal is also double. I begin with an effort to illuminate a moment in the history of literature, but by the end I hope to have recovered a piece of the history of medical ethics. One of the most important modern codifications of medical ethics, Thomas Percival's *Medical Ethics*, belongs to this period. Percival's text receives attention because it was the basis for many later codifications, including the Boston medical police and the American Medical Association codes of 1847, 1903, and 1912. The historian of medical ethics Robert Baker considers Percival's text a landmark, albeit not an enduring foundation. Baker considers Percival's *Ethics* a transitional text, mediating between a "character-based subjective ethics" and an "intersubjective morality of peer review, hospital rounds and collaboration."[58] As I hope to make clear in chapter two, I see this mixture of subjective and communal morality less as an artifact of "transition" and more as a product of the bitextual culture I have been describing. I find evidence for this particularly in the medical and imaginative literature of the period, a method which Baker himself endorses. In a review in which he regrets the dearth of scholarship on the history of medical ethics, Baker calls for a move from the "limited scholarly literature on medical ethics that focuses one-dimensionally on codes, oaths, and other formalizations" toward an examination of the "standards of medical propriety stated or implied in the law, in regulatory statutes, in the diaries and letters of practitioners and patients, in the columns of journalists, and in the lyrics of poets and playwrights."[59] Baker might well have included the mythic narratives like *Frankenstein, Sartor Resartus,* or *Wuthering Heights* that are the subject of the present study. These narratives took on lives of their own, with themes and fragments reproduced in many forms, because they made narrative sense (although not necessarily rational sense) of the strongest anxieties of the cultural moment. The way in which a culture creates narrative sense – the way it constructs and revises and reproduces stories – is an excellent indicator of its ethics. The texts that I examine here, from medical lectures to mythic narratives, all speak to a hermeneutic technique for evaluating ethical perplexities, oscillating between the two different ways of reading required by – in the terms of the Romantic materialists themselves – the Book of Nature and the Book of Scripture, God's work and his word.

This ethics is perhaps best described as a strategy for interpreting narratives; i.e. something more defined than an attitude or stance, but less prescribed than a method, algorithm, or set of principles. But lest we be left with no more to say than that this hermeneutics circles between two ways of reading, each chapter seeks to elucidate one important aspect of this interpretive strategy as practiced by the Romantic materialists.

The chapter on *Frankenstein* considers the problems of interpreting bodies in Mary Shelley's time, and demonstrates that, while Shelley alludes frequently to the contemporary vitalist-materialist controversy, she declines to take a position, demonstrating the importance of suspending judgment in the face of uncertainty. She speaks out strongly, however, for a new definition of sympathy as active reception. The bodily interpreter is not merely passively absorbing impressions, but actively making herself ready for the reception of difference. Bodily texts are problematic and require readerly work for completion, but at the same time the mental effort of the reader can be applied toward more acute reception of difference (instead of toward the projections or creations of the reader's own mind).

In *Sartor Resartus*, Thomas Carlyle uses the two-book language, but proclaims a unity between the books, and a difference only in the ways of reading them, throwing the emphasis on a dualism of interpretation rather than a dualism of substance. Here he shows a similarity to his scientist friend Richard Owen. Owen's transcendental anatomy is much like Carlyle's both-and, naturally supernatural world, which yields a different appearance when read prophetically than when read scientifically. For both, the world is not disjunct, but our ways of reading are necessarily so. This is important to note because Carlyle is so often read as a devotee of German idealism, but his emphasis on "clothes" and "work" throughout the text reminds us of his commitment (however often he indulges in self-satire) to materiality.

In the two chapters that follow I look at the effect of bitextual natural theology on the fictional worlds of Emily and Charlotte Brontë – which of course also later become absorbed by the British reading public. I look particularly at the influence of domestic medicine on Emily's vision of childhood, and the tension in her life between the purely physical child portrayed by domestic medicine and the bookish child she herself (also) was. Both Brontës, I argue, gain much of their imaginative power through upending the priorities of conventional Christian dualism, emphasizing materiality over spirituality – much as John Donne did with his "volitional materialism." In terms of interpretation, this often means applying reading strategies commonly reserved for the Book of Nature to the Book of Scripture. I examine Charlotte Brontë's use of literalization to argue that Romantic materialism permeates her innovative style and explains her powerful effect on her readers. Brontë reinterprets Biblical ethics, bringing a latent materialism to life in her emphasis on scenes of conflict in the Book of Scripture. Brontë finds revelation only and necessarily through the conflicts common to embodied experience.

In the chapter on Charles Darwin's *Autobiography*, I argue that Darwin owes his style of thought to Romantic materialism. He traces his debt in particular to the Romantic medicine practiced by his father and grandfather, and, although he does not explicitly tell us how that gave rise to his theory of natural selection, the narrative structure suggests a strong connection.

In the course of his *Autobiography*, Darwin rhetorically performs what I refer to as "narrative Darwinism," i.e., he amasses a quantity of rich, whimsical, and seemingly aimless stories from which he selects certain themes that contribute to the increasingly sharp focus of his mental development. As a narrator, Darwin alternates between a Romantic receptiveness to the fantastic and a utilitarian economy of logic, in which, unfortunately, the Romantic becomes a sort of fuel expended by the process. Thus, ironically, although Darwin is a great practitioner of Romantic materialism, he in the end offers a unitextual or naturalistic explanation of life, and effectively puts an end to the bitextual hermeneutics of earlier natural theology.

The final chapter uses George Eliot's *Middlemarch* as a lens to examine the later impact of Romantic materialism. Eliot specifically chooses to set her novel in the 1830s and to use Lydgate's medicine both as plot material and as the source of the book's reigning metaphors of optics and tissues or webs. I argue that Eliot is exploring the roots of German higher Biblical criticism in Romantic hermeneutics, and recognizing its affiliation with the birth of British Romantic medicine. Reading the medical case histories of Eliot's chosen period, I demonstrate the beginnings of the bipartite history and physical format, and discuss some of the complications of integrating narrative and scientific ways of knowing – of which, I argue, Eliot is acutely aware. I suggest, finally, that Eliot's interpretive strategies may offer a fruitful way to rethink medical hermeneutics today.

CHAPTER 2

Science and sympathy in Frankenstein

Perhaps because the tale is familiar, we often forget how odd it is that *Frankenstein* began as an entry in a ghost-story contest. The monster, after all, is an unlikely candidate for a ghost – constructed by a scientist out of dead body parts into a grossly oversized, undeniably living organism. How did a hyper-physical creature come to stand in for a ghost? As Mary Shelley recalls in her 1831 preface, her "unbidden" imagination worked with the diverse materials at hand – which by chance included transcendental fantasy and reports of scientific experiment. A "wet, uncongenial summer," so the story goes, confined her party – including her husband Percy, Lord Byron, and his doctor, John Polidori – to the house. They entertained one another by reading aloud German ghost stories until Byron proposed that they "each write a ghost story." A few nights later, Mary was racking her brain for an idea when she listened in on a discussion between her husband and Lord Byron:

During one of these [conversations], various philosophical doctrines were discussed, and among others the nature of *the principle of life*, and whether there was any probability of its ever being discovered and communicated. They talked of the experiments of Dr. Darwin (I speak not of what the Doctor really did or said that he did, but, as more to my purpose, of what was then spoken of as having been done by him), who preserved a piece of vermicelli in a glass case, till by some extraordinary means it began to move with voluntary motion. Not thus, after all, would life be given. Perhaps a corpse would be reanimated; galvanism had given token of such things: perhaps the component parts of a creature might be manufactured, brought together, and endued with vital warmth.[1]

The discussion inspired Mary Shelley's famous waking nightmare of a scientifically manufactured monster, and that monster has been haunting imaginations ever since.

The anxieties aroused by the search for "the principle of life," however, were not merely accidental products of Mary's heated brain, nor of the Shelley circle's eclectic interests. Romantic natural philosophers and lay persons turned fresh interest toward the discovery of a so-called "vital principle," an explanation for that which separated animate matter from the inanimate. In part, the vitalist movement was a reaction against eighteenth-century mechanism, protesting that life could not be adequately accounted for by mechanical physics alone. In part, it was simply the beginning of biology, the science of life, a call for the study of the structure and function of organisms. But inevitably, perhaps more on the part of the lay public than on that of the natural philosophers themselves, metaphysical questions intruded. Was life, or the "vital principle," natural or supernatural? Of one substance with the organism, or distinct from it – superadded, so to speak? How was life related to the soul or spirit? Would a scientific explanation of life threaten the domain of religion?

THE SCIENCE OF LIFE

The most publicized vitalist controversy of the early nineteenth century was waged between surgeon John Abernethy and his erstwhile pupil William Lawrence. In 1814, Abernethy, a prominent member of the Royal College of Surgeons, gave a lecture in which he attributed life to a "subtile, mobile, invisible substance, superadded to the evident structure" of the organism.[2] Further, he proposed, "the phaenomena of electricity and of life correspond" – not that electricity and life are identical, as Abernethy later clarified, but rather that they are analogous.[3] Lawrence, in 1816 a newly appointed professor, responded, also in a lecture to the Royal College. Well-versed in French physiology, especially that of Xavier Bichat, Lawrence proclaimed: "Life is the assemblage of all the functions, and the general result of their exercise."[4] In other words, one need not invoke a "superadded" substance; physiological function itself equals life. A bitter exchange of lectures between Abernethy in 1817 and Lawrence in 1819 followed. The conservative press caricatured the debate as a duel between transcendentalist religion and materialist science.[5] Abernethy was promoted as a believing scientist, protecting the domain of the immaterial soul, whereas Lawrence was denounced as a French-influenced materialist, hostile to religion. Lawrence was disciplined – his membership in the Royal College suspended and the copyright of his lectures denied. But eventually, as he amended his public statements, he regained his Royal College membership and established himself as a fashionable surgeon who in later years attended none less than Queen Victoria.

Lawrence's story has received much attention from historians interested in "radical medicine," and has been presented by Adrian Desmond, among others, as the tragedy of a heroic radical disciplined by the fearful scientists who compromised with religion. Unfortunately, Desmond's interpretation of Lawrence's story reinforces the religion vs. science melodrama as constructed by the conservative press of the day. In fact, Abernethy and Lawrence were both so-called "vitalists," interested in using scientific methods to elucidate the nature of life. Susan Lawrence argues that the Lawrence-Abernethy debate offers a history lesson not about conservative scientists squelching the radicals, but about the tolerance within the clinical community in contrast to the intolerance of the lay public:

Both Abernethy's and Lawrence's reputations were rooted in clinical experience, in teaching, in participation in medical societies, in publication for professional audiences, and in the ineffable mantle of hospital authority. And both of them expressed and subsequently polarized physiological positions familiar to anyone who already knew their work, including members of the College's Council . . . Lawrence then displayed, albeit in tendentious terms, the vision of medical science as it was already done among his peers. Many of them . . . eschewed appeal to mind, soul, or ephemeral vital powers as they went about experimenting, even if they may have believed that immaterial vital forces were necessary to living things . . . What Lawrence misjudged was not his surgical audience, but the power of lay opinion.[6]

The Lawrence-Abernethy debate – prior, at least, to its redaction in the lay press – represents not so much a philosophical struggle between materialism and transcendentalism as a suspense of that debate within clinical circles.

British medicine of the period was characterized by both deep interest in and ultimate deferral of metaphysical commitments. Whatever their convictions on the subject of religion, both Abernethy and Lawrence considered science a separate sphere or – to use the reigning "two books" language – a different text than that of religion. Abernethy thought electricity a possible "analogy" for life, a useful model rather than a reductive explanation. And Lawrence, though not personally religious, resorted to a typical natural theological defense of his inquiries. Like Bacon, he eschewed an "unwise mixing" of the "two books" of science and religion:

[The] theological doctrine of the soul, and its separate existence, has nothing to do with this physiological question but rests on a species of proof altogether different. These sublime dogmas could never have been brought to light by the labours of the anatomist and the physiologist. An immaterial and spiritual being could not have been discovered amid the blood and filth of the dissecting-room.[7]

Of course, this possibility – this "unwise mixing" of dissecting room and the spiritual being – is exactly what Mary Shelley had imagined one year previously in the writing of *Frankenstein*. Had Lawrence read the novel? It is possible, but it is more certain that both shared a cultural anxiety, taking seriously the materialist vision, and weighing the imagined consequences.

At the time of Mary Shelley's composition of *Frankenstein*, Percy Shelley was undoubtedly well-versed in the early stages of this debate. He began surgeon's training at St. Bartholomew's Hospital, and attended Abernethy's anatomy lectures. By 1815, he had consulted Lawrence as his personal surgeon and engaged him in intellectual exchange. Extrapolating from this evidence, Marilyn Butler argues that, in the 1818 text, Mary Shelley adopts Lawrence's position:

Frankenstein the blundering experimenter, still working with superseded notions, shadows the intellectual position of Abernethy, who proposes that the super-added life-element is analogous to electricity. Lawrence's sceptical commentary on that position finds its echo in Mary Shelley's equally detached, serio-comic representation.[8]

Butler moreover concludes, through comparing the 1818 text with the 1831 revisions, that Shelley revises her early materialism into a more respectfully religious stance. Thus Shelley's course from radical to moderate parallels Lawrence's, "[b]oth writers submitt[ing] to respectable middle-class opinion, in ways that allowed them to rescue what they could of their intellectual property."[9]

Neither version of the novel, however, aligns very well with either a strictly materialist or a purely transcendentalist stance. The vitalist question certainly pervades the novel, but Shelley seems to hover between philosophical positions. Frankenstein's "spark of being" does look like Abernethy's electricity, but his charnel-house raids allude to the grave-robbing, dissection, and vivisection popularly associated with radical science. The account of the monster's developing mind draws equally on materialist rhetoric of "sensations" which are "impressed" on nervous tissue, and on the transcendental language of the innate goodness of the natural child. The monster's character, as revealed by his narrative, tells such a different story to that of his body that he seems a hopelessly disjunct being, almost as if he were a product of matter and mind at war with one another. Furthermore, the monster himself teeters between declaring himself an immortal soul and a mere body, reducible to ashes. At the close of the novel, the monster, imagining his own fiery suicide, anticipates the "extinction" of feeling and the return to nature, his "ashes . . . swept into the sea by the winds." But is that all? "My spirit," he adds, "will sleep in peace; or if it thinks," he equivocates, "it will not surely think thus" (F, 220–221).[10]

Frankenstein's first readers, although they recognized the terms of the vitalist debate, were also unsure which side Shelley was on. Butler claims that most readers would have associated the novel's anatomical themes with Lawrence's position, but acknowledges that, even before Shelley revised *Frankenstein*, play versions and reviews had begun to interpret it as falling on Abernethy's side of the debate. From a very early date, the popular imagination interpreted *Frankenstein* as a cautionary tale warning against the presumptions of a purely materialist science.[11]

I propose that, like the clinical community portrayed by Susan Lawrence, Mary Shelley suspends judgment on the philosophical questions, allowing materialist and transcendentalist speculation to work side by side. Fearless in physical detail, *Frankenstein* endorses the value of matter, yet questions the ethical consequences of a wholly materialist vision. Half in love with sublimity, Shelley nonetheless deplores transcendental egotism and irresponsibility. But if she hovers between philosophical positions, it can't be entirely from youthful confusion or a welter of influences, as suggested by her 1831 preface. The novel argues for – something. Readers past and present have realized that *Frankenstein* has the force of a moral tale of mythic proportions, like Coleridge's *Rime of the Ancient Mariner*, to which Walton's frame tale alludes. What is the ethical issue of *Frankenstein*? I hope to show that Shelley's primary concern is redefining *sympathy*, a contested term in Romantic ethics and physiology. And finally I hope to show that Shelleyan sympathy is intimately related to the suspense of metaphysical commitments as practiced by both Shelley and the clinical community.

SYMPATHY

Over the last few decades, the field of biomedical ethics has claimed *Frankenstein* as its classic narrative, a cautionary tale warning that science divorced from ethics will produce monsters. But *Frankenstein* is a critique not so much of an amoral science, as of a conflation of scientific and moral theory – in the theory of physiologic sympathy. In *Frankenstein's* strange world, both scientifically modern and Gothically melodramatic, everybody is searching for sympathy, which functions as both a natural, material principle and the highest ideal of social interaction. The theory of physiologic sympathy, however, posits fragile bodies, susceptible to contagion and collapse. Under this model, social sympathy is safe only for people of nearly identical psychological and somatic constitutions. In *Frankenstein*, Shelley critiques the attempt to resolve science and ethics into a theory of physiologic sympathy, which she depicts as a narcissistic reduction, impatiently and prematurely synthetic in its demand for universal similitude, harmony, and unity.

Sympathy, judging from the word's frequency and weight in the text of *Frankenstein*, is the major theme and recurrent problem of the novel. Each narrator yearns for or mourns the loss of sympathetic relationship. Walton desires "the company of a man who could sympathize with me," and hopes he has found such a man when, with Frankenstein's arrival, the stranger's "constant and deep grief fills me with sympathy and compassion" (F, 13; F, 22). Walton's sympathy, however, is repulsed: "I thank you," Frankenstein replies, "for your sympathy, but it is useless" (F, 24). Frankenstein has already had such a friend in Clerval, whose "true sympathy" is now destroyed (F, 69). As for the monster, who claims he "was fashioned to be susceptible of love and sympathy," he "sympathizes" with the DeLaceys as he witnesses how they "sympathized with one another" (F, 217; F, 108; F, 127). After his unsuccessful self-exposure to the DeLaceys, the failure of hoped-for sympathy tortures him: "Finding myself unsympathized with, [I] wished to tear up the trees, spread havoc and destruction around me, and then to have sat down and enjoyed the ruin" (F, 132). The monster then pursues Frankenstein with the demand that he create a female monster, thinking he cannot live without the "interchange of those sympathies necessary for my being" (F, 140). Frankenstein, although finally coerced into agreement, flatly states "I could not sympathize with him" (F, 143). And after Frankenstein's death, the monster concludes: "No sympathy may I ever find . . . I am quite alone" (F, 218; F, 219). The search for sympathy amounts to an obsession for each narrator in this novel, and Shelley seems to be repeating that sympathy between individuals is impossible – or at least that it is a good deal more fragile than many Romantics assumed.[12]

For Shelley's generation, sympathy meant primarily fellow feeling – or, in David Marshall's definition, "the capacity to feel the sentiments of someone else."[13] But the word carried with it two other important historical connotations: of magical correspondence and of "modern" mechanical communication. Before the scientific revolution, sympathy implied powerful occult consonance that could occur on a variety of levels: celestial, between heavenly bodies; social, especially between friends, lovers, and relatives; physiological, between one's parts or organs, especially between mind and body; and elemental, between inanimate particles. For instance, in its oldest usage, sympathy was said to exist between the moon and the ocean, two lovers even at extreme distance, the liver and the mind, iron and a lodestone, and so on.[14] It seems that when correspondences were noted but unaccounted for – i.e., there was no clearly detailed or adequately understood mode of communication – sympathy became the explanatory concept.

In the eighteenth century, as physical science gained authority, mechanical explanations were offered for sympathy, and a crude materialism began to stand in for the previously occult attributes of sympathy. Following John Locke's empiricism, David Hume in moral philosophy and David Hartley in psychology used the rhetoric of "vibrations" and "impressions" to describe the communication of physical units of feeling. Tiny packets of information "impressed" themselves on the senses, and set up vibrations in the "aether," a supposedly airy substance flowing through the nerves. In his *Observations on Man*, David Hartley writes:

The Vibrations . . . are excited, propagated, and kept up, partly by the Aether, i.e. by a very subtle and elastic fluid, and partly by the Uniformity, Continuity, Softness . . . of the medullary substance of the Brain, Spinal Marrow, and Nerves.[15]

Of course, Hartley is not really explaining the physiology of the association of ideas – he is merely assigning physical substance to ideas, "confirming" their plausibility by constructing an ostensibly "scientific" account of how associations might imprint themselves on the body. In this attempt, however, he makes a significant move: the "free propagation of vibrations" requires "sufficiently uniform" substance. Repeatedly, Hartley invokes the "softness," "uniformity," and "continuity" – basically the passivity and the similarity of the substances necessary to provide for connection and communication of discrete impressions.

The softest, most responsive and resonant nerves, according to eighteenth-century moral philosophy and medicine, belonged to persons of "sensibility," or finely tuned physical sympathy. According to physician George Cheyne, "those *who govern*" were "mark'd out by Nature" from "those who *are governed*" by their "delicate and *elastic Organs* of *Thinking* and *Sensibility*." Thus, aristocrats were perfected in their "Heads, Faculties and Spiritual Nature," whereas the lower classes were designed for the "Exercise and Use of their Bodies, Limbs and Material Organs."[16] Erecting a physical basis for social difference, theories of sensibility operated to justify the privileges of the nobility. The supposedly exquisite delicacy of the person of sensibility, however, was thought to put him or her at risk for physical and mental derangement – such as melancholia, the vapours, hysteria, or hypochondria – and the rapid communication of illness between his or her mind and body.

Theorists of physical sympathy typically subscribed as well to a belief in social sympathy, or the literal transmission of sympathy from body to body.

Hume wrote in *A Treatise of Human Nature* that there is "a transition of passion" in any act of social sympathy, in which we not only imagine the experience of the other, but feel it on our nerves:

As in strings equally wound up, the motion of one communicates itself to the rest; so all the affections readily pass from one person to another, and beget correspondent movements in every human creature.[17]

Hume posited a direct, "instantaneous" transformation of the imagined idea into a neural "impression," reproducing "the very passion itself" in the onlooker through a rapid, unmediated transfer of identical information.

Although Hume proposed this immediacy as a foundation for moral behavior, fears of social contamination inevitably arose. The Earl of Shaftesbury, for instance, extolled sympathy within gentlemanly fellowship, but mistrusted sympathetic contact with the mob, whose "very looks" could be "infectious"; passion and panic might spread "from face to face."[18] Medical texts, such as the following by eighteenth-century physician Robert Whytt, regarded sympathy ambivalently, both as normal physiology and as susceptibility to disease:

[T]here is a remarkable sympathy, by means of the nerves, between the various parts of the body; and now it appears that there is a still more wonderful sympathy between the nervous systems of different persons whence various motions and morbid symptoms are often transferred, from one to another, without any corporeal contact or infection.[19]

Whytt's sentence quickly moves from admiration for the "remarkable" intra-body sympathy and the "still more wonderful" interpersonal sympathy, to anxiety about the consequences of sympathy, betrayed by his reference to "morbid symptoms" that leap from person to person with more efficacy even than an "infection." Michel Foucault takes this kind of ambivalence about sympathy as the sign of an epistemic shift, pronouncing that "[f]rom now on one fell ill from too much feeling; one suffered from an excessive solidarity with all the beings around one."[20]

Foucault's generalization has inspired most of the recent research on the history of sensibility.[21] But there was a prominent alternate medical and moral discourse about sympathy in later eighteenth-century and early nineteenth-century Britain, stemming from Adam Smith rather than Hume. According to Smith and his followers, this moral and physiological sympathy were not inextricably joined, and were not perpetually associated with contagion and illness. Smith argues contra Hume that sympathy is not a natural reflex, and cannot be explained by physiology alone:

As we have no immediate experience of what other men feel, we can form no idea of the manner in which they are affected, but by conceiving what we ourselves should feel in the like situation. Though our brother is upon the rack, as long as we ourselves are at our ease, our senses will never inform us of what he suffers. They never did, and never can, carry us beyond our own person, and it is by the imagination only that we can form any conception of what are his sensations.[22]

Smith argues that sympathy, contrary to popular fear, is not contagious, and that the senses can provide an account only of one's own pain, not that of another. Sympathy for another requires imaginative effort, and must be understood as moral action rather than as an automatic physiologic state.

Similarly, the new anatomists were more likely to abstract sympathy from its social and moral context and examine it simply as a physiological reflex of the healthy body. Both Abernethy and Lawrence, building on Bichat's tissue anatomy, considered sensibility (the capacity for sensation) and irritability (the capacity for motion) as the most fundamental properties of life. Identifying sensation with nerves and motion with muscles, Magendie and Bell first described the spinal reflex arc, and sympathy began to acquire its current physiologic association with the involuntary or "sympathetic" nervous system.

Just as the anatomists bracketed sympathy's moral connotation, the early medical ethicists bracketed its physiologic meaning. John Gregory, who wrote the first ethics for modern medicine, refused to speculate about mind-body sympathy. Granting the inherent interest to the physician of "the laws relating to the mutual influence of the mind and body upon each other," he warns against pursuit of such a subject

which, if we are not on our guard, is apt to lead us insensibly into a labyrinth of metaphysics. A student of genius should be watchful, lest his attention be too deeply engaged by this specious kind of philosophy, which gives so much room for imagination, and so little for experiment; apparently ingenious, but really trifling and useless: a philosophy in short, which by keeping the mind incessantly employed about subtleties of its own creation, soon renders it incapable of a patient and severe investigation of Nature.[23]

Arguing for humility in scientific investigation, Gregory suspends the long discussion of physiologic sympathy, categorizing it as one of the investigations as yet "beyond our reach."[24]

Although suspicious of the discourse of physiologic sympathy, Gregory promotes moral sympathy as the "chief" quality to be cultivated by doctors. Gregory introduces the idea that sympathy requires conscious effort, and is therefore a more complicated combination of feeling and action than previously thought. His model of sympathy requires attention – "attention to a thousand little circumstances that may tend to relieve the patient; an attention which money can never purchase" – and thus differs from the automatic or contagious models of sympathy. Furthermore, it accompanies, rather than counters, reasoned intelligence:

The insinuation that a compassionate and feeling heart is commonly accompanied with a weak understanding and a feeble mind, is malignant and false. Experience demonstrates, that a gentle and human temper, so far from being inconsistent with vigour of mind, is its usual attendant.[25]

Sympathy accompanies the "vigorous" rather than the "feeble" mind, functioning as a sign of mental health rather than of nervous illness, and, significantly, an attribute of the treating doctor rather than the disabled patient.

Gregory also treats scientific method, in addition to bedside practice, as a subject for the medical ethicist. A recurrent theme in his discussions of clinical practice and research methods is the "suspence" necessary to both sympathy and science. Just as sympathy hangs somewhere between imaginative "pity" and cool "composure," science is ideally constituted of warm "imagination" and cool "judgment." Gregory's ideal medical scientist is a man of "two characters": one character is "literary" and "disposed to attend to analogies"; the other is "calm, sedate and attentive to the difference of things seemingly alike."[26] In the best of circumstances, these two characters are "united in the same person":

One may possess that warm and lively imagination, so peculiarly fitted for invention, and, at the same time, a clear, accurate, and sound judgment, that candidly considers every objection to his proposed plans; and, according to the weight of evidence, can either reject them altogether, or preserve his mind in a proper degree of suspence, till their real merit is ascertained. This happy union of genius and understanding, which we so rarely see, constitutes a philosopher of the first rank and dignity.[27]

The scientist of dual character has the capacity to sustain himself in a state of "suspence" or toleration of uncertainty when his imagined theory encounters observed difficulties. Presumably, then, the scientist's imagination does not absolutely construct his observations, nor does his evidence passively impress itself on his mind. This possibility of conflict between expectation and observation requires a capacity to receive, tolerate, and weigh different kinds of knowledge. In these circumstances, the scientist cultivates a provisional, both-and posture, sustaining irresolution until more evidence tips the balance.

Whenever Gregory teaches this negotiation between two kinds of knowledge, he cites Bacon. Yet Gregory's description does not sound much like the strict inductivism usually attributed to Bacon; rather, Gregory recommends a dialectic of speculative and inductive thinking. This dialectical structure, harnessing two ways of knowing without each violating the integrity of the other, reflects a Baconian doctrine less celebrated than inductivism. As discussed in chapter one, Bacon, following Augustine, declared "two books of God": the Book of Scripture and the Book of Nature. Both books were authored by God, the Book of Scripture being his word and the Book of Nature being his works. In *The Advancement of Learning*, Bacon advocated the pursuit of both kinds of knowledge:

Let no man think or maintain that a man can search too far or be too well studied in the book of God's Word or in the book of God's Works, divinity or philosophy, but rather let men endeavour an endless progression of proficience in both.[28]

Bacon continues with a warning that we "not unwisely mingle or confound these learnings together."[29] Each book must maintain its own integrity. Ultimately, both, because they share the same author, will reveal the power of God. But, given the imperfection of current knowledge, each book must be read separately, without the reduction of one to the other. Particularly when examining the Book of Nature, the scientist must maintain a readiness to confess uncertainty:

[I]f in any statement there be anything doubtful or questionable, I would by no means have it surpressed [sic] or passed in silence, but plainly and perspicuously set down by way of note or admonition. For I want this primary history to be compiled with a most religious care, as if every particular were stated upon oath; seeing that it is the book of God's works, and (so far as the majesty of heavenly may be compared with the humbleness of earthly things) a kind of second Scripture.[30]

Studying the Book of Nature requires a humble, almost religious desire to get it right. Thus there is a moral imperative to air uncertainties, to "set them down" as issues that require further investigation. Bacon describes more than skepticism, more than the discarding of questionable evidence; rather, he recommends a state of not knowing, and being aware that one doesn't know – in short, a state of suspense.[31]

Perhaps because Gregory's *Lectures* were addressed to practicing doctors rather than the general public, it fell to nineteenth-century literary writers to develop a more widely accessible language of sympathy. Samuel Taylor Coleridge, like Gregory, worried about the moral consequences of conceiving of sympathy as an involuntary reflex. Steeped in both medical discourse and moral philosophy, Coleridge was concerned that materialist explanations could destroy the concept of moral will, as well as of creative imagination. In *Biographia Literaria*, he coined the famous phrase "the willing suspension of disbelief" as a description of the reader's state of mind. Borrowing possibly from notions of scientific suspense and from Locke's idea of the "will-in-suspense," Coleridge, in an interesting sleight of hand, turns the suspended will into the "willing suspension." Like Gregory, Coleridge makes suspense an activity, a product of the imagination, that permits reception of information. He also calls this suspension of disbelief "poetic faith" and "negative faith," a phrase that anticipates, perhaps, Keats's more difficult concept of negative capability.

Coleridge wrote his *Theory of Life* largely in response to the Abernethy-Lawrence controversy, and, though he was in general supportive of Abernethy, Coleridge considered both to be disappointingly materialist. Mind could be neither the "result of Structure" nor "a supervenient *Fluid*."[32] In his *Theory*, Coleridge again put forward his concept of the active imagination which he had developed in *Biographia Literaria*. For Coleridge, materialism necessitated a passively receptive mental substratum, whereas the imagination clearly "modif[ied] the objects observed." Coleridge offered the following illustration as an analogy for mental activity and passivity:

Most of my readers will have observed a small water-insect on the surface of rivulets, which throws a cinque-spotted shadow fringed with prismatic colours on the sunny bottom of the brook; and will have noticed, how the little animal *wins* its way up against the stream, by alternate pulses of active and passive motion, now resisting the current, and now yielding to it in order to gather strength and a momentary *fulcrum* for a further propulsion. This is no unapt emblem of the mind's self-experience in the art of thinking.[33]

Coleridge argued that the mind pulses between action and reception, both being equally important to thought. As Trevor Levere notes, Wordsworth, in conversation with Coleridge, moved in his poetry from a position that endorsed "wise passivity" of observation to one that embraced a world "half-perceived, half-created," similarly suspended between action and reception. Coleridge in turn complimented Wordsworth for combining "the fine balance of truth in observing, with the imaginative faculty in modifying the objects observed"[34] – both receiving truth from nature and actively molding the information he had gleaned.

Meanwhile, Hazlitt worried about the egotism implied in a Coleridgeo-Wordsworthian definition of the mind. Like Wordsworth and Coleridge, he deplored the passivity of the empiricist model of the mind, but objected to the recruitment of imagination solely for the expression of the self. To the model of an active mind, Hazlitt, in *An Essay on the Principles of Human Action*, added the possibility of active reception, which he called the sympathetic imagination, or disinterestedness. Paradoxical as it sounds, active reception was, by Hazlitt's definition, a mental activity that could be aroused for the detection of otherness. Thus, redefining sympathy as both voluntary and other-directed, Hazlitt found a way out of the automaticity of materialist sympathy as well as the egotistical, appropriative sympathy of the first generation of Romantic poets.

Keats's famous "negative capability" letter was heavily influenced by Hazlitt, whose lectures he was attending. In this letter, Keats defines negative capability as "when man is capable of being in uncertainties, Mysteries, doubts, without any irritable reaching after fact and reason."[35] The phrase "negative capability" implies both an "ability" or positive attribute, and also a "negative" – read receptive – quality, thus resembling Coleridge's "negative faith" as well as Hazlitt's notion of sympathy. In addition, the poet of negative capability is the "objective poet," mirroring Hazlitt's concept of disinterestedness. For both Hazlitt and Coleridge, the exemplar is Shakespeare, who is able to be at once "in" and "out" of his poetry – both the active, imaginative author and also the elusively absent one who defers to the full development of his characters. Recalling Keats's training as an apothecary-surgeon brings his definition of negative capability into further focus. Keats specifically opposes negative capability to "irritability," which for physiologists means the capacity to move, an inherent property of living tissue and a component of the reflex arc. Keats thus calls for an active suspension of reason analogous to the voluntary effort required to abort a motor reflex.

Of course, if Keats rejects physiologic models of sympathy, neither does he precisely embrace previous poetic models: he denounces both Coleridge and Wordsworth as egotists. He seems to be after an active and disinterested model of sympathy like Hazlitt's, but in his letters the concept remains abstract, without flesh. Keats's poems – most notably, "Ode on a Grecian Urn" and "Ode to a Nightingale" – often follow the trajectory of imaginative projection followed by frustration and retreat. It is as if Keats recognizes that identification with the object is both too easy and too egotistical, but runs out of time to generate a more viable model. Mary Shelley, I think, succeeds where Keats fails in elaborating a different kind of sympathy, one that suspends judgment and labors for the understanding of otherness.

THE TEXT OF *FRANKENSTEIN*

Moving between ghost stories and scientific research, and insisting on the validity of both Romantic and materialist points of view, Mary Shelley follows the same vein of Romantic materialism suggested by Hazlitt and by Keats. Her critique targets the variety of ideas about sympathy that relied on the insistent resemblance or identification, magically wrought, materially necessary, or egotistically imagined, between sympathetic participants. The problem with this kind of sympathy, according to Mary Shelley, was that it presupposed sameness and/or passivity as the necessary medium for such communication, and, as a corollary, an easy permeability between bodies and minds, and between people.

In good Gothic form, Shelley uses repetition of structure, doubling of characters, and suggestions of incest to evoke the fear of excessive similitude. The symmetries of *Frankenstein* contribute to a suffocating sensation of enclosure in the novel. The famous "frame" or "box-within-a box" structure of the novel, with Walton's letters to Mrs. Saville surrounding Frankenstein's narration, which in turn surrounds the monster's autobiography, gives this novel about monstrosity a perverse neatness. Of course, there is the well-known doppelganger effect of Frankenstein and his creature, pursuing and pursued by one another, exchanging the roles of master and servant. Similarly, if less overtly, Walton is included in this brotherhood, as each man's rhetoric resembles the others'. Each recounts his story in the same vocabulary and lofty, oratorical style so that, as Beth Newman writes, each narration is less a contrasting point of view than an echoic parallel.[36]

The theme of excessive similitude recurs in the incestuous suggestions regarding the Frankenstein family. Caroline Beaufort is the ward of Victor's father for two years before he marries her. Elizabeth and Victor in the 1818 edition are cousins, and, to Victor, she is his "more than sister." When Victor seems reluctant to marry Elizabeth, Victor's father suspects that Victor views her as a sister, and Elizabeth asks, "But as brother and sister often entertain a lively affection towards each other, without desiring a more intimate union, may not such also be our case?" As a whole, the Frankenstein family is itself a "circle" with all undesirable things "banished" from its enclosure:

Such was our domestic circle, from which care and pain seemed for ever banished. My father directed our studies, and my mother partook of our enjoyments. Neither of us possessed the slightest pre-eminence over the other; the voice of command was never heard amongst us; but mutual affection engaged us all to comply with and obey the slightest desire of each other. (F, 37)

The family's peace and equality is overshadowed by the perfection that prescribes a stultifying harmony, in which each member must "comply" and "obey."

Outside the family circle, each character searches for a reflection of himself, or, seen another way, for the engulfment or ownership of another. Walton desires a friend "whose eyes would reply to mine," wishes to "possess" the stranger Frankenstein "as the brother of my heart," and turns in his failure to seeking the sympathy of his sister, Mrs. Saville (F, 13; F, 22). Frankenstein's desire to create a species of his own stems from a desire for a relationship even closer, less diluted, than fatherhood:

A new species would bless me as its creator and source; many happy and excellent natures would owe their being to me. No father could claim the gratitude of his child so completely as I should deserve their's [sic]. (F, 49)

And, of course, the monster wants a partner just like himself, created by the same "father": "My companion must be of the same species," he warns Frankenstein, "and have the same defects" (F, 140).

Frankenstein incorporates this harmonic ideal into his search for knowledge. Shelley carefully details young Victor's early education, that "train of ideas" imparting "the fatal impulse that led to my ruin" (F, 33). Onto his son's occult reading of Cornelius Agrippa, Paracelsus, and Albertus Magnus, Victor's father superimposes corrective instruction in "modern" science. But modern science does not completely supplant alchemical pseudoscience, despite his father's practical lessons in electricity. Significantly, "by some fatality" (which Frankenstein alternately explains as resistance to paternal authority, disinclination for modern studies, and the "accident" of missing a lecture series), Victor arrives at the university well-versed only in the ancients. There, Victor's attraction to metaphysics continues to threaten his modern education. M. Krempe insists that Victor break with alchemy and embrace "modern natural philosophy." Krempe, a product of an "enlightened and scientific age," appears to be a thoroughgoing empiricist, and Victor rejects with "contempt" his study of dingy "realities" unadorned by metaphysical speculation (F, 41).

In pursuit of harmony, Victor finds his intellectual model in M. Waldman, the Romantic scientist who unifies ancient and modern knowledge for Victor. Waldman, as Anne Mellor demonstrates, resembles Humphrey Davy, the British chemist whose works Shelley had read just prior to writing *Frankenstein*.[37] According to historian of science D. M. Knight, Davy typifies the Romantic movement in science, especially its grand unifying schemes and resemblance to alchemy:

The widespread belief in the unity of matter, the view of chemical synthesis as a union of opposites, and the idea, implicit in Davy's *Consolations*, that the researches of the chemist can somehow cast light on the problems of the existence of God, freedom and immortality, all show an affinity with the alchemical scheme of things.[38]

Waldman wins Victor's confidence by affirming Victor's favorite alchemists: "[T]hese were men to whose indefatigable zeal modern philosophers were indebted for most of the foundations of their knowledge" (F, 42–43). In describing Frankenstein's "fatal" education as a reconciliation of chemistry and alchemy, Shelley reflects negatively on the synthesizing impulse of her Romantic peers – especially on the sort of conversation, mixing Gothic German ghost stories and modern galvanic experiments, that engendered her own dream of horror – the dream which, as she recounts in her 1831 preface, inspired *Frankenstein*.

The Krempe–Waldman contrast furnishes another form of haunting similitude as Frankenstein examines each man's "physiognomy," or physical appearance. The pseudoscience of physiognomy held that the body, especially the face and posture, revealed, or was sympathetic to, the moral and emotional constitution. Thus M. Krempe, the materialist, is "a little squat man, with a gruff voice and repulsive countenance" whereas Waldman presents "an aspect expressive of the greatest benevolence," and a "voice the sweetest I had ever heard" (F, 41). Frankenstein makes harmony of body a criterion for the assessment of ideas: of Krempe he says "the teacher did not prepossess me in favour of the doctrine." By his own admission, Frankenstein is highly prejudiced by his "secluded" childhood, full of "old familiar faces," which "had given me invincible repugnance to new countenances" (F, 40). We are prepared then to expect Frankenstein – if he is "repulsed" by the realistic disharmony of Krempe's ideas and appearance – to be incapable of tolerating the disjunctions of his creature.

When the assumptions of physiognomy were coupled with the notion that the person of sensibility should be highly impressionable, the result was a belief that the sensible body would be soft and susceptible, and extraordinarily responsive to the mind. Throughout *Frankenstein*, characters sicken from mental depression. Beaufort dies of grief, with no other apparent illness, and Frankenstein's father's stroke is precipitated by Elizabeth's death. But Frankenstein himself is the prime exemplar of this model. He palpitates and trembles as he plans his monster, falls into a nervous fever after creating him, and nearly dies after he is accused of Clerval's murder.

A similar physical fragility ruins the DeLacey family after they see the monster. Agatha faints, Safie flees, and Felix is overwhelmed by his terror.

When the monster returns to the cottage he overhears Felix report that "the life of my father is in the greatest danger, owing to the dreadful circumstance that I have related. My wife and my sister will never recover [from] their horror" (F, 134). The very beauty and tender sensitivity that attracted Felix and Safie to one another, promising a sympathy that overleaps racial and linguistic differences, renders them both susceptible to crippling illness.

Sympathy of mind and body can also, however, operate to Frankenstein's advantage. Although Frankenstein's body predictably collapses when he is overwrought, his mind is also capable of directing his body to do its will. When he is accused of Clerval's murder, for instance, he at first sinks with distress and fatigue, but then thinks "it politic to rouse all my strength, that no physical debility might be construed into apprehension or conscious guilt" (F, 171). Later, on his deathbed, Frankenstein reanimates when his spirit soars to admonish Walton's mutineers. Walton writes:

Frankenstein, who had at first been silent, and indeed, appeared hardly to have force enough to attend, now roused himself; his eye sparkled, and his cheeks flushed with momentary vigour. (F, 212)

Frankenstein's sparkling eyes and volitional reanimation contrast sharply with the monster's dull skin and eyes at the time of his creation, at which he is coerced into a life that he will regret.

Indeed, the monster's mind and body have a strangely tangled relation. The monster's mind arises from his material body, but matter does not in turn accurately express his mind. Miserable as he is, he continues to be excessively healthy, easily withstanding extreme cold and hunger, able to cross oceans and scale mountains with incredible speed and dexterity. Psychologically sensitive but somatically impervious, the monster violates the assumptions of sensibility theory.

For men of sensibility who must confront the monster's physical body, it is this lack of correspondence between mind and materiality that is most horrifying; in fact, there is some suggestion that the beholder projects bestiality onto the monster for no other reason than that he cannot tolerate this disjunction. Frankenstein labors to create a "beautiful" creature, and doesn't consider the "lifeless form" ugly; it is only after the creature opens his eyes that Frankenstein is repelled. Note the "contrast" between the "luxuriances" of the monster's body and the "watery" eye, the organ of speculation or consciousness:

How can I describe my emotions at this catastrophe, or how delineate the wretch whom with such infinite pains and care I had endeavoured to form? His limbs were in proportion, and I had selected his features as beautiful. Beautiful! – Great

God! His yellow skin scarcely covered the work of muscles and arteries beneath; his hair was of a lustrous black, and flowing; his teeth of a pearly whiteness; but these luxuriances only formed a more horrid contrast with his watery eyes, that seemed almost of the same colour as the dun white sockets in which they were set, his shrivelled complexion, and straight black lips. (F, 52)

This "horrid contrast" is repeated whenever Frankenstein or Walton observes the monster's facial expression. Walton is also most horrified by the mismatch of the monster's partly decayed flesh and the vitality apparent in his face. Approaching the monster from behind, Walton notes the "mummy"-like texture of the monster's hand. But he is calm until the monster turns and Walton sees his face: "Never did I behold a vision so horrible as his face, of such loathsome, yet appalling hideousness" (F, 216). The men of sensibility in the novel cannot fathom a mismatch of mind and body, or cannot tolerate the disjunction between a body that calls attention to its materiality and a mind that attempts nonetheless to reveal itself through the opacity of that medium.

The plot of *Frankenstein*, then, repeatedly dramatizes the failure of social sympathy. Oddly, however, *Frankenstein*'s readers, from the Romantic period to the present, have uniformly sympathized with the monster. Is reading *Frankenstein* a heuristic exercise, teaching a different kind of sympathy than that posited by Victor Frankenstein and company? I think Shelley may be redefining sympathy as an active reception of difference, rather than a passive transmission necessitating similarity, particularly whenever Shelley emphasizes listening to language, as she does in every near-sympathetic encounter permitted in the novel. Unlike the automatic uniformity of contagious physiologic sympathy, sympathetic listening, or straining to hear what one cannot see, does not happen naturally, but only through attentive exertion. It does not demand identification, but rather accommodates difference.

Shelley is working against a Romantic tradition in which the auditory was used to signify a transcendence of difference. Thomas Frosch points out that the Romantic poets frequently choose "anti-visual images," especially auditory images, in order to stimulate a reformulation of perception. Wordsworth uses mist and light to break down "the eye's hunger for boundaries"; and in the Snowdon episode of *The Prelude* the mist-covered mountain is translated into a roaring sea, visual images dissolving into an aural symphony. Coleridge figures imagination as the Eolian harp, on which Nature plays directly, without mediation. Blake and Shelley "are fond of images that are so complex visually that the eye is unable to follow them securely."[39] Their shifting metaphoricity appeals to all of the senses, according to Frosch, but the fluidity of images requires a "synesthesia," an undifferentiated perception that leaks out of neat perceptual categories.

In celebrating the auditory, Romantic poets were undoubtedly building on eighteenth-century sensibility theory, which often used musical analogies to explain the sympathetic transmission of feeling. G. J. Barker-Benfield notes that George Cheyne repeatedly compares the "sensorium" to a "*Musician*" and the nerves to "*Keys*," and that Newton's vibrations in the ether of the nerves became popularized as "thrills" along "heartstrings."[40] Shelley uses such Romantic analogies in describing the development of her monster's consciousness, but later portrays a mature state in which the monster's sensorium must accommodate conflictual rather than harmonious reception.

In his immature state, the newly created monster experiences fresh, "indistinct" sensorial acuity:

A strange multiplicity of sensations seized me, and I saw, felt, heard, and smelt, at the same time; and it was, indeed, a long time before I learned to distinguish between the operations of my various senses. (F, 97)

Synesthesia here is a developmental stage from which one must learn to "distinguish" differing sensations. One of the first distinctions the monster makes is between the fluid beauty of a bird's song and the "uncouth and inarticulate sounds" in which he tries "to express [his own] sensations" (F, 99). Later, he notes the contrast between the DeLaceys' music, so "divine" as to "enchant" him, and Felix's speech, "sounds that were monotonous, and neither resembling the harmony of the old man's instrument or the songs of the birds" (F, 105). Language, though heard, is not analogous to music, but impure, discordant, and mundane – and ultimately, as the monster learns, more effectual.

Of course, it is not only the difference between language and music, but the more dramatic difference between language and vision that convinces the monster that the evidences of the senses frequently conflict with one another. As Peter Brooks writes, the novel rehearses "the opposition of sight and language, of the hideous body and the persuasive tongue."[41] The eloquent monster presents himself to blind DeLacey, who responds to the monster's verbal overtures with "I am blind, and cannot judge of your countenance, but there is *something in your words* which persuades me that you are sincere" (F, 130, italics added). With the intrusion of the sighted characters, vision interrupts the beginnings of a sympathy based on listening to the persuasive words of the monster.

In fact, listening to language is instrumental in every near-sympathetic encounter with the monster. The monster begs Frankenstein to "hear" him tell his tale; within the space of two pages, I count nine pleas of "Listen to me" or "Hear my tale" (F, 96–97). But, lest we (or Frankenstein) miss the message, the monster touchingly mimes it. Frankenstein narrates his monster's cry for sympathy:

"Thus I relieve thee, my creator," he said, and placed his hated hands before my eyes, which I flung from me with violence: "thus I take from thee a *sight* which you abhor. Still thou canst *listen to me*, and grant me thy compassion." (F, 96, italics added)

Frankenstein is persuaded "at least to listen," and after the tale he admits:

His words had a strange effect upon me. I compassionated him, and sometimes felt a wish to console him; but when I looked upon him, when I saw the filthy mass that moved and talked, my heart sickened, and my feelings were altered to those of horror and hatred. (F, 143)

When Frankenstein hears, he "compassionates," but when he "looks" he is horrified.

Shelley repeats the motif of a hand placed before the eyes in the monster's encounter with William: "As soon as [the child] beheld my form, he placed his hands before his eyes." The monster, intending to "educate" the child, "drew his hand forcibly from his face, and said, 'Child, what is the meaning of this? I do not intend to hurt you; listen to me'" (F, 139). But William, predictably, cannot sort out the difference between the monster's appearance and his verbal appeal – cannot suddenly learn to compartmentalize his visual and verbal sensations – and the encounter ends in his death.

Walton must also shield his vision in order to feel for the monster. "I shut my eyes," writes Walton, and he wisely "dared not again raise my looks upon his face, there was something so scaring and unearthly in his ugliness." As the one sighted person who voluntarily averts his gaze, Walton hears the monster's "voice [which] seemed suffocated." Now Walton's "duty of obeying the dying request of my friend" is "suspended by a mixture of curiosity and compassion" (F, 217). The volitional act of listening interrupts the automatic horror of the man of sensibility, the man looking for harmony in the face of the like-minded. He "suspends" his former associations, tolerating the "mixture" of his uneven response. In this state of active reception, Walton listens to the monster's final speech, which Walton deems a "final and wonderful catastrophe" without which his tale would not be complete. In keeping with the rule of fragile sympathy in the novel, however, Walton "again cast[s] his eyes on the lifeless form of my friend" and "indignation" is "kindled within" him (F, 218).

The reader is, in the end, more successful in sympathizing with the monster than is Walton. Might the blind DeLacey or self-blinded Walton, both temporarily capable of sympathetic listening, be analogues for the reader, demonstrating the active reception involved in construing a text from words alone? If so, then Shelley has more completely articulated a reception theory than has Keats in his more famous theory of negative capability. Shelley, I think, more completely evokes the horror of the "egotistical sublime," and advocates the effort required to suspend sensations in the interests of acting ethically. Combating the narcissism of Romantic theories of physiologic sympathy, Shelley invites the reader to a kind of sympathy based not on identification, but on active accommodation of difference.

CHAPTER 3

Natural supernaturalism in Thomas Carlyle and Richard Owen

If *Frankenstein* articulates the frustrations of an apparent mismatch between body and mind, *Sartor Resartus* promotes a productive dialectic between these two conflicting ways of encountering the world. Carlyle broadens the terms of the specifically human body/soul dichotomy into a dualism of the entire cosmos, and translates those terms into two ways of viewing the world: the natural and supernatural respectively. For Carlyle, the natural perspective alternately conceals and reveals the supernatural, which in turn continually makes and remakes the natural. Although the natural and supernatural points of view are frequently at odds, they neither cancel one another out nor tie one another up in an endless stalemate. Rather, a dialectical conversation between the two modes of explanation produces an organic, continually developing body which gives shape and tangibility to the inner, living experience of the holy. The tailor is retailored; makers are themselves remade. In comparison to Mary Shelley's vision in *Frankenstein*, Carlyle's practitioner of sympathy not only tolerates the conflict between inner and outer points of view, but also finds in their interaction the source of transformation and renewed meaning.

This chapter will argue that Thomas Carlyle, in *Sartor Resartus*, and Richard Owen, in his anatomical writings, both employ two ways of reading one infinite world. Both of them accept – even revel in – disjunctions between prophetic and natural ways of knowing, using those differences to reinvigorate some of the outdated metaphors of natural theology. Both men subscribe to a form of philosophical dualism which destabilizes the traditional hierarchy between spirit and matter. Neither a secularization of religion nor a demonization of matter, Carlyle's natural supernaturalism and Owen's transcendental anatomy both describe a vigorous dialectic between scientific and religious ways of thinking.

Carlyle's oxymoronic shorthand for this interaction – "natural supernaturalism" – has provoked a variety of interpretations, none of which to date adequately captures the dialectical nature of Carlyle's creed. Most influentially, M. H. Abrams, in *Natural Supernaturalism*, adopts Carlyle's phrase to designate a secularization of Christian mythological structures. Rather than apprehending "natural supernaturalism" as a paradox, Abrams reads it as a usurpation, assuming "a displacement from a supernatural to a natural frame of reference."[1] The problem, however, with substituting secularization for natural supernaturalism is that it risks making Carlyle sound too monological, too lopsidedly naturalistic, when in fact *Sartor* exasperatingly breeds dualism after dualism: paradox, irony, dialogue, Nay and Yea, descendentalism and transcendentalism, "glancing from Heaven to Earth and back again," as Carlyle himself described the book. If secularization implies that the supernatural has been subsumed or discarded, the term is inadequate to Carlyle's notion of natural supernaturalism.

Presenting an alternate paradigm to Abrams's natural supernaturalism, Anne Mellor claims *Sartor Resartus* for English Romantic irony, which she defines as "a way of thinking about the world that embraces change and process for their own sake." Philosophically, Mellor writes, the Romantic ironist "sees the world as fundamentally chaotic";[2] artistically, he both enthusiastically creates and skeptically deconstructs his own work. Using the terms set out by Stanley Fish in his *Self-Consuming Artifacts: The Experience of Seventeenth-Century Literature*, Mellor designates *Sartor Resartus* a self-consuming artifact, its salient feature being its medicinal, purgative effects as the self-correcting rhetoric brings the reader to a painful conversion. Although Mellor acknowledges that Carlyle's commitment to teleological change differs from Fish's model, she does not adequately supply an alternative to the "self-consumption" so central to Fish's concept as well as to her own chapter on *Sartor*. As wasteful, conflictual, and intricately dialectical as *Sartor* is, it gets somewhere, and continues to inspire differing Victorians in a similar direction: to a redefinition or remodeling of religious sense. "Be no longer a Chaos," intones Teufelsdrockh, but "Produce! Produce!" and further, "produce it in God's name!" (SR, 149).[3] Clearly, Carlyle is not promoting a system, but he is in *Sartor* elaborating a creed of recognizable shape and substance, as well as calling people into a particular sort of experience and action. Because *Sartor* becomes a social and philosophical chap-book for so many Victorians to follow, because of its aphoristic power and its irritating tendency to lodge its textual idiosyncrasies in the mind, we can hardly call it self-consuming. Carlyle's alternations of prophecy and deflationary critique do not so much cancel as hone one another. The fervor that survives self-critique is infectious indeed, as Carlyle's Victorian readers were soon to demonstrate.

Carlyle's ethical concerns present another problem for making *Sartor Resartus* a prime example of Mellor's version of Romantic irony. In reviewing Clyde Ryals's attempt to extend the genre of Romantic irony into the Victorian period, Mellor raises an objection that applies equally to her own writing on *Sartor*. Ryals has side-stepped, according to Mellor, "the ethical problem implicit in the stance of the romantic ironist: the impossibility of making an enduring commitment to a particular political or moral program that might over time produce greater social or legal justice."[4] The Carlyle of *Sartor Resartus* was certainly committed to a moral program, despite the doubtful justice of his later social and political views. German Romantic ironic "hovering" may indeed preclude ethical commitment, but Carlyle's irony leads less to suspension of judgment than to an injunction to work in the world.

One strand of Carlyle criticism has associated his Romantic irony with the possibility of ethical commitment, crediting *Sartor Resartus* with both the ironic "double vision" that results from the differing voices of Teufelsdrockh and his editor, and the mutual transformation of philosopher and editor by the end of the book. Janice Haney describes the double vision of *Sartor Resartus* as "an empirical self, the editor, facing a metaphysical and aesthetic self, Teufelsdrockh."[5] But they face one another in a dynamic exchange, rather than a static face-off. Although the English editor begins with bluff empirical practicality, he ends by adopting Teufelsdrockh's visionary rhetoric:

What a result, should this piebald, entangled, hyper-metaphorical style of writing, not to say of thinking, become general among our Literary men! . . . Thus has not the Editor himself, working over Teufelsdrockh's German, lost much of his own English purity? (SR, 221)

Similarly, Teufelsdrockh takes on some of the editor's practical concerns, descending from his German tower and traveling to London to take up a new phase of work among the English. Thus the double vision or, perhaps better, dialogue between the two points of view effects a transformation in each.

Focusing also on the exchange between the editor and Teufelsdrockh, Wolfgang Iser reads *Sartor Resartus* as a paradigm for cross-cultural discourse. The dialogue produces not an "overarching third dimension" but "an interlinking network" that defies existing generic categories.[6] This discourse is transformative, in that neither of the cultures concerned remains the same. In *Sartor*, Teufelsdrockh's transcendentalism meets the editor's empiricism, each defamiliarizing and restructuring the other.

"Transcendentalism," writes Iser, "is neither assimilated nor appropriated, but 'clothed' in such a manner that its repatterning can serve the self-regeneration of an empirically oriented culture."[7] Iser is concerned with the encounter between German and English cultures, but his characterization of each culture suggests a cross-fertilization between primarily scientific and primarily religious ways of thinking.

The religious and ethical impact of *Sartor Resartus* is particularly impressive in the testimonies of a number of Victorian scientists. The scientific publicists in particular – men like T. H. Huxley, John Tyndall, Francis Galton, Herbert Spencer, and John Morley – were, by their own admission, deeply influenced by *Sartor Resartus*. Huxley, for instance, remembered "the bracing wholesome influence of [Carlyle's] writings when, as a very young man, I was essaying without rudder or compass to strike out a course for myself."[8] And Tyndall wrote that "through three long cold German winters Carlyle placed me in my tub, even when ice was on its surface, at five o-clock every morning – not slavishly, but cheerfully, meeting each day's studies with a resolute will."[9] Carlyle, however, was no advocate of science or scientists. *Sartor* opens, after all, with a diatribe against the piercing light of "the Torch of science":

Man's whole life and environment have been laid open and elucidated; scarcely a fragment or fibre of his Soul, Body, and Possessions, but has been probed, dissected, distilled, desiccated, and scientifically decomposed. (SR, 3–4)

In his first two paragraphs, Carlyle sets up his philosophy of clothes against the cutting light of modern anatomy. Why then should Carlyle have proved so inspirational to these scientists? Frank Turner argues convincingly that Carlyle's appeal to the scientists arose from "his call for a new social and intellectual elite."[10] Feeling themselves superior in talent and in moral truthfulness to their opponents in the Church, these men were empowered by Carlyle's anti-clerical brand of spiritualism and his charged call to work in the world. But, like M. H. Abrams, Turner interprets Carlyle's "Natural Supernaturalism" as a secularization without distinguishing extra-ecclesiastical spirituality from materialism. Failing adequately to take into account the incessantly metaphysical quality of Carlyle's thought, Turner claims that, by using religious language to affirm the natural world, Carlyle "eased the transition from a religious apprehension of the universe to a scientific and secular one."[11]

Of course it is possible that the scientific publicists willfully misread Carlyle, or adapted his thought to their own purposes. But there remains a religious element in their testimony. As Huxley famously wrote, Carlyle taught him "that a deep sense of religion was compatible with the entire absence of theology."[12] Perhaps we need to reformulate the relationship between that "sense of religion" and scientific naturalism. There is one prominent scientist, for instance, vocal on the issue of maintaining a sense of religion in science, whom Turner has overlooked: Sir Richard Owen. Carlyle and Owen shared personal and intellectual respect for one another, exchanging social visits and consulting one another professionally. Carlyle, rarely complimentary to scientists, said of Owen that "hardly twice in London have I met with any articulate-speaking biped who told me a thirtieth-part so many things I knew not and wanted to know."[13] Owen, as famously cantankerous as Carlyle, for his part evinced a "delight in Carlyle" which one diarist found "refreshing to witness."[14] As a friend and a philosophical collaborator of Carlyle's, Owen should be considered in any reexamination of natural supernaturalism, particularly one that asks how nineteenth-century scientists interpreted Carlyle.

Owen was arguably the foremost British naturalist of the pre-Darwinian period, the founder of the Museum of Natural History – then the natural history department of the British Museum. But because he was an antagonist of Darwin's, Owen's history has been nearly obliterated by the Darwin Industry. Admittedly, Owen makes an unglamorous subject for historical inquiry. He was possessed of a passionate temper, and was by some accounts professionally jealous and vituperative. Moreover he espoused, from our point of view, the "wrong" theories, at first his transcendental anatomy and eventually, contra Darwin, a theistic evolution. In his version of continental transcendental anatomy, Owen grafted idealist philosophy onto keen scientific observation of the natural world. Owen compared vertebrate skeletons in an effort to construe an "archetype" or ideal plan underpinning the various actual skeletons of different species. For Owen, the archetype was a schematic model which expressed the concept in the mind of God, "what Plato would have called the 'Divine Idea,'" out of which the variety of species were created.

Like Carlyle, Owen was a devout believer in God (although, more explicitly than Carlyle, he was a practicing Christian). His motto when knighted was: "Scientia et Pietate," or science and piety.[15] And his most ostentatious monument, the Natural History Museum, gives us Owen in a nutshell. Designed by Waterhouse, the building has the architecture "of a Romanesque cathedral . . . complete with side chapels," yet it was stuffed full of fragments of dead matter, documenting the changing history of nature.[16] This is not to say that Owen resembled at all what Americans would later call the creation scientist. He refused to sign a theological treatise defending Biblical literalism from scientific investigation. On the other hand, he opposed Darwin on the grounds of his materialism, rather than on the grounds of his evolutionary theory. Owen was for rigorous, serious science and equally serious, if entirely unconventional, faith.

Espousing an equable co-existence between science and religion, Owen belonged to the tradition of natural theology. However, he revised the old Paleyan, and even the more recent Cuvierean, versions of natural theology. While Paley found evidence of God in the contrivances which suited organisms to their surroundings, and Cuvier, more specifically in the functional relationships which demonstrated that suitability, Owen emphasized the morphological similarities which to him suggested a unified "Divine Idea" overarching the species of vertebrates. As Nicolaas Rupke aptly summarizes,

By changing from functional to transcendental anatomy, Owen placed the argument from design on a new footing. With his notion of archetypes, he shifted the evidence for the existence of a Supreme Designer from concrete adaptations to an abstract plan . . . Divine contrivance was to be recognised, not so much any more in the characteristics of individual species, but in their common ground-plan. God was no longer the Supreme Watchmaker, but the Supreme Architect who had personally conceived the blueprint of nature but employed natural laws for the actual construction work.[17]

Rupke emphasizes Owen's revision of the design argument: God is Owen's "Supreme Architect" but he uses "natural" methods, playing out his divine plan via the operation of physical "laws." The plan is transcendental, the operation natural.

Owen achieved this dual formulation in part by grafting German idealism onto English empiricism. As Adrian Desmond writes,

Owen needed a sensible alternative to transmutation embedded in a non-materialist framework, and he too turned to German transcendentalism, which he blended and muted with a liberal appeal to law. Far from the sterile hybrid that [T. H.] Huxley would have us believe, the union was astonishingly productive . . . [I]t gave him the ideal Archetype, the "primal pattern" on which all vertebrates were based.[18]

But, as with Carlyle, the transcendental-empirical hybrid was bound to be awkward. Owen opens his influential essay *On the Nature of Limbs*, written in 1849, with a confession of his difficulty in communicating German ideas to a British audience:

A German anatomist, addressing an audience of his countrymen, would feel none of the difficulty which I experienced. His language, rich in the precise expression of philosophic abstractions, would instantly supply him with the word for the idea he meant to convey; and that word would be "Bedeutung."[19]

Owen wants to discuss the *Bedeutung* – the signification or essential meaning – of limbs, but he finally settles on the English "nature." Here he signals the English tradition of natural history, and even more specifically natural theology, which persisted much longer in England than on the Continent. Owen probably succeeded in importing transcendental anatomy largely because natural theology provided him with a pre-existing British model for integrating religion and science.

As discussed in my first chapter, one of the central doctrines of natural theology was that God provided "two books" for human study, the Book of Scripture and the Book of Nature. Owen appreciated the possibilities offered by a specifically textual formulation of traditional Christian dualism. That is, instead of envisioning two separate realms, the natural and the supernatural, Owen emphasized two texts providing *two ways of reading* one world. In a speech to the YMCA, Owen chastises Christians for fearing the advance of scientific knowledge:

Has aught that is essentially Christian suffered – have its truths ceased to spread and be operative in mankind – since physical doctrines, supposed or "declared contrary to Holy Writ," have been established? Cease, then, to take alarm at each new ray of light that dawns upon the field of Divine Power, till now dark to our comprehension: for be assured, there remain many others yet to be illuminated by His predestined instruments. The light, bright as it is, contrasted with the darkness it has dispersed, penetrates but a short way into the illimitable theatre of the operation of infinite power. The known is very small compared with the knowable.[20]

For Owen there is no strict division between the realms described by the two books: there is simply the "known," the potentially "knowable," and between them the shifting cusp of scientific knowledge. Both known and knowable, though as different in appearance as light and dark, belong to the "field of Divine Power." What changes is simply the degree of human comprehension. But, Owen cautions, however long human science marches forward, the infinite world will exceed its comprehension – not because of some difference in kind, but because of the huge scope of infinitude that will forever shrink the human perspective. Owen is both pro-science, countering dogmatic Christian fears, and yet humble about its prospects.

In the final paragraph of *On the Nature of Limbs*, Owen suggests a theist evolution by employing one of Carlyle's central metaphors, that of clothes for outward appearances. Owen casts the various species as temporal clothing for the divine archetype. He writes:

We learn from the past history of our globe that she has advanced with slow and stately steps, guided by the archetypal light, amidst the wreck of worlds, from the first embodiment of the Vertebrate idea under its old Ichthyic vestment, until it became arrayed in the glorious garb of the Human form.[21]

Owen reconciles his archetype with evolutionary theory by differentiating between the unchanging divine idea and its manifold expression as a succession of species. This textual form of Platonic dualism becomes a tool for Owen's insight into evolutionary change.

Although Owen was in the end an antagonist of Darwin's, his archetypes nonetheless demonstrated the "homologies" (similarities of anatomical form between species) which Darwin later attributed to common evolutionary descent rather than divine plan. It might be helpful at this point to differentiate Owen's transcendental anatomy from Darwin's later natural selection because it is difficult to shed our Darwinian perspective when thinking about the anatomical relationships between animals. From a post-Darwinian point of view, the similarities between different vertebrate species indicate their close relationship in the evolutionary tree. For instance, vertebrate species have a more recent common ancestor than invertebrate species, which show greater morphological difference. That is, anatomical relationships are explained by the evolutionary proximity or distance between species, rather than by a transcendental pattern in the divine plan. The key difference is Darwin's introduction of change over time – the notion that species have a history. In the back of his personal copy of *On the Nature of Limbs*, Darwin had jotted: "I look at Owen's Archetypes as more than ideal, as a real representation as far as the most consummate skill & loftiest generalization can represent the parent form of the Vertebrata" – in short, it was the best guess at what the real ancestor had looked like.[22] Neatly substituting the real for the ideal, the archetype becomes for Darwin a real parent – "more than ideal," clearly a more satisfying theory to Darwin's taste. As Adrian Desmond puts it, Owen's archetypes become Darwin's ancestors. For Darwin, the archetype is merely a representation of a less differentiated – and therefore earlier – evolutionary type.

Desmond credits Owen and his transcendental circle (whom he designates the "medical Coleridgeans") with laying the groundwork for evolution through the use of Biblical and organic imagery: "With their tree of life, the medical Coleridgeans had unwittingly established a metaphoric image ready for a definitive Darwinian gloss."[23] Complimenting Owen on the contribution he made to evolutionary thinking, he writes:

In practical terms [the archetype] was simply a picture of a generalised or schematic vertebrate; but this in itself provided him with a *standard* by which to gauge the degree of specialisation of fossil life, and in 1853 he saw it as an indispensable aid in determining the true pattern of emergence "of new living species."[24]

That Owen was in 1853 contemplating, in Owen's own words, "new living species" reflects his belief in successive stages of creation, itself closer to evolution than to orthodox Biblical literalism.

Owen may indeed have been on the verge of some model of transmutation, but was it inevitable that transcendental anatomy should have been discredited by Darwinian evolution? Nicolaas Rupke demonstrates that the concepts of archetype and ancestor did coincide briefly for some thinkers. He quotes the following from an article on "Vertebral patterns" in an 1863 issue of the *Medical Times and Gazette*: "We rather prefer to believe that the archetypal vertebrate skeleton, whatever exact form it might have possessed, was once manifested in the flesh, as an objective entity, than conceive it merely as a process of the Creator's thought."[25] Rupke then goes on to comment that transcendental anatomy and evolutionary theory were not of necessity mutually exclusive:

The article in the *Medical Times* demonstrated that it was possible to think of Owen's vertebrate archetype as both an ideal blueprint and a real ancestor; or – to translate this into terms of personalities – that one could bring Owen and Darwin together, at least on this crucial point.[26]

Difficult as it is for post-Darwinians to imagine, it is important to recognize the prevalence in the mid-nineteenth century of this both-and position (both archetypes and ancestors; both science and religion) without necessarily dismissing it as a last-ditch, bad-faith effort of natural theologians to make peace with the Darwinians. Many seemed genuinely to find no contradiction in holding both positions without reducing one to the other.

Often the scientists who occupied the inclusive position with regard to archetypes and ancestors were doctors, and often readers of Carlyle. Nicolaas Rupke, finding an ideological explanation for this alliance, names the group "metropolitan, upwardly mobile Carlyleans."[27] According to

Rupke, these physicians were in the middle, between the Oxbridge natural theologians and the radical materialists:

The emphasis on "form", by being part of the wider acceptance of German Roman-ticism, provided Owen and his London colleagues with a suitable philosophical framework for a metropolitan, as opposed to Oxbridge, intellectual culture. There were only two philosophies of nature in Victorian Europe in which religious belief was given a place. One was the increasingly antiquated-sounding natural theol-ogy, the other was some form of Romantic *Naturphilosophie*. Owen and many of his Edinburgh- and Paris-educated *confrères* were not irreligious, yet at the same time they did not belong to the Oxbridge establishment; they were "MDs", not "DDs".[28]

The upwardly mobile city doctors were not only part of a rising middle class, they were also occupying a middle ground between the traditional professions of physician and surgeon. General practitioners, many of whom were followers of Owen, were trying to combine the philosophical approach of the physician with the hands-on intervention of the surgeon. They were, in effect, philosophical dualists with a growing regard for the body as the locale for health and for disease. They realized the body – especially the corpse – held the answers to many questions originally posed as philo-sophical problems. Anatomy, for them, supported rather than supplanted transcendental philosophy.[29] It revealed affinities of form that suggested archetypal resemblances.

Owen's transcendental anatomy not only sounds like Carlyle's natural supernaturalism, they are at bottom the same doctrine: what I have been calling Romantic materialism. Reading Owen and his camp confirms that there was a prominent middle position between traditional religionists and radical materialists. General practitioners, comparative anatomists, and many early evolutionary theorists sustained a both-and regard for religion and natural science, particularly in the form of a transcendental-empirical hybrid. Judging from the understanding between Carlyle and Owen, and the influence both exercised on pre-Darwinian culture, this position was not so inconsistent, not so paradoxical as it appears to the post-Darwinian reader.

Sartor Resartus, though fully a fiction, remains the most extensive expo-sition of the philosophical position underpinning Romantic materialism. What then, does "Natural Supernaturalism" mean in Carlyle's discourse? In his chapter entitled "Natural Supernaturalism," Carlyle plunges scientific and religious language into ironic juxtaposition. Taking a page from the book of Job, Carlyle transforms the scientist into a Job figure, the righteous man with a justifiable complaint. Just as Job, who requests an explanation for his undeserved suffering, is answered by the voice of God in a litany of questions, so also is the "scientific individual" met with a series of rhetorical questions:

Was man with his *Experience* present at the Creation, then, to see how it all went on? Have any deepest *scientific* individuals yet dived down to the foundations of the Universe, and gauged every thing there? Did the Maker take them into His counsel; that they read His ground-plan of the incomprehensible All; and can say, This stands marked therein, and no more than this, Alas, not in anywise! These *scientific* individuals have been nowhere but where we also are; have seen some handbreadths deeper than we see into the Deep that is infinite, without bottom as without shore. (SR, 194; my emphases)

Empirical man ("the man with his Experience") errs, not by exploring his "handbreadths" into the Deep, but by assuming that his empirical perspective could encompass, or establish a set of laws for, the infinite. Useful as the human perspective may be, the divine trumps it for Carlyle: the voice from the whirlwind silences even the most righteous (insofar as he goes) scientist.

A contrast is raised, not between Nature, ruled by scientific law, and "Supernature," ruled by religious law, but between human and divine perspectives on the same Nature/Supernature. Teufelsdrockh fields the following question which he imagines from the lips of the conventionally religious: "But is not a real Miracle simply a violation of the Laws of Nature?" (SR, 194). He replies, "What are the Laws of Nature? To me perhaps the rising of one from the dead were no violation of these Laws, but a confirmation; were some far deeper Law" (SR, 194). Teufelsdrockh blurs boundaries between natural and supernatural realms by arguing that the supernatural can be attributed to the natural once its laws are discovered, and that the supernatural is also law-abiding, even if humans are not acquainted with this "deeper Law." Nature and the supernatural become one continuous fabric, divided only by the shifting cusp of human knowledge. As the Duke of Argyll suggested in his interpretation of Carlyle, the two texts might more properly be labeled the "human" and the "super-human," with the divide resting between the humanly explained and the as-yet beyond human knowledge, which extends infinitely.[30]

If we interpret natural supernaturalism with less emphasis on an inevitable secularization, and more on the possibilities of a religio-scientific bitextuality, much of Carlyle's thought that has eluded understanding becomes startlingly clear. His position on religion, for instance, seems less inscrutable. In a letter to John Sterling, Carlyle responds to Sterling's concern that Teufelsdröckh does not believe in a "personal God." "A grave charge," writes Carlyle, "an awful charge: to which, if I mistake not, the Professor laying his hand on his heart will reply with some gesture expressing the solemnest denial." Carlyle is coy, certainly, and we suspect that he has Teufelsdröckh engage in a degree of mock solemnity. But Carlyle was an earnest friend of Sterling's; Sterling wrote Carlyle's biography, appreciating his friend's doubts as well as respecting his sometimes unorthodox faith. In a more serious mood, Carlyle reassures Sterling that "I am neither Pagan nor Turk, nor circumcised Jew, but an unfortunate Christian individual resident at Chelsea in this year of Grace." Carlyle stipulates in highly particular terms his own historical situation: his "unfortunate" state of mind, his "Christian" religious affiliation, his "Chelsea" neighborhood, and his date "this year of Grace," which the letter tells us is 1835. At the same time, Carlyle admits to only the vaguest of creeds. He writes, "By God's blessing, one has got two eyes to look with; also a mind capable of knowing, of believing: that is all the creed I will at this time insist on." Note his phrase "two eyes": here is Carlyle's famous double vision, boiled down to knowing and believing, historical specificity and faith in a divinity beyond time and space.

Of course, this insistence on both history and faith closely follows the pattern that German hermeneutic philosophers like Ast and Schleiermacher dubbed the hermeneutic circle. According to these thinkers (discussed at length in chapter one), interpretation of texts required endless tacking back and forth between research into the historical context and a more spiritual or intuitional "divining" of the intent of the writer. As most critics agree, Carlyle wasn't so much concerned with a faithful translation of German thought, but rather with adapting it to his own British audience. Suzy Anger argues that Carlyle blends German hermeneutics with Calvinist textual exegesis:

In Carlyle's hand, transcendental idealism takes a decidedly textual turn . . . Carlyle grafts onto the ideas he finds in idealism the notion of the world as a text, and the synthesis becomes a formula for the necessity of unending interpretation in pursuit of the meaning of the divine text.[31]

Anger attributes Carlyle's textual turn to his native training in Biblical exegesis. Although Anger examines primarily the way in which Carlyle treats history as a text requiring endless interpretation, the same can be said of Carlyle's treatment of science. In *Sartor Resartus*, the Book of Nature demands endless interpretive activity.

Carlyle identifies science and religion as two languages in intimate dialogue about the same infinite world, and in this he subtly alters the bitextual position of natural theology: rather than two texts – the Book of Scripture and the Book of Nature – he proclaims one text with two different modes of interpretation. One of his goals is to reveal the complexity of nature as a text, and the difference between scientific and religious modes of interpretation:

We speak of the Volume of Nature: and truly a Volume it is, – whose Author and Writer is God. To read it! Dost thou, does man, so much as well know the Alphabet thereof? With its Words, Sentences, and grand descriptive Pages, poetical and philosophical, spread out through Solar Systems, and Thousands of Years, we shall not try thee. It is a Volume written in celestial hieroglyphs, in the true Sacred-writing; of which even Prophets are happy that they can read here a line and there a line. As for your Institutes, and Academies of Science, they strive bravely; and, from amid the thick-crowded, inextricably intertwisted hieroglyphic writing, pick out, by dextrous combination, some Letters in the vulgar Character, and therefrom put together this and the other economic Recipe, of high availing Practice. That Nature is more than some boundless Volume of such Recipes, or huge, well-nigh inexhaustible Domestic-Cookery Book, of which the whole secret will, in this wise, one day, evolve itself, the fewest dream. (SR, 195–196)

Nature and the supernatural – both authored by God – thus become one very thick, complicated, and continuous text, beyond complete human understanding. The Book of Nature, considered by natural theologians to be the province of science, becomes in Carlyle's vision more properly a volume for the prophets. Science produces merely an "economic recipe" extracted from the hieroglyphs of nature. Prophets likewise glean only "here a line and there a line," but Carlyle suggests their narrative procedure is more promising an approach for the "grand descriptive Pages, poetical and philosophical . . . written . . . in the true Sacred-writing." The scientific recipe, in its concise "economy," is undoubtedly for Carlyle of "high availing practice," but prophets are better equipped to plumb the deep text of nature.

Of course, dualisms – of essence and appearance, spirit and matter, mind and body – whether Platonic, Christian, or Cartesian, are currently so out of favor that it may seem perverse to revisit them. Do we merely find, in Owen and Carlyle, the same old Western dualism that demeans matter, and that has long been deployed for the oppression of women, minorities, and the working class? George Levine worries that this may be the case, but nonetheless recognizes the ways in which Carlyle departs from Descartes. According to Levine, Carlyle serves an apprenticeship with Cartesian thought in "seeking to transcend the body." But, despite his heritage of Cartesian and religious mind-body dualism, Carlyle reluctantly returns to bodily language:

[Carlyle] invented a narrative that, by confronting the body directly, might be able ultimately to conquer it. Through metaphor and narrative, rather than through abstract philosophical discourse, he tried to find a way both to accept the inescapable reality of the body and to transcend it. So his prose reflects an obsession with things bodily, a very powerful sense that the body is always there, always in danger of taking command.[32]

Levine formulates Carlyle's difficult position as a fundamental distaste for the unfortunately necessary body. I think, particularly if we read the last three chapters of *Sartor* closely, we find that Carlyle is a dualist with a penchant for the material world. If Cartesian dualism prefers the mind, Carlylean dualism conversely elevates the body. True, in the chapters preceding and culminating in "Natural Supernaturalism," Carlyle shows the "Actual" bodily yearning toward the "Real" spirit. But when ethical push comes to shove, matter matters more. The final, seemingly miscellaneous chapters show the spirit caring for the ethically compelling body. Carlyle not only needs the body, as Levine argues, but he also affirms it.

I find in natural supernaturalism – as expounded by Carlyle and Owen – a special kind of mind-matter dualism in the tradition that Elaine Scarry has named "volitional materialism."[33] The volitional materialist consistently chooses the body, a choice that Scarry finds breath-taking precisely because the dualist has, at least in theory, the option of insisting on spiritual primacy. In conventional dualism, matter is real, but the world of the spirit has moral authority. For the volitional materialist like Carlyle, these functions are reversed: the spirit has ontological authority, and the body has ethical priority. When it comes to epistemology, true knowledge is possible only when each way of thinking is *for* the other. This amounts to being *for* matter rather than restricted to it. Matter matters, but not because it adequately accounts for the sum of all existence; rather, it matters because it points beyond itself. Conversely, the spirit is incessantly solicitous of the material world. Ontology and ethics become inverse operations, both necessary for right knowing.

Carlyle's movement from the transcendental high of "Natural Supernaturalism" to the descendental satire of "The Dandiacal Body" and "Tailors" has been remarked by a few but not yet fully considered. Let me briefly recap Carlyle's own version of natural supernaturalism, particularly in his chapter by that name, before discussing at more length his perplexing descent and farewell.

Carlyle first emphasizes how completely natural supernaturalism differs from scientific naturalism. His chapter summary begins: "Deep Significance of Miracles. Littleness of human Science." This is not, however, because

miracles are phenomena apart from the natural order, but because of the
"Divine Incomprehensibility of Nature." The bulk of chapter eight focuses
on how Space and Time are "appearances only; forms of human thought"
(SR, 248). For Carlyle, Time and Space are the ultimate clothes to be
removed. He envisions the world's apocalyptic divestment of temporal and
spatial attire:

> Thus, like a God-created, fire-breathing Spirit-host, we emerge from the Inane;
> haste stormfully across the astonished Earth; then plunge again into the Inane.
> Earth's mountains are levelled, and her sense filled up, in our passage: can the
> Earth, which is but a dead vision, resist Spirits which have reality and are alive?
> On the hardest adamant some foot-print of us is stamped in; the last Rear of the
> host will read traces of the earliest Van. But whence: – O Heaven, whither? Sense
> knows not; Faith knows not; only that it is through Mystery to Mystery, from God
> and to God. (SR, 201–202)

Shucking off these final clothes, Carlyle careens through a compressed
narrative time, defying spatial volume and mass alike. "We" – that is, the
whole parade of human "Spirits" – level the Earth and impress it with
burning footprints. "Can the Earth," asks Teufelsdrockh, "which is but a
dead vision, resist Spirits which have reality and are alive?" Spirits are real,
for Carlyle; they leave footprints. The supernatural perspective is, bizarrely,
the most solid and sound one.

Although "we" humans become "Spirits" more real than the "Earth" in
Carlyle's compressed vision, he swiftly deflates any sense he might have
created of human primacy. Turning to Shakespeare, he quotes:

> We *are such stuff*
> As Dreams are made of, and our little Life
> Is rounded with a sleep!
>   (SR, 202, italics Carlyle's)

In *The Tempest*, of course, "We are such stuff / As dreams are made *on*."
Carlyle, whether carelessly or intentionally, makes us thoroughly and inextricably *both* stuff *and* dreams (and his italics particularly emphasize the
"stuff"). Like Byron's formulation "half dust, half deity," Carlyle's rendering of Shakespeare is a form of Romantic irony. In contrast to Byron's wry
wit, Carlyle's is the irony of Shakespearean tragicomedy. Human "Life"
(though capitalized in Carlyle's version) is "little," and circumscribed – but
how gently, in Shakespeare's treatment, how delicately "rounded with a
sleep!" (The exclamation mark, needless to say, is also Carlyle's.) And this
is how Carlyle closes chapter eight, with uncharacteristic modesty, letting
Shakespeare have the last word. At the transcendental height of "Natural

Supernaturalism," the poet-prophet, the ultimate interpreter of the supernatural, shrinks time and space and human presence – and this, according
to Carlyle, is the "Real" perspective.

After Carlyle has pierced the clothes of time and space in his chapter entitled "Natural Supernaturalism," he returns to the confusion of the body and
the present time. Carlyle envisioned his chapters on Dandies and Tailors as
a shift toward the practical implications of natural supernaturalism. In the
summary of the chapter immediately following "Natural Supernaturalism,"
entitled "Circumspective," he writes, "Practical inferences enough will follow" (SR, 248). And, in a transitional paragraph between his thoughts
on dandies and tailors, he writes, "Thus, however, has our first Practical
Inference from the Clothes-Philosophy, that which respects Dandies, been
sufficiently drawn; and we come now to the second, concerning Tailors."
Of course, given the genre, Carlyle may simply be mocking the practical.
Dandies and tailors, as "cloth-animals, creatures that live, move, and have
their being in Cloth," may be no more than a comic literalization of the
clothes philosophy, rendered with Biblical overtones. But commentators
have tended to agree that Carlyle descends from the heights of theory to
the grass roots of practice in these final chapters. Haney, Anger, and Levine
sense that Carlyle sets out a practical ethics. But what exactly is Carlyle
advocating? I propose that Carlyle, in addressing these cloth-animals, aligns
himself absurdly with the anatomist in caring deeply enough about the
minutiae of material life to cut to its core. Furthermore, he aligns himself
even more fully with the transcendental anatomist, like Owen, in cutting
only for the purpose of re-fabricating, as does the tailor, a sense of the whole.
If the dandy is a "Clothes-wearing Man," then the tailor is a Clothes-making
Man (SR, 207). And, in Carlyle's vision, making, or tailoring, is an obsession with matter, or things made, for the purpose of reimagining spirit, or
a holistic sense of purpose.

In "The Dandiacal Body," Carlyle first lampoons the materialist dandy
who fetishizes clothes. The editor foolishly raises the dandy to the status of
poet, the "Poet of Cloth," who demonstrates a similarity to the "Prophetic
character" ennobled by Teufelsdrockh's philosophy. "Is there not," writes
the editor, "in this Life-devotedness to Cloth, in this so willing sacrifice
of the Immortal to the Perishable, something (although in reverse order)
of that blending and identification of Eternity with Time, which, as we
have seen, constitutes the Prophetic character?" (SR, 207). It is a minor
difference, according to the editor's silly logic, this reversal of priority that
makes the Perishable more important than the Immortal – otherwise, there
is a good deal of similarity between the dandy and the prophet of natural

supernaturalism. Teufelsdrockh then ironically tops the editor's blindness
with his discussion of dandyism as a religious sect, so devoted to literal
clothes as to commit a new "Fetish-worship" in the old tradition of "that
primeval Superstition, *Self-Worship*." He pronounces "*Fashionable Novels*"
their sacred texts, and ransacks Bulwer-Lytton's *Pelham* for the dandy's
"Articles of Faith." It now becomes clear why Carlyle uses the title "The
Dandiacal *Body*" rather than simply "The Dandy" for this chapter. If in fact
matter becomes all important, then why not apply the scientific tools of
material knowledge to the dandy himself? The editor transforms the dandy
into a cadaver, a "(stuffed) parchment-skin" and wonders why "Him no
Zoologist classes among the Mammalia, no Anatomist dissects with care:
when did we see any injected Preparation of the Dandy, in our Museums;
any specimen of him preserved in spirits?" (SR, 207, 208). Similarly,
Teufelsdrockh wishes to lay "fully open" the "physiognomy and physiology of the Dandiacal Body" (SR, 211). The dandiacal *body* scores as much
satire as dandiacal religion.

Before he closes the chapter, however, Carlyle balances his critique. Not
only does he laugh at the materialist as a fetishist, he also savages the dualist who neglects material human need. Carlyle is at his most cutting in
the final half of "The Dandiacal Body," when he has Teufelsdrockh divide
England between the mock-religious "Dandiacal Sect" (who choose to worship clothes) and the mock-mock-religious "Poor-Slaves" (who "choose" to
"worship" an entirely different set of "clothes"):

[The Poor-Slaves] appear to imitate the Dandiacal Sect in their grand principle of wearing a peculiar Costume . . . Their raiment consists of innumberable
skirt, lappets, and irregular wings, of all cloths and of all colours . . . It is fastened
together by a multiplex combination of buttons, thrums, and skewers; to which
frequently is added a girdle of leather, of hempen or even of straw rope, round the
loins. To straw rope, indeed, they seem partial, and often wear it by way of sandals.
(SR, 213)

Rags receive the kind of curious and detailed attention that Carlyle heaps
on the elaborate toilette of the dandy. Carlyle's irony in treating dandyism
as a religion is doubled in treating poverty as a similarly religious choice. In
Teufelsdrockh's diatribe, poverty and obedience become voluntary religious
offerings, rather than injustices suffered by the poor:

Something Monastic there appears to be in [the Poor-Slaves'] Constitution: we
find them bound by the two Monastic Vows, of Poverty and Obedience; which
Vows, especially the former, it is said, they observe with strictness; nay, as I have

understood it, they are pledged, and be it by any solemn Nazarene ordination or not, irrevocably enough consecrated thereto, even *before* birth. (SR, 213)

Like Swift's narrator in "A Modest Proposal," Carlyle's narrator in "The Dandiacal Body" is affecting tone deafness – suggesting mildly and modestly what in fact makes the author's blood boil – the double injustice of the entire spiritual failure to comprehend material injury in the first place.

In "The Dandiacal Body," Carlyle also formulates the fear of class warfare that later animates Disraeli's discussion of "the Two Nations": "To me it seems probable that the two Sects will one day part England between them; each recruiting itself from the intermediate ranks, till there be none left to enlist on either side" (SR, 216). Before he closes the chapter, Teufelsdrockh as poet-prophet works himself into a more apocalyptic mode than he reached even in "Natural Supernaturalism." Comparing the two classes to the oppositely charged poles of an electric battery, "Drudgism the Negative, Dandyism the Positive," Teufelsdrockh rages:

[O]ne attracts hourly towards it all the Positive Electricity of the nation (namely, the Money thereof); the other is equally busy with the Negative (that is to say the Hunger), which is equally potent. Hitherto you see only partial transient sparkles and sputters: but wait a little, till the entire nation is in an electric state; till your whole vital Electricity, no longer healthfully Neutral, is cut in to two isolated portions of Positive and Negative (of Money and of Hunger); and stands there bottled up in two World-Batteries! The stirring of a child's finger brings the two together; and then – What then? The Earth is but shivered into impalpable smoke by the Doom's-thunder-peal; the Sun misses one of his Planets in Space, and henceforth there are no eclipses of the Moon. – Or better still, I might liken (SR, 217)

At this point the editor cuts Teufelsdrockh off with "Oh! Enough, enough," complaining that Teufelsdrockh is "still scenting out Religion" in everything, most unfittingly in "the *Dandiacal Body*!" (SR, 217). Of course, for Carlyle, this is where religion counts the most – in its attention to material human circumstances.

Carlyle's voice emerges most plainly in the chapter entitled "Tailors," in which the editor, whose opinion finally "happily quite coincides with that of Teufelsdrockh himself," allows Teufelsdrockh to "speak his own last words, in his own way." Teufelsdrockh here could be Carlyle, asking rhetorically, "What too are all poets, and moral Teachers, but a species of Metaphorical Tailors?" (SR, 219). In this figure he means to ground poets and prophets in the guild of makers, cutters, and sewers of material fabric, but makers with a moral purpose. Teufelsdrockh complains first of the injustice done to tailors, that they are considered to be parts rather than the ones who divide into parts. He rails against the "rooted Error, that Tailors are a distinct species in Physiology, not Men, but fractional Parts of a Man" (SR, 218). Carlyle is back in the metaphorical territory of "Physiology," objecting that tailors are anatomized when they should be recognized as the ultimate anatomists, who cut and rearrange the fabric of human experience. This is not to deny the corporeality of tailors, but rather to consider them as complete bodies who succeed in making: "Nevertheless, need I put the question to any Physiologist, Whether it is disputable or not? Seems it not at least presumable, that, under his Clothes, the Tailor has bones, and viscera, and other muscles than the sartorius?" (SR, 219). That is, the tailor is more than just the strap muscle of the thigh named "the sartorius" because it permits the cross-legged sitting position traditionally used by the tailor at his trade. Reaching again for a metaphor for a thorough participation in and attention to corporeality that nonetheless finds its end in fabricating something supra-corporeal, or at least epi-corporeal, to cover the body, Carlyle returns to anatomy. The tailor is not only the familiar figure of the anatomist anatomized, but also the anatomizable anatomist who can, through clothes-making, transform the fabric of the human body. The poet's words are both *from* and *for* matter, but succeed in impacting the body (mysteriously) through their rearrangement of an immaterial meaning.

Carlyle has Teufelsdrockh close the chapter with a descendental illustration of the tailor's high ambition:

[I]n the Scottish Town of Edinburgh, I came upon a Signpost, wheron stood written that such and such a one was "Breeches-Maker to his Majesty"; and stood painted the Effigies of a Pair of Leather Breeches, and between the knees these memorable words, SIC ITUR AD ASTRA.[34] (SR, 220)

Notably, Teufelsdrockh has made it to Carlyle's Scottish home territory, only to find that the "way to the stars" is between the knees of a pair of Scottish leather breeches. Moreover it is the tailor's "covering Art" that makes the "Unhol[y]" groin holy (SR, 220). Carlyle hasn't given up on the supernatural, but reminds us that we must descend to the material to get there. Carlyle's irony doubles back on itself, serving up absurdity as an ultimate truth. He lampoons the artist as a lowly tailor, yet elevates him to the highest of callings – the tailor is in the service of "his Majesty," the king.

Some commentators have worried that *Sartor* loses its ironic tension near its end, with a merging of Teufelsdrockh and his editor. Others have noted that the editor and Teufelsdrockh seem to have changed places, the editor taking on the tone of Teufelsdrockh's transcendentalism, while Teufelsdrockh is suspected of traveling to London to assume practical work in the British style. In this way, the editor and Teufelsdrockh maintain distinct identities: the empiricist uttering prophetic cries, the transcendentalist taking up practical work in the urban center. Each shifts toward the other's previous position, and taken together they describe a hermeneutic circling between transcendentalism and empiricism.

Moreover, the editor, initially friendly to his British audience, ends on a pugnacious note. He suspects that his "British readers consider him, during these current months, but as an uneasy interruption to their ways of thought and digestion, not without a certain irritancy and even spoken invective" (SR, 225). Having grown more secure through the course of the book, the editor succeeds by the end, like Teufelsdrockh, in welcoming dissent. In Teufelsdrockhian mode, the editor embraces "one and all of you, O irritated readers" with "outstretched arms and open heart" (SR, 225). Of course, Carlyle has set the stage for valuing quarrel, remarking in an earlier chapter,

Our Life is compassed round with Necessity; yet is the meaning of Life itself no other than Freedom, than Voluntary Force: thus have we a warfare; in the beginning, especially, a hard-fought Battle. For the God-given mandate, *Work thou in Welldoing*, lies mysteriously written, invisible, acted Gospel of Freedom. And as the clay-given mandate, *Eat thou and be filled*, at the same time, persuasively proclaims itself through every nerve, – must there not be a confusion, a contest, before the better Influence can become the upper? (SR, 140)

The meeting of Necessity and Freedom results in "warfare ... a hard-fought Battle." "Confusion" and "contest" dominate a world-text split for Carlyle between the "God-given" and the "clay-given" mandates – the supernatural and the natural. A conventional reader might assume that Carlyle's "better Influence" is the supernatural, but in *Sartor Resartus* it seems to depend on the particular contest. Certainly Carlyle was concerned that in the instance of the "Poor-slave" we should worry more about the "clay-given mandate" that "persuasively proclaims itself through every nerve." The urgent claims of the body, according to Carlyle, should sometimes win the battle.

Perhaps Carlyle's frustrated farewell is in part an acknowledgment of the difficulty of performing a dualist affirmation of the material world. But, like Blake, Carlyle values a friendship of opposition, characterized by contrariness in the interest of progression. Carlyle's dualism has no orderly hierarchy, but performs instead a perpetual dialectic. He affirms that reader and writer have "traveled some months of our Life-journey in partial sight of one another" and so have "lived together, though in a state of quarrel!" (SR, 225). This is the best we can do, according to Carlyle – keep each other in "partial sight" as we engage in both quarrel and camaraderie, "living together" as irritable co-travelers on a mutual "Life-journey." As with the editor and Teufelsdrockh, however, we can hope that both writer and reader are transformed by the process.

The editor and Teufelsdrockh, writer and reader, and – to return to the issue of Carlyle's relationship with the scientific naturalists – scientist and prophet all participate in a Blakean friendship of opposition. If Carlyle and Owen, both cantankerous, were friends in remarkable agreement with one another, then Carlyle and Huxley, for instance, were theoretical enemies with an undeniable affinity. That similarity, however, does not lie – as Frank Turner has argued – in an incipient naturalism detectable in Carlyle's writing. Rather, Huxley, who early on appreciated the "sense of religion" apparent in Carlyle's affirmation of matter, betrays an ongoing attraction to dualism that resurfaces in his 1893 Romanes lecture, "Evolution and Ethics." Turner recognizes the "striking" "Carlylean features" of this lecture, but passes over the fundamental dualism apparent both to Huxley's contemporaries and more recently to Huxley critic James Paradis. Paradis writes that, in "Evolution and Ethics," Huxley sets ethical thought at odds with the natural laws established by science. Just as people cultivate gardens in defiance of nature, writes Huxley, humankind must develop and nurture an ethical code in resistance to the natural forces of instinct. Huxley, like Carlyle, figures the opposition of morality and nature as a battle:

The more we learn of the nature of things, the more evident is it that what we call rest is only unperceived activity; that seeming peace is silent but strenuous battle. In every part, at every moment, the state of the cosmos is the expression of a transitory adjustment of contending forces; a scene of strife, in which all the combatants fall in turn.[35]

Paradis reminds us that Huxley's contemporary readers saw this insistence on an antagonism between nature and human culture as a dualistic betrayal of his past naturalism. Christian writers, while acutely aware of Huxley's agnosticism, welcomed his dualism of instinct and ethics. Paradis writes:

Henry Drummond, the Scottish naturalist and evangelical writer, noted the widespread surprise at Huxley's dualistic drift: "For by an astonishing *tour de force* – the last, as his former associates in the evolutionary ranks have not failed to remind him, which might have been expected of him – [Huxley] ejects himself from the world order, and washes his hands of it in the name of Ethical Man". . . And an anonymous reviewer in *The Athenaeum* marveled at Huxley's dexterity in promulgating a doctrine that made no mention of Christianity, yet "in its essential character was an approximation to the Pauline dogma of nature and grace."[36]

Huxley's return to a dualist frame recapitulates the Romantic materialism of his youth: his appreciation of Carlyle's natural supernaturalism, his training as a surgeon and his practice aboard the *Rattlesnake*, his involvement in comparative anatomy. Huxley, one of the most prominent scientific naturalists, flirts seriously – early and late – with this middle position between traditional religionists and radical materialists, the Romantic materialism of Richard Owen and Thomas Carlyle.

CHAPTER 4

Wuthering Heights *and domestic medicine:*
the child's body and the book

On first consideration, Emily Brontë may seem out of step with the medical thinking of the period. She was personally averse to any form of medical treatment, and during her final illness she rebuffed her sisters' attempts to send for a doctor. Charlotte, nearly desperate, wrote that Emily "has refused medicine, rejected medical advice; no reasoning, no entreaty, has availed to induce her to see a physician."[1] Although Emily never explained her aversion, we may see some clue to it in her portrayal of a country surgeon in *Wuthering Heights*. Kenneth is a morose, pessimistic visitor at the deathbed, who refuses hope to Frances and family, pronouncing, according to a servant girl, that "mississ must go . . . I heard him tell Mr. Hindley . . . she'll be dead before winter" (WH, 49).[2] When Lockwood gets a cold, he complains of Kenneth's "terrible intimation" that "I need not expect to be out of doors till spring!" (WH, 70). Nelly tells us that doom-and-gloom Kenneth, called to Catherine in her grief after Heathcliff's departure, makes swift work of his attendance:

> Mr. Kenneth, as soon as he saw her, pronounced her dangerously ill; she had a fever.
>
> He bled her, and he told me to let her live on whey and water gruel; and take care she did not throw herself down stairs, or out of the window; and then he left, for he had enough to do in the parish where two or three miles was the ordinary distance between cottage and cottage. (WH, 68)

Kenneth, as overworked country surgeon, proceeds with grim prognostication, fierce intervention, and abrupt departure. In the world of *Wuthering Heights*, one's best hope is to maintain a hardy constitution and avoid the doctor whenever possible.

Perhaps this is why health, and keeping in good health, does become a major concern in the novel. Among the contrasting terms critics have applied to Wuthering Heights and Thrushcross Grange – storm and calm, "raw" and "cooked," id and superego – one might add physically weak and strappingly healthy. One of the central questions of the novel, I will argue, is: can one be both strong and good? Can one bring together the robust physical health of the Earnshaws with the Lintons' gentle manners, book-learning, and Christian virtues of pity and charity? Cast in the language of natural theology, can one bring together the teachings of "good books" that Catherine and Heathcliff reject, and of the Book of Nature that they know so intimately?

At least for the first generation of those who lived at Wuthering Heights, the answer seems to be a resounding "No." The robust natural health of the children at the Heights, "half-savage, and hardy and free," trounces the coddled weakness of the children at the Grange. In part this represents, as often noted, a Blakean reversal of value on good and evil, heaven and hell. But particularly because the emphasis is on the *physical* constitution of *children* it should be no surprise to find as well a strong undercurrent of early pediatric medical ideas in *Wuthering Heights*. Emily Brontë may have been distrustful of surgical intervention, but she seems to have fully absorbed a strain of early nineteenth-century medical teaching about childhood. Her personal devotion to, and fictional treatment of, childhood reflects not only the Romantic elevation of the child, but more particularly a Romantic materialist location of value in a prolonged, physically robust childhood.

The medical profession began seriously to address child-rearing in the late eighteenth century with the publication of William Buchan's *Domestic Medicine*, which appeared in several editions and remained popular throughout the first half of the nineteenth century. Paul Starr describes the rise of these household medical manuals, written by doctors expressly for the lay public:

[T]he distance of domestic from professional medicine began to narrow in the late eighteenth and nineteenth centuries, as physicians published guides to domestic practice. The most widely read of these domestic medical manuals had a remarkably self-conscious political as well as practical character. The two aspects were insepa-rable. Written in lucid, everyday language, avoiding Latin or technical terms, the books set forth current knowledge on disease and attacked, at times explicitly, the conception of medicine as a high mystery.[3]

From what we know of Emily Brontë's attitude toward doctors, it is likely that this democratizing of medical knowledge would have appealed to her. The Brontë family's medical reference books apparently included Buchan's *Domestic Medicine* (which does not survive in the Brontë Parsonage library, but is mentioned in Patrick Brontë's annotations) and a later text in the same tradition, also entitled *Domestic Medicine*, by Thomas John Graham,

M. D.[4] We know that Graham's *Domestic Medicine* figured significantly in the Brontë family's lives, in part because it is heavily annotated by Patrick Brontë, and in part because Charlotte was later to include parts of Graham's name in that of her doctor-hero of *Villette*, John Graham Bretton. Buchan and Graham, both physicians, encouraged lay participation in medicine, promoted natural health, and discouraged the more vigorous forms of medical intervention such as copious bleeding, blistering, or purging. In part they drew on an eighteenth-century tradition of patient participation in medical decision-making; in part they (Graham especially) integrated a strain of the new therapeutic nihilism which acknowledged the futility of a good deal of past medical treatment, and relied on supporting the body's own healing process. With regard to child-rearing, their natural approach amounted to a revolution in domestic advice. They advocated maternal nursing and a childhood as prolonged as possible by exposure to natural elements.

Graham's advice on "the management and treatment of infants and young children" recommends feeding children a "sparing" quantity of food, clothing them in a shift "perfectly loose and easy, so as to allow free motion of the limbs" (this rather than the older tradition of swaddling), promoting regular exercise in the open air and "dipping" the child in cold-water baths three times a week to "impart vigour to the muscles and nerves, and promote alacrity and cheerfulness of mind. In a striking manner does the cold bath preserve and promote the health of the infant race."[5] Conversely, writes Graham, warm dressing, bathing, over-feeding, and coddling will produce a weak and sickly child. It's not hard to find these prescriptions echoed in *Wuthering Heights*, with the strong children Catherine and Heathcliff running barefoot on the moors, and the weak child Linton reclining by the fire bundled in furs. Kenneth remarks on Cathy's resistance to illness, "A stout, hearty lass like Catherine does not fall ill for a trifle" (WH, 125). Cathy and Heathcliff fall ill only when they will it, and only because their strong wills are stronger than their strappingly healthy bodies.

There is nothing necessarily new in noticing Emily Brontë's preoccupation with childhood. Many have remarked that the Heights is a sort of never-never land, ruled by the id, in which even the supposed adults indulge in childish behavior. Juliet Mitchell goes so far as to claim that

[T]here are no mysteries in *Wuthering Heights*. The nature and actions of every character in the drama are fully intelligible because they are always related to the total biographical development of the person and, above all, to what we now know to be the most critical phase of life: childhood.[6]

Reading *Wuthering Heights* as a novel fundamentally about childhood does explain many of the so-called mysteries. If childhood is central to the novel, we see the bond between Cathy and Heathcliff arising from childhood loyalty and interdependence, a refusal to individuate into self-sufficient adulthood. Their childhood symbiosis then explains their strangely innocent yet hungrily demanding love. Instead of assuming that Cathy's and Heathcliff's love is purely transcendental, we can understand it as prepubertal camaraderie, full of physical if not specifically sexual urgency. Finally, this perspective answers one of the puzzles of Lockwood's dream, a puzzle which Emily Brontë plants for us and calls our attention to. When the child-ghost identifies itself as "Catherine Linton," Lockwood asks himself "why did I think of *Linton*? I had read *Earnshaw* twenty times for Linton." Why indeed should this married adult "Catherine Linton" who dies at the age of twenty-one, and has been wandering the moors for twenty years, return as a child-ghost to her childhood home? Brontë seems to suggest that Cathy is always first and foremost a child.

Although the possibility that Cathy and Heathcliff are perennial children has been frequently mentioned, it has almost as frequently been dismissed. For instance, Terry Eagleton writes, "But it won't do to see [Cathy and Heathcliff] merely as children eternally fixated in some Edenic infancy: we do not see them merely as children."[7] Literally true, but neither, I would argue, do any of the characters mature in any meaningful sense. They grow physically larger, they marry, but they remain emotionally preadolescent, unwise, demanding, and unswervingly loyal. Brontë signals through incessant references to childhood and childishness that, in this enclosed little corner of Yorkshire, nearly all of the players remain children. Lockwood sees the second Catherine, already married and widowed, "in a pet, her forehead corrugated, and her red under-lip pushed out like a child's ready to cry" (WH, 9). Hindley and Francis, though heads of the household, are said to make love "like two babies" (WH, 16). Nelly warns Edgar that his intended bride is "dreadfully wayward, sir! . . . As bad as any marred child" (WH, 66). After Heathcliff's departure, Cathy mourns violently, "beat[ing] Hareton, or any child, in a passionate fit of crying" (WH, 66). Cathy in turn describes Isabella and Edgar as "spoiled children" even after she marries into the family. Nelly concurs, calling the eighteen-year-old Isabella "infantile in manners," while Heathcliff calls her a "child" in his "custody" (WH, 78; WH, 118). The first Catherine dies "like a child reviving and sinking again to sleep." Only Joseph and Nelly demonstrate adult psychology, and Joseph is old when the world of *Wuthering Heights* begins. Nelly grows into the role of nurse/mother, inimical to childhood, except in one rare moment, when she thinks she sees Hindley's child-ghost. Then, she says, "a gush of childish sensation flowed into my heart," and "I felt an irresistible yearning to be at the Heights" (WH, 84). Even Nelly can recover a child's sensation near Wuthering Heights, the powerful locale of childhood experience.

Emily Brontë probably delighted more in her childhood than traditional Brontë mythology leads us to expect. In her recent biography of the Brontë family, Juliet Barker revises the myth – which dates back to Elizabeth Gaskell's biography of Charlotte – of Patrick Brontë as the cruel and uncaring father, and Aunt Branwell as a forbiddingly austere foster-mother. Drawing on an account by Sarah Garrs, one of the Brontë's servants, Barker concludes that, excepting the loss of their mother, "the Brontës had a perfectly normal childhood . . . Their home life was secure and stable, with their father always ready to spend time with them, despite the pressures of his own work. Their aunt, too, was an affectionate mother, supervising their lessons and their household work and nursing the infant Anne."[8] In her biography of Emily, Winifred Gérin points out that Emily's experience of childhood may have differed significantly from her sisters', given her young age at her exposure to the privations of the Clergy Daughters' School at Cowan Bridge:

Emily's extreme youth [that is, six] gave her a favoured position; on the later evidence of the Superintendent, Miss Evans, she was "quite the pet nursling of the school". Miss Evans's additional recollection, to the effect that Emily "was a darling child" explains no doubt Emily's happy isolation in the midst of the general misery. To this fact may be attributed her intellectual as well as her physical survival from the ordeal of Cowan Bridge, which hastened the deaths of her two eldest sisters, and marked Charlotte for life.[9]

Whatever her response to Cowan Bridge, we know that Emily perpetuated her childhood fantasy world of Gondal at least into her twenties, and probably until her death. In contrast to Charlotte, who wrote her farewell to Angria somewhere around age twenty-three, Emily was still playing Gondal at twenty-seven. Recording a rare journey with Anne to York she enthuses: "during our excursion we were Ronal Macalgin, Henry Angora, Juliet Augusteena, Rosbella Esmaldan, Ella and Julian Egremont, Catherine Navarre, and Cordelia Fitzaphnold, escaping from the palaces of instruction to join the Royalists who are hard driven at present by the victorious Republicans."[10] Anne's diary entry at that time indicates that for her Gondal has faded irrevocably, but for Emily the Gondals are "flourishing bright as ever."[11]

Wuthering Heights *and domestic medicine*

73

Stevie Davies affirms the "never-say-die of her [Emily's] fantasy games" as a radical posture. Acknowledging the probable early trauma caused by Emily's mother's death, Davies forwards nonetheless the proposal that Emily's rejection of adulthood was "a consciously embraced choice, linked with the radicalism of her philosophic attitudes." At least in the first half of *Wuthering Heights*, Davies's "radical" Brontë "licences the childish and anarchic against the police-state of social and religious establishment." Thus Davies converts a possible pathology into a political act, emphasizing Brontë's intolerance of social division and her perversely child-like refusal to settle for compromise. Furthermore, Davies claims that the novel's power lies in its ability to awaken the reader's own experience of childhood: "Part of the novel's magnetic effect on generations of readers derives from its power to regress us, activating the child we have left for dead, so as to assume adult identity and responsibilities."[12]

Davies goes on, predictably enough, to relate Brontë to the Romantic "cult of the child" of which Emily Brontë is undeniably a member. But it should be emphasized that Brontë's treatment of the child differs significantly from Blake's or Wordsworth's in several important ways. First, Brontëan children have neither the innocence of Blake's "Songs" nor the wisdom of Wordsworth's child-philosophers; rather they are violently, foolishly headstrong and erring, veritable bundles, as Joseph would put it, of original sin. Second, Emily Brontë's children are not individualistic, but rather have difficulty defining boundaries between one another and the natural world. To be natural, for Brontë, means not to be fully differentiated, not to distinguish between one's own interest and that of another, to find one another, as Cathy says, not delightful, but "necessary" (WH, 64). As Cathy famously claims: "I *am* Heathcliff." Furthermore, there is none of Wordsworth's neoplatonism in Emily Brontë's vision: the Brontëan child doesn't arrive in the world a fully formed spiritual being, "trailing clouds of glory," but learns through difficult, sometimes brutally physical experience. Finally, where Wordsworth would have us recollect childhood in mental tranquility, Brontë would have us, quite literally, prolong it.

Perhaps most significantly, Emily's poetry attests to a prolongation of childhood experience, or at least an uncanny ability to access it at will. One of Emily's best poems begins with a confident, defiant recurrence to childhood that would have made Wordsworth envious: "Often rebuked, yet always back returning / To those first feelings that were born with me." Significantly, those "first feelings" lead her to a natural, earthly home:

I'll walk where my own nature would be leading:
It vexes me to choose another guide:
Where the grey flocks in ferny glens are feeding;
Where the wild wind blows on the mountain side.

What have these lonely mountains worth revealing?
More glory and more grief than I can tell:
The earth that wakes one human heart to feeling
Can centre both the worlds of Heaven and Hell.[13]

The speaker's earliest feelings ground her in the earth, to which she imputes a spectacular agency. The earth inspires human feeling, awakening the child in Brontë, instead of nursing it to sleep and forgetfulness, as in Wordsworth's Immortality Ode. Moreover the earth "centre[s]" both Heaven and Hell. If Brontë has like Blake reversed the values of Heaven and Hell, she has also introduced a vital third term, the earth which suspends the child between poles, a world charged with both "glory" and "grief."

These features that Brontë brings to the Romantic child – a more social, empirical, physical, literal version of childhood – can be found in the domestic medical texts which function as a sort of secular scripture in the Brontë household. T. J. Graham cribbed heavily from William Buchan, and in his *Domestic Medicine* Buchan is quite open about his philosophical source: Jean-Jacques Rousseau. When Buchan promotes maternal nursing, for instance, he quotes Rousseau:

"Would you have mankind return all to their natural duties," says the eloquent ROUSSEAU, in one of his fine sallies of sentimental enthusiasm, "begin with mothers of families: you will be astonished at the change this will produce . . . [S]hould mothers again condescend to NURSE THEIR CHILDREN, manners would form themselves: the sentiments of nature would revive in our hearts: the state would be re-peopled: this principal point, this alone would re-unite every thing."[14]

Buchan Anglicizes Rousseau into a sentimental gentleman, but he is careful to preserve his social vision: if mothers would "NURSE THEIR CHIL-DREN," "the state would be re-peopled." The child, here, is father of the State (rather than, as in Wordsworth, father of the Man). According to Rousseau – and Buchan – the practice of maternal nursing could "re-unite" the populace, supplying a foundation for social reform.

Buchan also recommends, again via Rousseau, the literal exposure of children to experiences of physical pain:

He [Rousseau] then begs of mother to attend to nature, and follow the track she has delineated: "She continually exercises her children, and fortifies their constitution by experiment of every kind; inuring them betimes to grief and pain. In cutting their teeth, they experience the fever; griping colics throw them into convulsions; the hooping-cough suffocates, and worms torment them; surfeits corrupt their blood; and the various fermentations to which their humours are subject, cover them with troublesome eruptions: almost the whole period of childhood is sickness and danger. But in passing through this course of experiments, the child gathers strength and fortitude; and, as soon as he is capable of living, the principles of life become less precarious."[15]

In Buchan's translation, Rousseau's key terms are solidly empirical: nature "exercises" the child via "experiment" and "experience." The trial and error of empiricism inevitably involves "sickness and danger." Rousseau seems almost to revel in the variety of pain available in nature: convulsions, suffocation, torment, corruption, etc. "This," Buchan adds, "is the law of nature. Why should you act contrary to it? Do you not see that, by endeavouring to correct her work, you spoil it, and prevent the execution of her designs?"[16] Nature, though harsh, batters the child only to render him stronger – and the wise caretaker will actually cooperate with nature's "experiments."

Buchan quotes from Rousseau's *Emile*, often cited as a highly influential text in the cultural formation of the Romantic child. In *Emile*, Rousseau argues for the postponement of moral and emotional education until the age of thirteen. Thus the first two books of *Emile* (covering birth through age twelve and entitled, in the manuscript plan, the "Age of Nature") focus on the physical education of the child, and advocate "natural" learning through experience. Education in these early years should be "merely negative," writes Rousseau. "Leave childhood to ripen in your children . . . beware of giving anything they need today if it can be deferred without danger to to-morrow." Moreover, Rousseau justifies his system by describing the child's sensate experience as completely alien to that of the adult: "childhood has its own ways of seeing, thinking, and feeling." And finally, the period of this radically different experience for Rousseau is both delightful and fleeting, a fitting object of nostalgia.

Love childhood, indulge its sport, its pleasures, its delightful instincts. Who has not sometimes regretted that age when laughter was ever on the lips, and when the heart was ever at peace? Why rob these innocents of the joys which pass so quickly, of that precious gift which they cannot abuse? Why fill with bitterness the fleeting days of early childhood, days which will no more return for them than for you?[17]

If childhood becomes a "precious gift," all the more reason to "leave child-hood to ripen," to allow the child to linger in enviable pleasures of "sport" and "instinct."

The ideal of a prolonged childhood shows up as well in conduct books addressing the difficulties of adolescence – particularly of female adolescence. E. J. Tilt, in his 1851 *On the Preservation of the Health of Women* writes "[T]he art of educating girls in order to bring them to the full perfection of womanhood, is to retard as much as possible the appearance of first menstruation."[18] Later in the century, E. H. Ruddock, in *The Common Diseases of Women*, echoes Tilt's advice, and modifies Graham's prescriptions for infants, which are now applied to teenage girls:

Probably the most successful mode of rearing girls, so as to bring them to the full perfection of womanhood, is to retard the period of puberty as much as possible, at least until the 14th or 16th year . . . It is the duty, therefore, of the mother to enjoin on her daughter to frequent use of cold baths, free exercise in the open air, or in cool, well-ventilated rooms, to provide plain and digestible diet for her.[19]

By this time, the link between the child and nature is so strongly forged that natural treatment like outdoor exercise, scant diet, and liberating clothing is supposed to fend off maturation and menarche.

To what extent did the Brontë family follow the pediatric prescriptions of domestic medicine? It is difficult to know precisely, especially because Patrick Brontë, who made copious annotations in his copy of T. J. Graham's *Domestic Medicine*, made none in the section on childhood. This is not surprising, since Graham's text wasn't published until Anne, the youngest, was already six years old. (Patrick Brontë's note on the title page of Graham suggests that he consulted Buchan's *Domestic Medicine* when the children were younger, but, as noted earlier, Brontë's own copy of Buchan does not survive.) But reading Patrick Brontë's annotations in the other sections of Graham's volume gives us insight into the role that domestic medicine played in the family's life. Unfortunately, most who have read Patrick's annotations so far have been quick to interpret his remarks as controlling of his children simply because he comments most copiously about conditions from which they suffered – hardly surprising in a family medical reference book. Nor does he focus any less minutely on his own medical conditions – indigestion and cataracts – than on his children's. I find less evidence of medical surveillance than of a father's concern for his children's health, and a responsible clergyman's lay interest in medicine. Clergymen in Brontë's time were expected, in the absence of an apothecary or surgeon, to dispense lay medical advice, attending to the body as well as the soul. Domestic medical texts were intended, as their title pages announce, "for the use of clergymen, families and medical students."[20] Clearly Patrick Brontë respected medical authority, but he also considered himself a competent judge of conflicting opinions. On the front page of *Modern Domestic Medicine*, Patrick writes: "I have read many works, of Dr. Elliotson, and the ablest medical writers, and found this book, as far as it goes, perfectly to accord with them, both in its description of the symptoms of diseases, and their causes and remedies. P. B." Brontë first announces himself well-read in medicine, and proceeds to render his educated lay opinion with an authority that may seem pompous to the current medically disenfranchised lay population. His annotations include pasted-in newspaper articles and references to other medical texts, as well as carefully detailed notes about his own experience, which he sometimes adduces in critique of Graham's prescriptions. The Rev. Brontë clearly endorsed the teamwork of doctor and clergyman as co-defenders of the body and of the soul.

The dualism of matter and spirit is, as I have been arguing throughout, one of the major premises of natural theology: the Book of Scripture and the Book of Nature are written in two very different languages, after all, even if they should ultimately agree with one another. Patrick Brontë was an avid reader and interpreter of natural theology, which became the subject of a number of his sermons and articles.[21] For instance, after the Crow Hill Bog Burst, in which a gas eruption and torrent of mud destroyed crops, a mill, and a bridge near Haworth, Patrick preached a two-part sermon which first detailed the natural causes of earthquakes (as he categorized the bog burst), and second argued that, in the Bible, God sometimes uses earthquakes for spiritual purposes.[22] That his children absorbed the teachings of natural theology is evident from Charlotte's performance when catechized by her father. In this famous incident, recorded by Elizabeth Gaskell, Patrick provided his children with a mask and posed piercing questions, expecting them to answer more boldly from behind the cover of the mask. "What is the most important book?" he asked. "The book of Scripture," answered Charlotte. "And the second?" queried Patrick. "The book of Nature," Charlotte replied. Patrick then turned to Emily. What should she do, her father asked her, when her brother Branwell was naughty? "Reason with him," Emily replied, according to Elizabeth Gaskell's account, "and when he won't listen to reason, whip him."[23] The question Patrick posed to Emily seems at first glance unrelated to Charlotte's, pertaining more to household conduct than to natural theology. But the two-part structure of the Rev. Brontë's questions, and of Emily's reply, attests to a parallel, if more specific lesson. When a child is naughty, one first attempts mental reform, and if unsuccessful one resorts next to corporal persuasion. Emily follows a "first mind, then body" checklist that echoes the "first, the Word, then Nature" succession of Charlotte's answer. Her reply demonstrates both a respect for the primacy of language and a doubt as to its effectiveness – no wonder, given Branwell's resistance to all the reason his family had to offer.

Emily's toughness, her grim awareness of physical violence, has been chronicled by her biographers. We get a picture of Emily the crack-shot, encouraged by her father to practice with his guns, and of Emily, the passionate dog-lover, capable nonetheless of nearly throttling her favorite dog for the sake of its discipline. This is the side of Emily that Charlotte Brontë memorialized in the eponymous heroine of *Shirley*, who was Charlotte's vision of what Emily might have been if she were born to wealth and privilege. Emily's writerly attention to animals, and especially the cruelty and competition of the animal world, has been noticed since an early review subtitled her novel "Life in the Kennel."[24] Barbara Munson Goff has recently revisited the long-noticed rhetoric of animality in *Wuthering Heights*, adding a number of persuasive biographical examples of the Brontë family's interest in pre-Darwinian natural history:

Charlotte Brontë lists "Bewick and Audubon and Goldsmith [the *History of Animated Nature*] and White's *Natural History* [*of Selborne*]" in her recommended reading for Ellen Nussey. Emily copied drawings from Thomas Bewick's *British Birds* (1797), and all three sisters did naturalistic portraits of the family pets. Given their obvious interest in natural history, it is probably a persistent sentimentalism (and possible sexism) regarding the Brontës' intellectual isolation that has prevented us from seeing them relatively aggressively pursuing scientific interests. Charlotte Brontë remarks on this very point in a letter to Ellen Nussey concerning the lectures given by her father and the curate William Weightman at the Keighley Mechanics' Institute, at least one of which the girls were allowed to attend: "[B]oth are spoken of very highly in the newspaper, and it is mentioned as a matter of wonder that such displays of intellect should emanate from the village of Haworth, situated amongst the bogs and mountains, and, until very lately, supposed to be in a state of semi-barbarism. Such are the words of the newspaper."[25]

After making a strong case for the contributions of natural theology to the Brontës' family life, Goff claims that Emily Brontë, like Charles Darwin, uses the examples accumulated by natural theologians in order to topple natural theology. For both Brontë and Darwin, writes Goff, "unnecessary cruelty was the distinct feature of human behavior. In nature, death and destruction on a massive scale are necessary for the proliferation of life and variety."[26] Goff further proposes that Heathcliff is the "mechanism," which, like Darwin's natural selection, supplants the providential God of natural theology.

Although Goff's is certainly a new and interesting approach to the mystery of Heathcliff, her associations between Brontë and Darwin are highly speculative, depending on the possibility that Brontë may have read texts available to her at the Keighley Mechanics' Institute, and that she may have presciently anticipated Darwin's master stroke simply because, as often so loosely argued, evolutionary ideas were "in the air." Beyond this, Goff's argument depends heavily on what she interprets as Brontë's endorsement of cruelty in *Wuthering Heights* and on what she reads as the misanthropy of Emily Brontë's Brussels devoirs. Here Goff fails, I think, to distinguish adequately between misanthropy and the conviction of original sin.

Goff argues, for instance, that Brontë's essay "The Cat" pushes "beyond natural theology to Darwin's rebuttal of anthropocentrism," because it argues that "humanity's fall was not shared by the more pristine animals, with the single exception of cats."[27] But this interpretation skates over Brontë's introductory statement of intent: "I can say with sincerity that I love cats; furthermore I am going to give very good reasons why those who hate them are wrong."[28] Brontë goes on to compare cats and humans to conclude that both are loveable despite, or even because of, their shared fallenness. Her argument follows a logical structure, beginning with the assumption that we love humans, proceeding to the evidence that cats are like humans in behavior, and concluding that we should therefore love cats as well. Brontë's view of human nature – created good but deplorably fallen – is a centrist Christian position. Her innovation in this essay is the extension of this valuable-but-fallen human nature to the feline species. "The Cat" is therefore as anthropocentric a defense of cats as one could imagine.

Goff similarly sees in "The Butterfly" a critique of anthropocentrism (and therefore of natural theology), but I think that this essay again demonstrates Brontë's commitment to the two books of natural theology. Brontë's natural theology, as presented in "The Butterfly," is hyperbolic, plunging into the depths of pessimism, and is therefore perhaps unrecognizable to the reader scanning for the gentle observation and wonder of earlier natural theologians like Gilbert White. Her essay begins with the speaker in a "black humour" in which "the entire creation" seems utterly "meaningless." Observing a maggot destroying a flower as one small sample of the daily destruction in nature, the speaker complains that

Nature is an inexplicable problem, it exists on a principle of destruction; it is necessary that each be the tireless instrument of death to the other, or cease to live itself; . . . [A]t this moment the universe seemed to me a vast machine constructed solely to produce evil.[29]

Although the universe appears evil to her, the speaker addresses her doubt to God, whose existence she does not question. She does, however, question his goodness: "I almost doubted the goodness of God, for not annihilating man on the first day of his sin." She takes it upon herself to crush the maggot, participating in the destruction she has read in the Book of Nature – and wishing that God himself had done likewise with his newly created man.

But the depths of Brontë's pessimism about natural cruelty are matched by the heights of an apocalyptic prophecy of the justice to come. Just as she kills the caterpillar, she espies a butterfly "with wings of glowing gold and purple: it only shone a moment before my eyes, then reascending among the leaves, it vanished in the height of the azure vault." In a dramatic reversal, the speaker then condemns her prior "blind presumption" in "blaming Omniscience":

[T]he creature should not judge the Creator . . . God is the god of justice and mercy; then certainly each penalty which he inflicts on his creatures, be they human or animal, rational or irrational, each suffering of our unfortunate nature is only a seed of this divine harvest which will be gathered when sin having expended its last drop of poison, Death having dealt its last stroke, both will expire on the pyre of a universe in flames and will leave their ancient victims to an eternal empire of happiness and Glory.[30]

The speaker's grim pessimism is replaced by a prophetic vision of the triumph of good over evil, the eradication of death, and the reign of an "eternal empire of happiness." The violence of this end may obscure, for the modern reader, its insistent theocentricism and belief in the redemption of humankind. But what might look like misanthropy to the post-Darwinian reader can be more adequately described as Brontë's Romantic materialism, her participation in a radical version of natural theology that suspends the resolution of the Books of Nature and of Scripture. To Brontë, the Book of Nature spells cruelty, and the Book of Scripture the victory of justice. She denies neither, but sustains the conflicting evidence of both ways of knowing.

While some nineteenth-century natural theology fell prey to a simplistic, hasty, or patently absurd reconciliation of science and religion, the two-books doctrine did permit a radical both-and posture. What is perhaps not typically noticed about natural theology is the freedom it allowed for incommensurate epistemologies to co-exist within the same discourse. Clergymen amateur scientists often contentedly pursued natural philosophy without immediate regard for its theological implications, trusting that ultimately natural philosophy would yield results to the glory of God. Many were able to suspend the urge to correlate the languages of nature and revelation, tolerating and working back and forth between dueling epistemologies. The Brontë family participated in this form of natural theology, discussing with some sophistication the science of medicine and that of natural history, but adhering devoutly to the doctrines of Christianity – often appreciating, or even delighting in, the problematic conflicts between these two ways of thinking.

I am suggesting, then, that the model of natural theology, which accommodates two incongruous languages, may explain the incorporation of competing medical and religious ideas into Emily's vision of childhood. Together, the medical and theological teachings of the day regarding childhood created a very mixed message: the child was the site of both natural health and original sin. Hugh Cunningham, in his review of the history of childhood, emphasizes the conflict between the Rousseauian ideal of the natural child and the Puritan doctrine of original sin, particularly following the eighteenth-century Evangelical revival. He writes, "In 1799 the *Evangelical Magazine* advised parents to teach their children that 'they are sinful polluted creatures', and in the same year Hannah More, one of the leading figures in the Evangelical revival, warned against the prevalence of treating children as if they were innocent."[31] Certainly, between the Rousseau-influenced domestic medical texts and Evangelical Christianity, the Brontë children heard this double message in their household, that children were both inherently sinful and naturally good. And they may very well have heard the strange implications of the double message – that children's souls were polluted, but their bodies were naturally good. This is quite the inversion of the more familiar Christian view of a sinful flesh and a redeemable soul, and one applicable only and especially to childhood. When Jane Eyre, for instance, is asked by the Evangelical Brocklehurst what she must do to avoid hell, she replies, "I must keep in good health and not die."[32] The healthy body is the only hope for a fiery child like Jane, whose sinful rage blazes out against the Reed family. As I will argue in this and the following chapter, this inverted dualism of good body/bad soul permeates all of Charlotte and Emily Brontë's work.

Emily Brontë's emphasis on the material world has long been noted, of course, by Marxist critics. Patsy Stoneman's review of the political criticism of *Wuthering Heights* demonstrates that materialist readings have been nearly as durable as transcendental interpretations. As early as 1947, David Wilson set the novel in the context of Yorkshire's "West Riding social history," presenting evidence that the Brontës were intimately aware of the deprivations that industrialism thrust upon their neighboring hand-loom weavers.[33] In 1951, Arnold Kettle took critics more broadly to task for placing *Wuthering Heights* within the genre of mystical romance:

ing Heights is about England in 1847. The people it reveals live not in a never land but in Yorkshire. Heathcliff was born not in the pages of Byron, a Liverpool slum. The language of Nelly, Joseph and Hareton is the language of Yorkshire people. The story of *Wuthering Heights* is concerned not with love in the abstract but with the passions of living people, with property-ownerships, the attraction of social comforts, the arrangement of marriages, the importance of education, the validity of religion, the relations of rich and poor.

There is nothing vague about this novel; the mists in it are the mists of the Yorkshire moors; if we speak of it as having an elemental quality it is because the very elements, the great forces of nature are evoked, which change so slowly that in the span of a human life they seem unchanging. But in this evocation there is nothing sloppy or uncontrolled. On the contrary the realization is intensely concrete: we seem to smell the kitchen of Wuthering Heights, to feel the force of the wind across the moors, to sense the very changes of the seasons. Such concreteness is achieved not by mistiness but by precision.[34]

Wuthering Heights is not only carefully situated in time and in locale, concerned with inheritance and property, attentive to human physical comfort and brutality, and literally crawling with animals, but it also casts the metaphysical back into physical terms. Cathy's image of heaven is conspicuously earthly; Heathcliff by name and reputation is a piece of nature, "an arid wilderness of furze and whinstone," and Heathcliff needs Cathy's physical presence so much that he exhumes her corpse. Even in Lockwood's dreams, Cathy's ghost bleeds as if it were embodied. These undeniably spiritual or metaphysical concerns are deeply intertwined with the material elements.

As critics have with increasing eclecticism tried to manage both the novel's mythic elements and its patent materialism, it has become almost standard to read *Wuthering Heights* as a disjunct novel. In the classroom, many have welcomed such ambiguity as fodder for classroom discussion. Is Heathcliff, we ask, a supernatural interloper whose diabolical machinations exceed realist explanation, or a realistic Liverpool street kid, molded by his environment? Is Cathy a female Romantic, charged with the visionary energy of the moors, or is she a crass little capitalist, intent on climbing the social ladder? Certainly, on the critical level, *Wuthering Heights* has frustrated most recognizable ways of reading mid-century British novels, deflecting especially the categories of Gothic romance on the one hand and Victorian social realism on the other. Nancy Armstrong, for instance, argues that the novel poses questions in one genre that cannot be answered by the other.[35] And J. Hillis Miller thinks that *Wuthering Heights* is constructed to lure the reader further in with false promises of a secret meaning, but finally, and repeatedly, to frustrate those readerly expectations.[36]

Without denying the uncanny repetitions of the text, or the fruitful ambiguity of its generic borrowings, I wish to place *Wuthering Heights* firmly in the Romantic materialist tradition, which provides a logic for its disjunctions. The late Romantic two-book culture, in which the Brontës participated, specifically features both an intimate interrelationship and an untranslatability between the natural and supernatural worlds. An unexpected twist complicates this otherwise typical Christian dualism: the soul becomes an untrustworthy monitor while the body becomes the site of authenticity and justice. Furthermore, locating childhood as the realm of the bad soul/good body frustrates the common expectation that a nineteenth-century novel should be some approximation of a bildungsroman. *Wuthering Heights* is not a children's story, but fully to understand it one must read *for* the child in it – that is, one must resist declaring the novel ultimately frustrating if child logic turns out to furnish a better explanation of the book than the logic of maturation.

How does one revalue the child's body, usually considered the inferior husk from which our privileged adult psyche emerges? How do you make the surface into the core? Emily Brontë's answer is to enshrine the child body in a book. As a Romantic materialist, Brontë doesn't deconstruct the binary of body and soul, outside and inside, but rather inverts the traditional priority in order to reawaken the strangeness of the dualism. The result is a mythic novel that enshrines within it the healthy child body – "half-savage, and hardy and free" – as well as its material locale, the West Riding of Yorkshire, with its values of fierce loyalty and flat-footed impatience with compromise. The sense of formal unity is, I believe, more than an elaborate illusion; the concentric frames of narrative function to build desire for the core, investing it with value as the central concern of the novel. As Beth Newman writes of frame narratives: "As we pass from teller to teller, peeling back one story to discover another as though peeling an onion, we progress not only through time but also toward some goal that seems the more powerful and important for being so palpably *within*."[37] What is startlingly original is that the inner experience for which this text provokes desire is not that of the psyche, nor that of transcendental mystery, but rather that of the full, ravenous physicality of childhood.

The enshrining of a child body within a book presented a unique problem for the Romantic materialist in that the natural child supposedly resisted learning from books. In addition, the parents should prevent early reading: books might corrupt the natural child, accelerating maturation. To return briefly to child-rearing literature, we find E. J. Tilt advising a strict avoidance of imaginative literature. In this passage Tilt turns his attention from the girl's natural environment to the girl's household environment, i.e., the nursery.

> If there be any possibility of effecting this purpose [the prolongation of girlhood], it must be by maintaining in its integrity an essential English institution – the nursery. The nursery . . . means the absence of sofas to lounge on – the absence of novels fraught with harrowing interest; it means the absence of laborious gaiety, of theatres, and of operas – the absence of intimacies which are of a too absorbing nature.[38]

Tilt aligns the nursery with nature, banning the corruption of art and civilization from this natural sanctum. For Tilt, urban luxuries, like sofas, parties, and balls, blend into those of art: theatre, operas, and above all novels. Novels are too "absorbing" for young girls, and apt to stimulate a precocious sexuality. Best to leave such books alone (as well as the lounging attitude of reading them), either retreating to the unadorned nursery, or venturing out of doors into the bracing elements.

This tension between books and the natural child is particularly apparent in the first generation of *Wuthering Heights*. Upon inspecting the books in Cathy's childhood bedroom, Lockwood wryly notes that

> Catherine's library was select, and its state of dilapidation proved it to have been well used, though not altogether for a legitimate purpose; scarcely one chapter had escaped pen and ink commentary – at least, the appearance of one – covering every morsel of blank that the printer had left. (WH, 16)

Although this passage has been used as evidence of Cathy's "interpretive" capacity, we shouldn't miss Lockwood's thickly applied irony.[39] Cathy's "library" consists of a handful of "select" Evangelical treatises which she deplored; they are not merely "well used" but "dilapidated," and her "commentary" (or, according to Lockwood, the tongue-in-cheek "appearance of one") of course has nothing to do with Christianity, except to chronicle her rebellion against it, or to draw an "excellent caricature of Joseph, rudely yet powerfully sketched" (WH, 16). Cathy and Heathcliff rebel against Joseph's attempt to make them read "good books" on the Sabbath. In her marginal diary, one of the innermost core narratives, Cathy writes, "I took my dingy volume by the scroop, and hurled it into the dog-kennel, vowing I hated a good book. Heathcliff kicked his to the same place" (WH, 17). When punished by confinement to the back-kitchen, Cathy proceeds to deface another "good book" by writing her own text in the margins:

> I reached this book, and a pot of ink from a shelf, and pushed the house-door ajar to give me light, and I have got the time on with writing for twenty minutes; but

my companion is impatient and proposes that we should appropriate the dairy woman's cloak, and have a scamper on the moors, under its shelter. (WH, 17)

Cathy's own writing, like the partially opened door, helps her to pass the time, but Heathcliff's proposal to "scamper on the moors" wins out over her own assertive rewriting over good books.

Even as an adult, in the childish petulance of her final illness, Cathy seems to think that Linton's library, and his books, are diametrically opposed to her own desire for the open window and the wind that blows from her childhood home. After Cathy's fit and three-day fast, Nelly tells her that Edgar spends his time closed up in his library. "What, in the name of all that feels," Catherine rages, "has he to do with *books*, when I am dying?" (WH, 94). Linton attempts to assist her recovery by placing books in front of her. As Nelly tells us, "A book lay spread on the sill before her, and the scarcely perceptible wind fluttered its leaves at intervals. I believe Linton had laid it there, for she never endeavoured to divert herself with reading" (WH, 121). Cathy repeatedly chooses windows over books, the childhood world of the Heights over the adult world of the Grange's library, the promise of a threshold opening out toward nature over the inward journey of reading books.

Examining this opposition between thresholds and texts, Carol Jacobs has argued that texts lie at the center of Lockwood's three dreams, and thus at the center of *Wuthering Heights*. She traces Lockwood's journey into Cathy's oak-paneled bed at Wuthering Heights, often considered to be the inmost "penetralium" of the novel's world:

Having reached the very center of Wuthering Heights, Lockwood finds it inhabited by texts . . . Each dream incorporates one of the three texts. In the first appear the spectre-like letters etched on the sill. The second concerns the pious discourse of Jabes Branderham, which Lockwood had just begun reading. The third personifies the child Cathy, who speaks from the pages of her diary.[40]

Although all three of Lockwood's dreams feature texts in some way, I do not find these texts as central to the novel as does Jacobs. In fact, each of Lockwood's dreams features the book-destroying natural child, as if Lockwood, with uncharacteristic perception, has by sharing child Cathy's bed-closet been drawn into her youthful, anti-textual world.

In the first dream, Catherine's various names scratched on the sill "swarm" confusedly in front of Lockwood's eyes. This writing of "nothing but a name" (for Lockwood, hardly a text) is the product of Cathy's rebellious and destructive passing of time as she wishes herself out of the window. As Lockwood rouses himself "to dispel the obtrusive" words, he finds that, by resting his forehead on the sill, he has knocked the candle over and "roasted" the "calf-skin" book-covers, thus participating in Cathy's carelessness with her books. This is less a dream about texts than an idle tracing of names on Cathy's part, and a resistance to those names on Lockwood's – both resulting in a literal destruction of texts.

In the second dream, inspired by the mildewed copy of Jabes Branderham's sermon, Lockwood practically becomes (for once, and at his best) a Yorkshire natural child, impatiently fidgeting and squirming like Catherine when subjected to endless scriptural commentary:

Oh, how weary I grew. How I writhed, and yawned, and nodded, and revived! How I pinched and pricked myself, and rubbed my eyes, and stood up, and sat down again, and nudged Joseph to inform me if he would *ever* have done! (WH, 19)

Branderham's sermon, entitled "Seventy Times Seven, and the First of the Seventy-First" is a commentary on Matthew 18: 21–22, in which Jesus teaches limitless forgiveness, not just the seven times that Peter proposes, but "until seventy times seven." In this hilarious dream sermon, Branderham takes Jesus literally, perversely preaching that the first of the seventy-first sin is therefore unforgivable. At this, Lockwood refuses to forgive Branderham the sin of excessive exposition (ironically, upon Branderham's arrival at the "first of the seventy-first" point), and Branderham refuses to forgive Lockwood the yawning which "gapingly contort[ed] thy visage" seventy-one times. This absurd misinterpretation of Matthew dissolves into a lusty brawl involving everyone in the chapel – and results finally in Lockwood's awakening.[41] The second dream derives its irrepressible comedy from the perverse literalization of texts, rather than an appreciative interpretation of them.

For Carol Jacobs, the third dream signals Lockwood's trust in "the good text to exorcise an evil."[42] She quotes the passage in which the ghost-child is persuaded to let go: "The fingers relaxed, I snatched mine through the hole, hurriedly piled the books up in a pyramid against it" (WH, 20). If this is a case of the "good" text versus the "evil" ghost, it is also an instance of the book versus the child body. This is of course the dream which most readers remember for Lockwood's gruesome slicing of the dream-child's wrist across the broken window, with the dream-ghost expressed in such literal, bodily terms that we almost feel the spurt of blood that "ran down and soaked the bedclothes" (WH, 20). Lockwood dreams of adults-turned-children and ghosts incarnate. And Cathy's embodied child-ghost is definitely in opposition to books. Lockwood may pile up the books against the window, but they do not succeed in protecting him from trouble. "I've been a waif for twenty years," the child wails from the other side of the book-barricaded window. Lockwood tells us "Therat began a feeble scratching outside, and the pile of books moved as if thrust forward. I tried to jump up, but could not stir a limb; and so yelled aloud, in a frenzy of fright. To my confusion, I discovered the yell was not ideal" (WH, 20). To our confusion, much of Lockwood's dream turns out to be not altogether ideal. We learn later that Lockwood has dreamed much of what he cannot possibly know, things that Nelly will only later corroborate. Her later narrative reveals that the dying Catherine, like the dream-child, begs to have a window open, remembers the knock of the "wind sounding in the firs by the lattice," yearns to return to her "oak-panelled bed at home," and is reduced, according to Nelly, to "no better than a wailing child" (WH, 96–97). If we make the mistake of taking Lockwood's dreams literally, we are certainly teased into it by Brontë's own suggestions throughout the course of the novel.

Jacobs explicates Lockwood's dreams, arguing for the centrality of texts, in order to demonstrate ultimately the disruption between Lockwood's framing narrative and the self-deconstructing texts at its center. The excommunication of Lockwood from the text of *Wuthering Heights* reflects a "fundamental estrangement . . . between signs and meaning, an impasse of interpretation."[43] While I quite agree that Lockwood functions as the estranged outsider, I think his anti-heroism serves as a strong interpretive marker for the meaning of the text. Lockwood's framing text functions as a foil to the center, which turns out to be the anti-textual child body. *Wuthering Heights* has this in common with *Frankenstein* and *Sartor Resartus*: the outer frame is told by a weak or dependent narrator with faulty judgment. We are to understand the meaning of the text in *contrast* to that construed by Walton, Teufelsdrockh's editor, and Lockwood. The reader compares her interpretive acuity with that of the frame narrators, and comes to understand herself to be a better interpreter, in on a secret, deeper truth. Lockwood's outsider status helps us to envision what Brontë places at the core, with the framing texts gesturing toward what is finally beyond the capacity of language, beyond the capacity of complete conscious reconstruction, but deeply embedded in each reader's sensory memory – that is, a kinesthetic trace of childhood experience.

Although Lockwood is an inexperienced young man, he is the antithesis of Brontë's natural children in that he is both bookish and closed to sensate experience. U. C. Knoepflmacher, in his study of *Wuthering Heights*,

notes both Lockwood's young age and his "linguistic self-consciousness."
Knoepflmacher deftly captures Lockwood's speech patterns as those of

a youth who refers to pots and pans as "culinary utensils," who calls a front entrance
the "penetralium," who prefers "canine mother" to "bitch," [and] who feels com-
pelled to furnish a pedantic definition of the "significant provincial adjective" of
"Wuthering."[44]

Although Knoepflmacher is acutely aware of Lockwood's "circumlocutions,
his Latinisms, his fondness for ready-made phrases," he argues, strangely,
that Lockwood is unusually open to female experience, simply because
after reading Cathy's marginal scrawling, he identifies with her in one of
his dreams. In part, Knoepflmacher, as an expert in literature for and about
children, wants to claim Lockwood as a stalled adolescent, a Branwellian
figure who assists in Emily's imaginative play. But the evidence of his close
reading points more clearly to Lockwood's premature adulthood, as well as
to his preference for books over sensate experience.

Lockwood does, of course, attempt identification with Yorkshire
natives – particularly with Heathcliff – but Lockwood's narrative demonstrates how signally he fails. Through Lockwood, Brontë pokes fun at the
conventions of Romantic poems and tales such as *Frankenstein*, as Lockwood tries on the roles of, alternately, the Byronic hero and the man of
sensibility. He opens the novel by pretending to seek solitude in this "perfect misanthropist's heaven," so little desiring company that he considers
his landlord a neighbor to be "troubled with." Yet even in this first paragraph, our would-be misanthropist is so eager to identify with Heathcliff
that he pronounces him a "capital fellow" to whom his "heart warm[s]" in
fellow feeling. Lockwood fairly pushes his way into the house, commenting
that, "I felt interested in a man who seemed more exaggeratedly reserved
than myself" (WH, 3). Even at this early point, the reader notices that the
exaggeration is all on Lockwood's side, and the reserve all on Heathcliff's.

Although Lockwood uses the language of a man of sensibility, Brontë
makes it clear that he fails in that role as well. In the following oft-quoted
passage, Lockwood aspires to sympathetic identification with Heathcliff:

Possibly, some people might suspect him [Heathcliff] of a degree of underbred
pride: I have a *sympathetic chord* within that tells me it is nothing of the sort:
I know, by instinct, his reserve springs from an aversion to showy displays of
feeling – to manifestations of mutual kindliness. He'll love and hate, equally under
cover, and esteem it a species of impertinence to be loved or hated again – No, I'm
running on too fast – I bestow my own attributes over-liberally on him. (WH, 5,
my emphasis)

Lockwood attempts, through sympathetic intuition, to become a Byronic figure, averse to "showy displays of feeling." Next he arrests his fantasies, but gives a ridiculously unperceptive reason for doing so: "I bestow my own attributes over-liberally on him." Lockwood has it exactly backwards: it is Lockwood who wishes to bestow Heathcliff's attributes on himself. In some ways, of course, *Wuthering Heights* is a book about identification: "I am Heathcliff," as Cathy famously says. But Lockwood is the antithesis of Heathcliff, and his narrative serves as a contrasting frame to Cathy's and Heathcliff's childhood refusal to individuate.

Lockwood's digressive seaside love story reveals the source of his Byronic delusion. What Lockwood mistakes for misanthropy is really sexual terror at the threat of a non-scripted encounter with an embodied female. Attempting to cover his cowardice in a veneer of Romantic misanthropy, Lockwood retires to Yorkshire. His bursts of precious pseudo-literariness show that he is acquainted with the conventions of Romanticism, but he has little understanding of Brontë's Romantic materialism. Thus, even before Lockwood's excommunication from Wuthering Heights, we see him as an outsider, merely an armchair Romantic, with neither the capacity for sympathetic understanding nor the courage to risk physical experience.

In keeping with Brontë's system, in which the poor in natural experience are also weak in body, Lockwood displays the same kind of susceptibility to physical breakdown we saw in the characters of *Frankenstein*. In both of his visits to Wuthering Heights, Lockwood is cornered by a pack of dogs, requiring rescue by Zillah. He "trembles" with wrath, has a nosebleed, and becomes "sick exceedingly, dizzy and faint," so that Zillah puts him to bed. After his nightmare and involuntary scream from within Catherine's chamber, he is led to the Grange home with Heathcliff's reluctant assistance and arrives "feeble as a kitten" (WH, 25). The bulk of *Wuthering Heights* – that is, Nelly's tale – is in fact a tale told at Lockwood's sickbed to cure his fear-induced invalidism.

If Lockwood's narrative circles the perimeter of *Wuthering Heights*, Nelly Dean's tale, nested within Lockwood's frame, serves to mediate between robust child health and grown-up education, as well as between Yorkshire natives and mere visitors. Nelly demonstrates a reserve somewhere between Heathcliff's misanthropy and Lockwood's puppyish efforts to win friends: "We don't in general take to foreigners here, Mr. Lockwood, unless they take to us first" (WH, 35). While sturdily self-sufficient, Nelly demonstrates more give-and-take, more willingness to reciprocate human decency, than do the residents of the Heights. She functions literally as a go-between in numerous situations, carrying "tales" between virtually every member

households. We learn that she has been a sort of foster-sister to
y, neither quite servant nor family member. Not only does she nurse
n into adulthood, she also nurses other characters from illness to
health (or death). Nelly prides herself on raising Hareton and the second
Cathy, but at the same time, as earlier noted, retains her capacity to regress
into childhood yearnings. Nelly's tale signals that we've penetrated closer
to (but not yet arrived at) a genuine Romantic-materialist voice.

Just as Nelly hovers between the worlds of children and adults, she also
hovers between the worlds of nursery ballads and books. When rocking
young Hareton, for example, she sings:

> It was far in the night, and the bairnies grat,
> The mither beneath the mools heard that.
>
> (WH, 59)

The Norton edition translates "bairnies grat" as "little ones wept," and
"mools" as the "earth of a grave." Nelly rocks the motherless boy to sleep,
with songs not of heaven but of crying children whose mother, mouldering
in her grave, is helpless to assist them. Nelly's balladry acknowledges the
pain of earthly existence with an authenticity she usually avoids, as when
she utters such conventional phrases as "all children love their parents"
(WH, 157), and "People who do their duty are always finally rewarded"
(WH, 196). As Lockwood puts it, Nelly is "something heterodox," alternately spouting Christian teaching and Yorkshire superstition. Thus when
Cathy dies, and Nelly performs the ritual of "watch[ing] in the chamber of
death," Nelly muses:

To be sure, one might have doubted after the wayward and impatient existence she
had led, whether she merited a haven of peace at last. One might doubt in seasons
of cold reflection, but not then, in the presence of her corpse. It asserted its own
tranquillity, which seemed a pledge of equal quiet to its former inhabitant. (WH,
127–128)

Nelly knows that, according to orthodox doctrine, Cathy is in danger of
hellfire. But Nelly lets the "presence of [Cathy's] corpse" overcome the "cold
reflection" of orthodoxy – the physical presence of the dead body, for Nelly,
"asserted its own tranquillity" more powerfully than any system of thought.

Despite her heterodoxy, Nelly frequently returns to the teachings of good
books. Strangely, for a member of the servant class, she is book-learned, and
she deftly balances her practical Yorkshire common sense with a hard-won
education. As she explains to Lockwood:

"I certainly esteem myself a steady, reasonable kind of body," she said, "not exactly from living among the hills and seeing one set of faces, and one series of actions, from year's end to year's end; but I have undergone sharp discipline which has taught me wisdom; and then, I have read more than you would fancy, Mr. Lockwood. You could not open a book in this library that I have not looked into, and got something out of also, unless it be that range of Greek and Latin, and that of French – and those I know one from another: it is as much as you can expect of a poor man's daughter." (WH, 49)

Nelly's steadiness comes from living in the "hills" and experiencing their "sharp discipline" as well as from a thorough acquaintance with the English literature of the Grange's library.

Perhaps because Nelly's narrative mediates, combining conventional learning and Yorkshire legend, Nelly manages to bring even Lockwood to some glimmer of understanding of the world of the Heights. Her story, instead of lulling Lockwood to sleep, "rouses him to animation" (WH, 26). As it approaches eleven at night, Nelly prepares to leave, and when Lockwood protests she suggests skipping three years of the narrative. Lockwood declares himself in an "active" mood, and begs her to remain and "continue minutely." In this unusual state of animation, Lockwood exclaims:

They *do* live more in earnest, more in themselves, and less in surface change, and frivolous external things. I could fancy a love for life here almost possible; and I was a fixed unbeliever in any love of a year's standing. (WH, 48)

This is Lockwood's one fevered flash of insight, achieved as, like a child under Nelly's care, he demands yet more of the story – and here, although he's still posing as a once cynical "unbeliever," he recognizes what by now the reader takes to be the truth about the insiders at Wuthering Heights.

Unfortunately, Lockwood's month-long convalescence at the Grange, under Kenneth's surgical care, erases whatever affection for Yorkshire Nelly has raised in Lockwood. From here on, Lockwood, though he flirts with Yorkshire possibilities, evinces a distaste for local culture.

A charming introduction to a hermit's life! Four weeks' torture, tossing and sickness! Oh, these bleak winds, and bitter, northern skies, and impassable roads, and dila-tory country surgeons! And the terrible intimation of Kenneth that I need not expect to be out of doors till spring! (WH, 70)

Sick of "pills and draughts, blisters and leeches," Lockwood rings for Nelly. A winter in Yorkshire has taught him Emily Brontë's own hatred of "dilatory country surgeons"; he has instead become addicted to Nelly's healing stories.

Almost like a petulant Yorkshire child, Lockwood impatiently dismisses Nelly's gestures toward his medicines:

> "Away, away with it!" I replied. "I desire to have – "
> "The doctor says you must drop the powders."
> "With all my heart! Don't interrupt me. Come and take your seat here. Keep your fingers from that bitter phalanx of vials. Draw your knitting out of your pocket – that will do – now continue the history of Mr. Heathcliff, from where you left off, to the present day." (WH, 70)

Because he chooses "the history of Heathcliff" over "that bitter phalanx of vials," there may seem to be some hope for Lockwood. Indeed, Nelly is encouraged enough to try more mediation in the form of matchmaking between Lockwood and her beloved young Cathy. But Lockwood retreats, pronouncing "I'm of the busy world, and to its arms I must return" (WH, 195). We may not be able to imagine Lockwood as a vital participant in urban life, but it is a better backdrop for him than the Yorkshire moors. When Lockwood announces his plans for departure, Heathcliff wonders what brought this misfit to the moors in the first place. Lockwood replies, "An idle whim, I fear, sir . . . or else an idle whim is going to spirit me away" (WH, 230). Again pretending Byronic ennui, Lockwood tries to cover for his failed project of becoming Romantic – in fact for his total incomprehension of the Romantic materialism of Wuthering Heights.

If the first Cathy's narrative is resolutely anti-textual, reflecting the domestic medicine of the period, the second Catherine works through some of the problems introduced by domestic medical assumptions. Given that Emily Brontë was herself a child who read avidly and wrote prolifically, we would expect her to have a stake in reuniting the book and the natural child – and in fact, this seems to be one of the primary tasks of the second generation of *Wuthering Heights*. Having posed the question in the first generation, "How can one be both good and strong?", Brontë replies in the second: "Be a child who reads and writes." The second Cathy grows up amongst her father's books, and offers them as treasured gifts to her cousin Linton, and valuable bribes to her groom Michael (WH, 188). Once Cathy becomes the widowed Mrs. Heathcliff and an impoverished resident at the Heights, books are her only resource and the focus of her struggle with her new family. Various volumes are thus in turn smuggled from the Grange by Nelly (WH, 235), destroyed by Heathcliff, and appropriated by Hareton:

> "I was always reading, when I had them," said Catherine, "and Mr. Heathcliff never reads; so he took it into his head to destroy my books. I have not had a glimpse of one, for weeks. Only once, I searched through Joseph's story of theology, to his

great irritation; and once, Hareton, I came upon a secret stock in your room – some Latin and Greek, and some tales and poetry; all old friends. I brought the last here – and you gathered them, as a magpie gathers silver spoons, for the mere love of stealing! They are of no use to you; or else you concealed them in the bad spirit, that as you cannot enjoy them, nobody else shall. Perhaps *your* envy counselled Mr. Heathcliff to rob me of my treasures? But I've most of them written on my brain and printed in my heart and you cannot deprive me of those!" (WH, 228)

Even Joseph, jealous of his library of evangelical books, refuses to allow Cathy her own stock of literature, planning to seize any books left lying around until "Cathy threaten[s] that his library should pay for hers" (WH, 239).

Particularly in her relationship to Hareton, books are Cathy's cultural capital, which she alternately withholds or presents in gestures of rejection, flirtation, and reconciliation. After her initial scorn for Hareton's reading efforts, she decides to win him over to her side via the present of a book. Nelly tells us that

Catherine employed herself in wrapping a handsome book neatly in white paper; and having tied it with a bit of riband, and addressed it to "Mr. Hareton Earnshaw," she desired me to be her ambassadress, and convey the present to its destined recipient. (WH, 238)

The gift book succeeds where, earlier, a kiss had failed. After a brief interlude of negotiation, Cathy and Hareton have progressed beyond a truce to a silent pledge of faithfulness.

I overheard no distinguishable talk; but, on looking round again, I perceived two such radiant countenances bent over the page of the accepted book, that I did not doubt the treaty had been ratified on both sides, and the enemies were, thenceforth, sworn allies. (WH, 239)

Catherine, battered by the crew at Wuthering Heights into self-sufficiency, brought down from her sense of superiority, woos the already tempered Hareton into education. Books (despite their distancing capacity) and the wild child (despite its resistance to book-learning) finally come together. Lest we miss that we're to see Catherine and Hareton as children, Nelly describes Cathy and Hareton, bent over a book "animated with the eager interest of children; for, though he was twenty-three, and she eighteen, each had so much of novelty to feel and learn, that neither experienced nor evinced the sentiments of sober disenchanted maturity" (WH, 244). In Brontë's utopian second generation, children explore books without falling prey to "sober disenchanted maturity."

Although there is some satisfaction in watching Brontë work through the reunion of books and children, I, like most readers, do not think the story of the second generation puts to rest the more compelling desires and frustrations of the first. Nor, given the novel's structure, do I think that Brontë was after a resolution. Her closing of Lockwood's frame narrative serves not so much to tame the inner voices of the novel as to ensure their ongoing potency. We are reminded that even the educated second Cathy is more a child than Lockwood has ever been. Lockwood's incomprehension, as well as his envy, continues to build the reader's desire to claim an insider's acquaintance with the passionate world of the Heights. When Cathy doesn't appear to want to join Lockwood for his last dinner at the Heights, Lockwood in his vanity surmises "Living among clowns and misanthropists, she probably cannot appreciate a better class of people, when she meets them" (WH, 230). Then, upon departure, he cannot help fantasizing about carrying Cathy off to his busy world:

"How dreary life gets over in that house!" I reflected, while riding down the road. "What a realization of something more romantic than a fairy tale it would have been for Mrs. Linton Heathcliff, had she and I struck up an attachment, as her good nurse desired, and migrated together into the stirring atmosphere of the town!" (WH, 230–231)

Lockwood has transplanted his "romantic" "fairy tale" from rural Yorkshire to the town, but still he foolishly overestimates his courage and underestimates Cathy's. He does make one final visit to the Heights – supposedly a casual afterthought on his way to "devastate the moors of a friend, in the North" (WH, 231). Still we find him playing at country life, pluming himself on hunting skills which we by now doubt gravely. But his return is an important frame for the union of Cathy and Hareton. Lockwood voyeuristically spies on the two lovers with "a mingled sense of curiosity and envy" (WH, 233). Even now he pretends that he might have had a chance with Cathy: "I bit my lip, in spite, at having thrown away the chance I might have had of doing something besides staring at its smiting beauty" (WH, 233). Wisely, however, this outsider of outsiders keeps himself out of sight:

Then, they came to the door, and from their conversation, I judged they were about to issue out and have a walk on the moors. I supposed I should be condemned in Hareton Earnshaw's heart, if not by his mouth, to the lowest pit in the infernal regions if I showed my unfortunate person in his neighbourhood then, and feeling very mean and malignant, I skulked round to seek refuge in the kitchen. (WH, 233)

Lockwood's skulking around the house sets off the freshness, openness, and bravery of the new owners of the Heights. Upon the return of the "ramblers" Lockwood is by comparison in a very bad humor: "'They are afraid of nothing,' I grumbled, watching their approach through the window. 'Together they would brave Satan and all his legions'" (WH, 255–256). Lockwood, forced to acknowledge his unworthiness, again feels "irresistibly impelled to escape them." In the ridiculous position of being once again assumed by Joseph to be Nelly's suitor, Lockwood throws money at them both and ducks out of the Heights (WH, 256).

In the final pages of the novel, Nelly and Lockwood talk, giving voice to two options for understanding the Heights. Nelly appears, as Lockwood has noted before, particularly "heterodox," full of both local superstition and banal conventionality. She tells Lockwood that a local boy has seen Cathy and Heathcliff "*walk.*"

[The boy] probably raised the phantoms from thinking, as he traversed the moors alone, on the nonsense he had heard his parents and companions repeat – yet still, I don't like being out in the dark now; and I don't like being left by myself in this grim house. I cannot help it, I shall be glad when [Hareton and Cathy] leave it, and shift to the Grange! (WH, 255)

Yet when Lockwood makes an uneasy joke about her superstitions, she reverts to a more pious position: 'No, Mr. Lockwood,' said Nelly, shaking her head. 'I believe the dead are at peace, but it is not right to speak of them with levity' (WH, 255). Lockwood follows Nelly's lead – or *one* of her leads, the conventional one (and, for insiders, the wrong one) – to utter the memorable closing words of the frame, and of the novel:

I lingered round [the graves], under that benign sky; watched the moths fluttering among the heath and hare-bells; listened to the soft wind breathing through the grass; and wondered how any one would ever imagine unquiet slumbers for the sleepers in that quiet earth. (WH, 256)

These are perhaps Lockwood's wisest and most poetic lines. Here he seems most to know himself and to appreciate what he can appreciate, simply, about the Yorkshire graveyard. Yet for the Brontëan reader, Cathy and Heathcliff *walk*, precisely because Lockwood fails to imagine it. By surrounding the ravenous, physically passionate, child world of Wuthering Heights with a frame as insubstantial as Lockwood's, Brontë has made sure that the central myth will remain dangerous. Lockwood's unperceptive narrative provides both the sense of an ending and the sense of the soul of the novel living untamed, in all of its wild vigor, to recall to us the strong, healthy freedom and fast attachments of the earthly child.

In the end, then, Brontë transforms the teachings of earlier domestic medicine, communicating its vision of natural childhood within the covers of a book, suggesting it *through* a text rather than in lieu of it, evoking flesh through words. Deftly, she replaces the doctor's authority with the power of the narrative tale. Furthermore, she does this through a narrative technique that is difficult to describe without recourse to spatial metaphors: "nesting narratives" or "box-within-a-box narratives." Even the "frame" metaphor suggests the analogy between bodies and frames, both structures figured as supportive of, or in the service of, the art or the soul. However, Brontë's myth complicates our post-modern, often facile analogy between bodies and texts. Language gestures to, points to, embodiment, and the body back to language. Yet, for the Romantic materialist, each refuses a reduction to the other.

CHAPTER 5

Literalization in the novels of Charlotte Brontë

One of the most striking differences between the work of Emily Brontë and that of her sister Charlotte is found in their representations of childhood. For Emily, the natural child is "half-savage and hardy and free," rambling on the moors, breathing the dry, salubrious air of the high ground. For Charlotte, the child is plagued by privation and ill health, rarely escaping the unhealthy miasmas of symbolic prisons like Lowood. In part, this can be explained by the two girls' differing experiences at the Cowan Bridge School for Clergymen's Daughters, the institution that inspired Lowood. The healthy young Emily was the "pet" of the school and probably too young to be aware of the institutional neglect that hastened their elder sister Maria's death. But this experience marked Charlotte so completely as to mar forever her memories of childhood, despite her appreciation of its imaginative intensity and personal attachments. One might observe that if *Wuthering Heights* is a novel of regression, Charlotte Brontë's novels are about the struggle toward maturation. Charlotte's "Farewell to Angria" closes her apprenticeship to childhood romance and opens arguably one of the most important chapters in the development of the bildungsroman for the British tradition.

Perhaps because of her early acquaintance with privation and disease, Charlotte demonstrated less faith in the kind of natural health promoted by domestic medical texts, and exhibited less aversion to doctors and their interventions, than did Emily. More like her father in this way, Charlotte took a lay interest in medicine, particularly in the pseudoscience of phrenology. In Charlotte Brontë's fiction, doctors figure as friends offering crucial assistance and understanding. In *Jane Eyre*, the apothecary Mr. Lloyd revives the ailing Jane after her ordeal in the Red Room. He first fixes his eyes on her "very steadily," not so much in a Foucauldian gaze as in the kind of attentive receptiveness young Jane craves (JE, 22; chapter 3).[1] Lloyd then dismisses a meddling Bessie in order to have a private conference with the child. Jane seizes the coveted "opportunity of relieving grief by imparting it,"

and Lloyd is able to recommend "a change of air and scene," intervening
practically in Jane's circumstances by suggesting to her aunt the desirability
of sending her away to school (JE, 23, 25; chapter 3).

In *Villette*, of course, Dr. John Graham Bretton, named in part after
the author of Brontë's own domestic medical text, becomes Lucy Snowe's
first love interest. Much has been made of Bretton's disciplinary role as
Lucy's authoritarian doctor. Indeed, Bretton does dismiss much of Lucy's
inner experience, and (as will Lydgate after him) gravitates toward a doll
of a woman rather than the more complicated Lucy. But current criticism
has failed to remark upon Bretton's surprising status as an enduring ideal
for Lucy. *Villette* is one of the first British novels to consider a doctor as
a potential hero, remarkable at a time when a newly minted doctor had
little more prestige than a curate, that object of much Brontëan ridicule.
Lucy's consistent appreciation of the material world attracts her first to a
strappingly healthy, solidly practical John Graham Bretton, who pursues
the study of, and care for, the body. Although Lucy, after a long struggle,
recovers from her near-obsession with Bretton, she continues to enshrine
him within her imagination, to hold for him a "tabernacle" in her heart.

In contrast, then, to Emily's mythic elevation of the child body,
Charlotte's interest in the body extends beyond childhood, with less faith
in natural health, but nonetheless a deep affirmation of the Book of Nature
and those who study it. Both sisters are confirmed Romantic materialists,
but what Emily Brontë buries deep in the core of her text, Charlotte Brontë
disperses throughout hers. If Emily's material ghosts "walk" dangerously,
Charlotte's are too often missed, so integral are they to her use of language.
The means of divine revelation, for Charlotte Brontë, or even of revealing
one person to another, is typically a literalized battle between stubbornly
resistant parties, communicated in the language of bodily confrontation.
Whether in her figures of speech, her depiction of human relationships,
or her metaphysical world view, Charlotte Brontë emphasizes the difficult
but revealing conflict between two incongruous terms of comparison. This
linguistic wrestling, I will argue, attests to a deeply ingrained Romantic
materialism – a dualistic habit of thought that nonetheless revalues the
body and the material world.

This aspect of Charlotte Brontë's writing style has long been treated
as immature, both too perilously autobiographical and too violently passionate. There is a family resemblance between Matthew Arnold's disgust
at Brontë's "hunger, rebellion and rage,"[2] Virginia Woolf's wariness of
her "self-centered and self-limited" but "overpowering personality,"[3] and
Terry Eagleton's ambivalent acknowledgment that Brontë's novels, though

politically compromising, nonetheless contain a radical *"sexual* demand – an angry, wounded, implacable desire for full personal acceptance and recognition."[4] Each of these critics, to varying degrees, distrusts the personal and emotional as factors that pull Brontë (and her readers) too close to herself and too far away from either her social conscience or her art. Of course, in *The Madwoman in the Attic*, Gilbert and Gubar valorize rather than regret Brontëan rage, but they still emphasize the violent emotion, on the verge of spinning out of control, which pervades her "confessional art."[5] More recently, Janet Gezari notices the recurrence of bodily language in Brontë's novels, but interprets it as "defensive," a term that she seeks to recuperate but that nonetheless suggests more self-protection than stylistic innovation.[6]

Margaret Homans provides perhaps the most coherent theoretical framework for connecting Brontë's peculiar style with her social position. In *Bearing the Word*, Homans argues that nineteenth-century women's literature demonstrates a psycholinguistically intelligible combination of both attraction to and repulsion from *literalization*, which she defines as "a series of literary situations and practices . . . by which the relatively figurative becomes the relatively literal."[7] Unfortunately, in her chapter on Charlotte Brontë, Homans maintains that Brontë rejects literalization and "assert[s] her allegiance to her culture's dominant myth of language."[8] This "dominant myth," for Homans, is the Lacanian notion that the absence of the mother is necessary to the acquisition of the linguistic capacity for figuration. Focusing on Jane Eyre's foreboding dreams of wailing children, Homans argues that Brontë reveals Jane's unconscious fear of childbearing, which in turn betrays Brontë's own fear of being barred from figurative writing and restricted to the traditionally feminine realm of the literal.

Homans has presented a convincing argument for taking literalization seriously despite the denigration of the literal by mainstream Western culture. But my position with regard to literalization in Brontë is nearly 180 degrees from Homans's, which relies too heavily on brief and particularly ambiguous dream passages from one novel. Preserving Homans's general theory about nineteenth-century women's literature, but taking issue with her particular application of it to Brontë, I will argue that literalization is Brontë's forte rather than her fear, which explains such markedly Brontëan peculiarities as her stylistic "coarseness," her wryly ironic Biblical allusions, her fondness for phrenological psychology, and the seeming sadomasochism that she depicts in human relationships.[9]

There is one point about Homans's theory that I wish to clarify before turning to Brontë's works. At times Homans confuses literalization with "taking things literally."[10] But literalizing a metaphor, I will argue, recharges its metaphoricity. To take things literally is to abolish the difference between compared terms; to literalize is to enhance that difference, which is often absurdly or mystically heightened by emphasizing the conflict between the terms of the metaphor. The treatment of "dissonance" in Ricoeurean hermeneutics offers a method for a more precise theorization of literalization. In *Interpretation Theory*, Paul Ricoeur introduces his theory of split reference, arguing that "discourse cannot fail to be about something" but that the problematic referent constantly shifts between the self and the world.[11] Thus discourse refers at once in two directions, the reference being split to varying degrees between self-reference and other-reference.

In Ricoeur's view, discourse can "redescribe" the world because it moves in a dialectic between distancing and appropriating otherness. Mario Valdés explains the terms of Ricoeur's dialectic:

> By "distanciation" Ricoeur means the semantic autonomy of the text, which stands removed from its unknown multiple readers. By "appropriation" he means the process of making one's own what was not.[12]

To this I would add that in Ricoeur "appropriation" should not be confused with the current usage in literary theory – that cultural theft performed by a dominant group in the process of subjugating the other. Neither should it be confused with a Diltheyan interpretation of Romantic hermeneutics, the extreme against which Ricoeur pitches his argument in *Interpretation Theory*. In this text, Ricoeur is most concerned that his term "appropriation" should not be misconstrued as "the Romanticist claim to a 'congenial' coincidence with the 'genius' of the author":

> In other words, what has to be appropriated is nothing other than the power of disclosing a world that constitutes the reference of the text. In this way we are as far as possible from the Romanticist ideal of coinciding with a foreign psyche. If we may be said to coincide with anything, it is not the inner life of another ego, but the disclosure of a possible way of looking at things, which is the genuine referential power of the text.[13]

Ricoeur stresses that appropriation rescues the reader from complete "estrangement" from the foreign, whereas distanciation "preserves the cultural distance." The act of reading challenges "ownness" with "Otherness," and permits a difficult proximity.[14]

At the level of the sentence, Ricoeur's redescription, or refiguration, takes place through metaphor. Innovation comes through the tension generated by the conflict of similarity and difference within the metaphor itself. Drawing from Aristotle, Ricoeur claims that the maker of metaphors sees the similarities in things previously thought irretrievably different. The "semantic impertinence" of such an unexpected but felicitous linking of things thought different "shocks" the reader into a new conception of reality. "There are no live metaphors in a dictionary," Ricoeur points out. The "life" of a metaphor relies on the presence of both "dissonance" and "concordance" between the two things said to be "like" one another.[15]

For Ricoeur, then, there is no ultimate synthesis or resting place in dialogic exchange between the literal and the figurative, both of which are equally necessary for innovation in meaning. For the reader, "there are really not two significations, one literal and the other symbolic, but rather a single movement which transfers" him or her from one interpretation to another.[16] Here I add that this transfer is reversible, and, in the terms used earlier, the direction which points to the consonance in assumed dissonance is figuration, whereas the direction which reintroduces dissonance into presumed consonance is literalization. Literalization thus consists of the reawakening of a somnolent metaphor by insisting on the dissonance of its parts, releasing the disjunction or otherness, and thereby, according to Ricoeur, renovating the meaning of a traditional metaphor.

Homans sees literalization as a translation from idea to fact, whereas I propose that literalization takes the fact as primary, originary, crucial, and something that has been ignored – and insists on returning to it. And where Homans sees the delivery of the literal as the end and/or goal of the translation process, I would emphasize with Ricoeur that the literal is the midwife of a startling new figuration. Literalization is conservative in that it is a sort of back-translation, checking a figure against its literal components, but it is radical in its production of dissonance, usually in the form of comedy, irony, absurdity, or mystery.

One indication of Charlotte Brontë's major literary innovation is that epithet "coarse" which fellow Victorians most frequently hurled at her. The epithet surprised Brontë, and Harriet Martineau won Brontë's devotion by declaring that any coarseness was attributable to the minds of the readers.[17] Yet the word, with its connotation not only of sexual explicitness but also of rough insistence on the intransigence of matter and human bodies, captures a significant characteristic of Brontë's novels. Homans demonstrates that the literal haunts Jane's dreams, but she ignores the evidence that literal, tangible material goods are also Jane's conscious desire.

The third volume of *Jane Eyre*, detailing Jane's sustained conflict with St. John Rivers, revolves around the importance to Jane of earthly things. Though she respects St. John's spiritual ardor, she cannot marry without domestic love. When she inherits, she is glad of the money for what she can do with it, and when St. John inquires about her mission in life, she replies:

My first aim will be to *clean down* (do you comprehend the full force of the expression?) to *clean down* Moor-House from chamber to cellar; my next to rub it up with bees-wax, oil, and indefinite number of cloths, till it glitters again; my third, to arrange every chair, table, bed, carpet, with mathematical precision; afterwards I shall go near to ruin you in coals and peat to keep up good fires in every room; and lastly, the two days preceding that on which your sisters are expected, will be devoted by Hannah and me to such a beating of eggs, sorting of currants, grating of spices, compounding of Christmas cakes, chopping up of materials for mince-pies, and solemnizing of other culinary rites, as words can convey but an inadequate notion of to the uninitiated like you. (JE, 498–499; chapter 34)

Piling together enthusiastic quantities of bees-wax, coals, and currants in her ardor, Jane has reversed the sacramental order of spiritual over material. Doubtless offended by Jane's ironic use of the ecclesiastical language of "devotion" and "solemnizing rites" which are mystifying to the "uniniti-ated," St. John demeans these "commonplace home pleasures" and enjoins her to "look beyond" these "trite transient objects" (JE, 499; chapter 34). Yet, in a sense, her comic domestic litany looks *with* these valued objects toward a more than material meaning, a domestic energy signaled by the dissonance between currants and "solemn rites," a joy to which St. John is indeed uninitiate.

More pervasive throughout Charlotte Brontë's novels than this thematic insistence on domestic matter is the Brontëan trick of literalizing Biblical metaphors. Elizabeth Gaskell, one of Charlotte's staunchest supporters, worried about her supposed "profanity" in quoting Scripture, and *The Christian Remembrancer* charged that she "plays with [the Bible's] sacred pages, as though they had been given to the world for no better purpose than to point a witticism or furnish an ingenious illustration."[18] In *Shirley*, for instance, when Caroline is surprised by a sudden coldness in Robert's behavior, the narrator advises us to embrace maltreatment:

You expected bread, and you have got a stone; break your teeth on it, and don't shriek because the nerves are martyrized: do not doubt that your mental stomach – if you have such a thing – is strong as an ostrich's – the stone will digest. You held out your hand for an egg, and fate put into it a scorpion. Show no consternation: close your fingers firmly upon the gift; let it sting through your palm. Never mind: in time, after your hand and arm have swelled and quivered long with torture, the squeezed scorpion will die, and you will have learned the great lesson how to endure without a sob. For the whole remnant of your life, if you survive the test – some, it is said, die under it – you will be stronger, wiser, less sensitive. (S, 117–118; chapter 7)

This is an apparently ironical reference to one of Jesus' illustrations of divine love. Encouraging his listeners to "seek, and ye shall find," Jesus asks whether a father when asked for bread will give a stone, or when asked for an egg will give a scorpion. He caps these rhetorical questions with another, "how much more shall your heavenly Father give the Holy Spirit to them that ask him?"[19] Brontë perversely counters Jesus' rhetoric, pointing out that earthly fathers or at least friends are quite likely to give vicious "gifts," that the Heavenly Father does not intervene, and that we should therefore not so much "seek to find" as strive to endure – and she says this in brutally physical, painful, ugly terms.

Even today many readers find such language repellent, and some assume with Brontë's contemporaries that her narrator's bitterness is indicative of a loss, or at least a secularization, of faith.[20] Thomas Vargish admits that the providential aesthetic – the idea that God rewards goodness – has "undergone some sinister modifications" in *Villette*, and that in fact Brontë entirely "drops the convention of poetic justice." But he points out that, despite *Villette*'s darkness, that novel "puts itself forward as a Christian, even as a Protestant work," maintaining a rhetoric of divine intent.[21] Lucy refuses to deny God's ultimate justice, not to mention his loving presence, despite her exquisite (and exquisitely detailed) suffering. This results in a sort of reverse election in which some are specially chosen to suffer: Lucy recounts,

How I used to pray to Heaven for consolation and support! With what dread force the conviction would grasp me that Fate was my permanent foe, never to be conciliated. I did not, in my heart, arraign the mercy or justice of God for this; I concluded it to be a part of his great plan that some must deeply suffer while they live, and I thrilled in the certainty that of this number, I was one. (V, 198; chapter 14)

Vargish calls this "inverted election" a "variation of Protestantism in which divine favor reveals itself through a logic of reversal."[22] Images of inversion recur in the Bible: the high are brought low, the rich are sent away empty, the first are made last, servants become masters, the by-ways are scoured for the outcasts to celebrate the wedding feast. Moreover, notes Vargish, those who believe tenaciously despite a series of unexpected and undeserved reversals, "those who like Job, embrace pain as divinely sent and who embrace it not from choice but from compulsion," are granted "peculiar fulfillment."[23] Peculiar – in the sense of singular, special, strange, odd – is indeed an

appropriate word for the dissonance Brontë favors, given that it is her own
specially marked word. In her farewell to her beloved M. Heger, Brontë
wishes for him "peculiar blessings," and they are peculiar blessings indeed
that she grants Lucy in *Villette*.[24]

One of the traditional mechanisms for reversal in the Bible is insistence on the hyperbolic materiality of something presumed to be spiritual, or the immediacy of something assumed to be either past or in the
future. This tradition was maintained especially by Evangelical Protestants
through an emphasis on historical reality, the literal truth of the Bible,
and a strict application of the Bible to daily practice. Victorian Evangelicals
favored typological interpretation, in which certain people and events from
Hebrew Scripture were taken to be both historically true and prefigurations
of Jesus, the events of the New Testament, and the apocalypse of Jesus' Second Coming. Though an ancient interpretive method, typology had been
popularized by Protestant reformers as a corrective to the supposed deval-
uation of the literal in medieval allegorical readings. Its revival in Victorian
England, according to George Landow, was probably due to the promise
it held for reconciling spiritual teaching with the increasing importance
of scientific fact in industrial culture, as well as with the growing taste for
realism as an aesthetic value.[25]

Raised a Low Church Anglican, influenced by the Methodism of her
Aunt Branwell, Brontë was a fluent typologist. One pivotal instance of
Brontëan typology occurs in the third volume of *Shirley*, a volume written
amidst the fresh grief of Anne's death following hard upon Branwell's and
Emily's. Lyndall Gordon notes that Charlotte "appears to be thinking of
her sisters and only obliquely of her heroine."[26] Caroline Helstone nearly
dies in this chapter, which ends with the agony of her mother Mrs. Pryor
who "spent the night like Jacob at Peniel. Till break of day, she wrestled
with God in earnest prayer" (S, 497; chapter 24).[27] The next chapter opens
with the meditation that Jacob's experience was not representative of that
of all those who pray strenuously:

Not always do those who dare such divine conflict prevail. Night after night the
sweat of agony may burst dark on the forehead; the supplicant may cry for mercy
with that soundless voice the soul utters when its appeal is to the Invisible . . . And
after this cry and strife, the sun may rise and see him worsted. (S, 498; chapter 25)

Brontë's narrator is plainly challenging the universality of this tale of conflict
and revelation.

In the Genesis account, of course, Jacob does prevail against his unseen
opponent after wrestling through the night.[28] Although his hip is wrenched

in the process, Jacob tenaciously holds his opponent until he obtains a blessing, and then limps away at dawn claiming victory. The teaching frequently
drawn from this passage is that divine revelation often follows a difficult conflict, with wrestling becoming a type for strenuous prayer. Brontë's emphasis
is strange, however, for a typologist – she uses the passage specifically to
protest that one may wrestle prayerfully and to the limit of one's endurance,
not through one night, but "night after night," and yet God may remain
"Invisible," and "the sun may rise and see [the supplicant] worsted." Moreover, this reversed typology is superfluous, unnecessary because Caroline's
physical crisis passes the very night of Mrs. Pryor's prayerful wrestling.
Why this concrete, realistic, violent disturbance of the traditional typological relation? The obvious answer is that Brontë is distracted by her own
grief, that the autobiographical overwhelms the fictional. But this pattern
of concretizing and challenging typology is so frequent for Brontë that we
must either say, with some of her critics, that she is an incessantly and
distractedly autobiographical novelist, or that such a pattern constitutes a
significant part of her art.

Does Brontë's ironic reversal necessarily contradict the Jacob story? I
think her rendition of the struggle with God is a literalized and hyperbolic
vision rather than a counter-vision. Brontë makes a typological connection
between Jacob's struggle and Jesus' at Gethsemane. That the "sweat may
burst dark on the forehead" (or, in the uncorrected manuscript, "the heart's
dark sweat may burst red on the forehead"[29]) recalls the story of Jesus
sweating blood as he begs the Father to avert his death on the cross (S, 498;
chapter 25).[30] Brontë thus relates Jacob's triumphant struggle to Jesus' struggle in his Passion, and these to the possibility that the faithful may also suffer
and die. This updates and prolongs the dissonance already present in the
Genesis story, releasing the idea that revelation is a mystery, and that an
epiphany may not be so much a completed and comprehensible appearance
as an embattled interface between comprehension and confusion.

The curious dissonance in the Genesis story, especially when reviewed
through a Brontëan perspective, arises from the fact that Jacob's victory is
entirely dependent on his audacious claim and is otherwise somewhat questionable. The Biblical text never identifies the opponent, even emphasizes
that the opponent refuses to identify himself, and the struggle takes place
in complete darkness. Yet Jacob declares he has seen God "face to face," an
epiphany that, according to Hebrew belief, should have cost Jacob his life.
It is almost as if the material conflict itself constitutes the epiphany. Note
the crude physical terms in which the struggle is described: Jacob's opponent is "a man" who can be grasped and detained, who can put Jacob's hip

out of joint, bandy phrases with him, and send him away wounded. Even the blessing pales in comparison to the struggle – it is not enunciated by the text, nor is there an account of whether or how the blessing is fulfilled. Genesis has previously presented Jacob as a grasping man, and once again he seizes and shapes his own opportunity with a confident interpretation: to struggle in the dark (perhaps with God) is, according to Jacob, to see God face to face.

Like the Jacob story, Brontë's novels present conflict not as a mere preliminary to a final, transcendent synthesis, but as a revelation in and of itself. To engage in battle with a demanding opponent is to take the opponent seriously, as worthy to be known. For Brontë, it is only in pitched conflict that we see the friend/opponent face to face. Sometimes, as in *The Professor*, psychological warfare is literalized as physical wrestling, but more frequently the contest is one of reading faces, of scanning literal features for signs of character. The acute reading of facial features, especially if one can accomplish it without being read oneself, becomes the sharpest of Brontëan weapons.

The tendency for literalization to create dissonance is dramatically illustrated in Brontë's penchant for phrenology, a theory of a literalized mind, and in her depiction of the contests in which phrenologic readers engage one another. According to phrenological doctrine, personality could be read through tactile examination of enlargements and depressions of the skull. People were thought to wear literal, external signs of their psychological constitution. The mind, located in the brain, was supposedly differentiated into personality traits that were further localized into specific areas of the brain, with the skull molded around uneven distributions of such personality traits. Reading these signs required a trained examiner because each individual exhibited multiple and contrasting "propensities" (negative traits) and "faculties" (positive traits) arguing with one another. Sally Shuttleworth emphasizes the phrenological belief in the conflict within the individual psyche:

George Combe, the Scottish populariser of phrenology, observed, "Man is confessedly an assemblage of contradictions." ... The individual was, for the phrenologist, the site of warring forces.[31]

Just as the literalized mind is a "site of warring forces" for Brontë, so also is human relationship a wrestling between parties who try to know one another without themselves being known. Brontëan heroes and heroines are astute readers of character who mask and withhold information about their own characters, and who are most challenged and intrigued by other people whose characters are likewise difficult to decipher.[32]

In *The Professor*, Brontë reveals her most disturbing vision of difficult human relationships through a narrator who is himself isolated and self-protected, and who nonetheless aggressively probes those around him. William Crimsworth prides himself on his skill at reading character, and cruelly renders several of his students in the phrenological jargon of features and evil propensities, concluding that "in less than five minutes they had thus revealed to me their characters, and in less than five minutes I had buckled on a breastplate of steely indifference, and let down a visor of impassable austerity" (P, 86; chapter 10). Crimsworth's armor imagery already betrays his embattled defensiveness, but his reading of character really ripens into mutual contest when Crimsworth meets a more worthy opponent. Of his wily employer Mlle. Reuter, Crimsworth writes:

Her mere words could have afforded no clue to this aim [of discovering my character], but her countenance aided; while her lips uttered only affable commonplaces, her eyes reverted continually to my face. Her glances were not given in full, but out of the corners, so quietly, so stealthily, yet I think I lost not one. I watched her as keenly as she watched me; I perceived soon that she was feeling after my real character; she was searching for salient points, and weak points, and eccentric points; she was applying now this test, now that, hoping in the end to find some chink, some niche, where she could put in her little firm foot and stand upon my neck – mistress of my nature. (P, 89; chapter 10)

Heather Glen likens this interpersonal surveillance, which "chillingly replac[es] any more intimate conception of human interaction," to the Foucauldian gaze, claiming that, although "Charlotte Brontë is not primarily concerned with institutions," she nonetheless "charts the operation of such strategies in the most intimate recesses of the personality."[33] Of course Brontëan watching is blatantly a contest for power in which one tries to become master or "mistress of [another's] nature," but Glen misses the mutuality of many of these encounters, and the degree to which the gazing weapon counters rather than enforces the dominant social power. True, Brontë stereotypes French or Belgian Catholic "surveillance" as sinister because one-sided, imbalanced, and covert, but she promotes the forthright gaze (which she codes as Protestant) precisely because it invites confrontation. Finally, Glen ignores the strange, almost transcendent, intimacy Brontë implies when such gazing becomes increasingly open, increasingly difficult, and literalized as an acknowledged contest.

The antagonistic friendship between Crimsworth and Yorke Hunsden suggests both a natural friction between socially disparate individuals and a mysterious, supernatural bond between them. Elements of both comedy and fairy tale merge in the character of Hunsden, who, with his dark locks and masterful temper, may be a throwback to Charlotte's childhood hero Zamorna, the semi-supernatural king of Angria. Hunsden comes in and out of Crimsworth's life unexpectedly but especially at crucial times, a bit like a fairy godbrother, granting favors and suing for gratitude, a sort of trickster-deity. Socially, Hunsden is Crimsworth's opposite, a wealthy manufacturer to Crimsworth's impoverished aristocrat. As a captain of industry, Hunsden is at once a materialist and a part of a new upper class, which explains in part the mutual antagonism. But he is also "original," unpredictable, alternately generous and petty. His is the only face Crimsworth has difficulty deciphering. His features

were plastic; character had set a stamp upon each, expression re-cast them at her pleasure – and strange metamorphoses she wrought, giving him now the mien of a morose bull and anon that of an arch and mischievous girl; more frequently the two semblances were blent, and a queer, composite countenance they made. (P, 35; chapter 4)

Hunsden's plasticity, his androgyny, and the "queer composite" of his crude materialist pride and neo-aristocratic lordliness remain an undeveloped mystery in the novel, the significance of which is signaled by barely suppressed comedy and a suggestion of mysticism.

In the midst of barbed teasing, Hunsden and Crimsworth finally literalize their strange friendship in an archetypal wrestle:

[Hunsden] swayed me to and fro; so I grappled him round the waist; it was dark; the street lonely and lampless; we had then a tug for it, and after we had both rolled on the pavement and with difficulty picked ourselves up, we agreed to walk on more soberly. (P, 243; chapter 24)

Crimsworth gives no further commentary on this tussle in the dark. We only know it is intimate and hilarious in that they "agree" to walk on together "more soberly." But the antagonism is real enough as they part: "With a simultaneous movement, each turned his back on the other; neither said 'God bless you'; yet on the morrow the sea was to roll between us" (P, 244; chapter 24). No blessing comes from this struggle; if Brontë is alluding to Jacob's wrestle, she is following her pattern of ironic typological reversal. The hints at revelation are indeed meager in this novel; Brontë seems more concerned with establishing the conflictual nature of human relationship, and, as she writes in her preface, values the novel for its vision of strife. *The Professor*, she writes, has "gone through some struggles" in its publication and will wrestle even more strenuously with its audience in "its worst struggle and strongest ordeal," that of being read.[34]

In *The Professor*, Hunsden, the worthy, perhaps even supernatural opponent, is also the most difficult person to read phrenologically. I propose that Brontë uses phrenology as a literalization, often comic, which returns value to the plasticity of personality, especially when contrasted to a phrenologic materialist reduction. Most critics of Brontë have assumed that, because she used phrenologic jargon, she quite soberly adopted phrenologic belief. According to Sally Shuttleworth, phrenology offered the rising Victorian middle class a material confirmation of cherished theories about meritorious rather than class-based intelligence and moral capacity. But Brontë's personal and novelistic references to phrenology are frequently jocular, pointing out that the very literalization that offered reassurance was absurdly inflexible. Even phrenologic devotees often succumbed to the temptation to joke about it, an irrepressible humor arising from the idea that one's character was equivalent to one's "bumps." Certainly this humor surfaces in *Jane Eyre* when Rochester offers his forehead for Jane's reading:

He lifted up the sable waves of hair which lay horizontally over his brow, and showed a solid enough mass of intellectual organs; but an abrupt deficiency where the suave sign of benevolence should have risen.
"Now, ma'am, am I a fool?"
"Far from it sir. You would perhaps think me rude if I inquired in return whether you are a philanthropist?" (JE, 161; chapter 14)

Jane's teasing irony is effective because Rochester's capacity for loving people is infinitely more complicated, unpredictable, alternately stingy and extravagant, than the presence or absence of a smooth, "suave" sign could possibly communicate.

In *Villette*, the characters also watch and read each other incessantly, but reading is no longer a rigid or defining task. When M. Paul has concentrated all his physiognomic skill on the newly arrived Lucy, he pronounces "I read [her countenance]," but evades direct reply when asked what he sees in it saying he reads "bien des choses," many things, both bad and good. Questioned at length by Madame Beck,

Still he scrutinized. The judgment, when it at last came, was as indefinite as what had gone before it.
"Engage her. If good predominates in that nature, the action will bring its own reward; if evil – eh bien! ma cousine, ce sera toujours une bonne œuvre." (V, 91; chapter 7)

The "resolute" M. Paul, who gazes as if "a veil would be no veil for him," cannot give more than an "indefinite" prediction of Lucy's course. He is both a "diviner" and a "vague arbiter." He sees, but it is a mixed vision, and he cannot or will not do more than recommend the ethical performance of a "bonne œuvre," a good turn, regardless of Lucy's character. This is a remarkably different use of character reading than that which we see in *The Professor*. It is just as literal – M. Paul is consulted, gazes steadily, and draws conclusions from his observations of the shape of Lucy's face, and she is hired on these grounds, as historically some like her were. But the meaning of the literal is complicated and uncertain, framed in terms of value-laden potential rather than determined fact.

Villette's phrenologic language, when less rigidly determining, is also less humorous; but Lucy literalizes character via a related comic style, that of caricature. Francesca Kazan recognizes the importance in *Villette* of the caricature of M. Paul:

More often than not he is a formless body represented by three articles: his *lunettes*, his *paletot*, and his *bonnet grec* . . . To cite two arbitrary examples: a door bursts open and "a paletot, and a bonnet grec filled the void" (201); "that chair, and my desk, seized by the wild paletot, one under each sleeve, were borne afar" (492). To some extent this is comic relief in a tale of solitude. But it is more than that.[35]

Kazan concludes that this "more" than comic effect is that rendering of M. Paul as "a pure abstraction, a negative presence" that Lucy can then recreate by projecting her own memory of dialogue, ensuring "her own inviolate dominion."[36] Kazan's reading coincides with many that stress M. Paul's three-year absence and death as necessary to Lucy's growth and independence, and as somehow satisfying to the author as an exorcism of the memory of M. Heger, her beloved master at Brussels. Quite to the contrary, I read these episodes as comic literalizations of M. Paul that release, in addition to comedy, a sense of the fullness of his character. In Henri Bergson's theory, humor is produced by "something mechanical encrusted on the living"; the disjunction between the rigidity of the signifier and the supple life of the signified produces laughter, and an affirmation of that which cannot be captured so simply.[37] M. Paul is funny and endearing because his expansive generosity exceeds his irritable temper. In literalizing him, Lucy releases this excess, sparking a recognition of full character on the part of the reader. Rather than suppressing or controlling the expression of Paul's character, she allows its male, Roman Catholic, Spanish, French, and Belgian otherness free play.

Dissonance in *Villette* also continues to be the primary metaphor for human relationship: Lucy and M. Paul in particular engage in "sharp combat" (V, 509; chapter 30) or "strong battle, with confused noise of demand and rejection, exaction and repulse" (V, 516; chapter 30). When they battle over the question of religion, Lucy declares her faith:

[I] so widely severed myself from him I addressed – then at last, came a tone accordant, an echo responsive, one sweet chord of harmony between two conflicting spirits. (V, 611; chapter 36)

This rapport is not a fusion; they both utter their creeds in their native languages – and each as an assertion of a tough constancy of belief. But peaceful accord follows, in which M. Paul articulates his belief in the mystery of human trust despite clash and confusion. The largeness of God, beyond "Time," "Space," "Measure," or "Comparison," makes human difference insignificant, he says. Although M. Paul has a humble vision of an embattled "little" humanity, he claims that human constancy is more important than the cosmos, even to a high and inscrutable God, "that mighty unseen centre incomprehensible, irrealizable, with strange mental effort only divined" (V, 612; chapter 36). When Lucy and M. Paul have struggled to exhaustion and agreed only on the importance of humility and individual integrity, a visionary acceptance of mystery descends in the form of M. Paul's eloquent vision and the peace of his benediction: "God guide us all! God bless you, Lucy!" (V, 612; chapter 36).

Although the secretive Roman Catholic "surveillance of a sleepless eye" continues as in *The Professor* to be a sinister activity of the powerful, open confrontational looking becomes a positive acknowledgment and engagement of another. Part of the trouble between Lucy and Dr. John is that John does not see her, except at most as an "inoffensive shadow,"

according me just that degree of notice and consequence a person of my exterior habitually expects: that is to say, about what is given to unobtrusive articles of furniture, chairs of ordinary joiner's work, and carpets of no striking pattern. (V, 135; chapter 10)

When Lucy gapes at Dr. John in the recognition that he is Graham Bretton, his attention is finally "arrested" by her "direct, inquiring gaze":

I saw that his notice was arrested, and that it had caught my movement in a clear little oval mirror fixed in the side of the window recess – by the aid of which reflector madame often secretly spied persons walking in the garden below. (V, 136; chapter 10)

This confrontational mutual looking takes place in Madame's spying mirror, as if to emphasize the difference between secretive spying and the kind of looking that demands – even offensively – engagement.

Beginning with his phrenologic examination of Lucy's head, M. Paul is the one who seems fully to see her. He recognizes her potential as an actress, and consequently demands her participation: "I read your skull, that night you came; I see your moyens: play you can; play you must" (V, 185; chapter 14). She becomes more concrete and solid under his gaze, a sentient being full of untapped resources, to whom M. Paul exclaims:

> I know you! I know you! Other people in this house see you pass, and think that a colourless shadow has gone by. As for me, I scrutinized your face once, and it sufficed. (V, 216; chapter 15)

Lucy recognizes the cruelty of M. Paul's gaze on his most talented students, and literalizes it in a sustained analogy of the student as newly born being, emerging through conflict and longing to rest, but unprotected from M. Paul's scrutiny. Keeping "austerest police-watch" over the "pain-pressed" victims of his ordeals, M. Paul continues to torture through examination:

> And when at last [M. Paul] allowed [his student] rest, before slumber might close the eyelids, he opened those same lids wide, with pitiless finger and thumb, and gazed deep through the pupil and the irids into the brain, into the heart, to search if Vanity, or Pride, or Falsehood, in any of its subtlest forms, was discoverable in the furthest recess of existence. (V, 506–507; chapter 30)

Only after severe trial, "when the most corrosive aquafortis had been used, and failed to tarnish the ore," did M. Paul consider the metal genuine and then he, "still in clouded silence, stamped it with his deep brand of approval" (V, 507; chapter 30). Rest is won only at perilous cost, and even in the midst of silence M. Paul's approval sears the hardened metal. This is certainly one of Brontë's most violent series of images for interpersonal contest and engagement. Lucy, however, considers M. Paul's manner explicable – even admirable – and, though she at one point chastises him for undignified spying, she comes to trust his more direct literal and metaphorical scrutiny. In nearly the same phrase she uses for Catholic surveillance, she revels in "the assurance of his *sleepless interest* which broke on me like a light from heaven" (V, 703; chapter 41, my emphasis).

Contest and scrutiny, for the tough combatants Lucy and M. Paul, yield a remarkable understanding of one another, often expressed in the religious language of trust. "Fear not to trust in me – I am a man to be trusted," M. Paul tells her when he offers fraternal friendship (V, 588: chapter 35). When M. Paul defies Madame Beck, comforting Lucy before he sails away, he whispers, not "I love you," but, strangely, "Trust me!" (V, 695; chapter 41). As he takes her to view her own school, he asks if she will not "trust my shoulder as a safe stay?" (V, 697; chapter 41). Her response, likewise, is not "I love you," but the disciple's "Teach me," "I am ready," and "I will be your faithful steward" (V, 697, 704; chapter 41). Can Brontë really be suggesting that the little tyrant Paul Emanuel is a type for the divine?

Literalization offers a plausible explanation for the touching absurdity of M. Paul's alternately violent and tender, yet somehow trustworthy relationship with Lucy. M. Paul is hardly a recognizable Christ-figure, as his Hebrew surname Emanuel, meaning "God with us," might suggest, but he is a literalized, humanized reflection of Lucy's experience of a notably Hebraic God – often inscrutable, jealous, irritable because passionately loving, and commanding trust anyway. This literalization accents the dissonance between a New Testament, Greek conception of a perfect, all-knowing, heavenly Father-God, and the Hebraic tribal deity that argues and wrestles with his stiff-necked people. In the absurdity of comparing M. Paul to a transcendent God, Brontë rejuvenates the peculiar, even offensive tension latent in Old Testament metaphors of faith, reintroducing the force of Hebrew metaphor to the tamed imaginations of her largely Christian readers.

If the irritable trustworthiness of the Hebraic God is literalized in M. Paul, so also is the apparent arbitrariness of circumstance literalized as fate. "Fate" is the "great abstraction" which Lucy nonetheless immediately personifies as an individual "on whose wide shoulders I like to lay the mountains of blame they were sculptured to bear" (V, 265; chapter 17). Lucy "won't hear any one blamed" for her mental turmoil over the long vacation. In her bitterness, she will not blame Madame Beck, nor Dr. John, nor God – so she creates the personage of Fate. Lucy seems most incapacitated when she uses standard dying metaphors for her misfortunes, such as the shipwreck metaphor in which she mysteriously cloaks her family's misfortune earlier in the novel. She is strongest when she literalizes, when she is able to tear into her pain, and face it as she would a real person or thing. Shuttleworth notes that "the description of Vashti tearing hurt into shreds anticipates Lucy's later destruction of the figure of the nun."[38] Here are the two passages side by side:

[Vashti] does not *resent* her grief . . . To her, what hurts becomes immediately embodied: she looks on it as a thing that can be attacked, worried down, torn in shreds. Scarcely a substance herself, she grapples to conflict with abstractions. (V, 370; chapter 23)

All the movement was mine, so was all the life, the reality, the substance, the force; as my instinct felt. I tore her up – the incubus! I held her on high – the goblin! I shook her loose – the mystery! And down she fell – down all round me – down in shreds and fragments – and I trode upon her. (V, 681; chapter 39)

Literalization of abstractions becomes a weapon for Lucy's battle against resentment and blame. Like Vashti, Lucy finds that creating a tangible opponent gives her "life," "reality," "substance," and "force."

This fierce and funny battle with the "nun" (literally a dressed-up bolster that Lucy rips to shreds) is all the more powerful because it immediately follows, and deflates the drama of, a more likely scene for revelation, Lucy's magical, opium-laced wandering on the *nuit blanche*. As in *Jane Eyre*, in which Jane is "tempted" by St. John's inspired preaching on the Book of Revelation to "cease struggling with him – to rush down the torrent of his will into the gulf of his existence" (JE, 534; chapter 31) –, Lucy is similarly tempted to relax her struggle and be swept into revelation. Brontë's language throughout the *nuit blanche* sequence is remarkable for its uncharacteristically fluid images: the gate yielded as if with "some dissolving force," music "floated," and the noise of the crowd grew "like a strong tide, a great flow." Women wore gauze and drooping plumes, their "drapery floating." Lucy "drank the elastic night-air," the pool appeared "tremulous and rippled," and the concert sounded "as a sea breaking into song with all its waves." Even the movement of the crowd like a "swaying tide swept this way, and then it fell back." The scene was "impressed" on Lucy's mind, with "a dream-like character; every shape was wavering, every movement floating, every voice echo-like" (V, 656; chapter 38). Intoxicated with opium-heightened perception, Lucy floats easily into Villette society, almost magically invisible amongst her friends, like a visitant spirit.

If we forget the Brontëan pattern of conflict and revelation, all this fluid harmony seems a set-up for revelation. Lucy expects it – and is disappointed – twice. First she expects a metaphysical revelation, as she hears that "Justine Marie" will soon appear. She uses St. Paul's language of apocalyptic revelation: "[H]itherto I had seen this spectre only through a glass darkly; now was I to behold it face to face" (V, 671; chapter 39).[39] Lucy's life stands still as she waits, holding her breath, but "the crisis and the revelation are passed by" as, instead of the nun, M. Paul's ward appears, cut "from the homely web of truth" (V, 672; chapter 39).

Understandably, Lucy next expects a revelation to be had from the real. Again she uses the language of seeing the face of the divine: "I always, through my whole life, liked to penetrate to the real truth; I like seeking the goddess in her temple, and handling the veil, and daring the dread glance" (V, 674; chapter 39). "Truth" and "Fact" become the objects of revelation as she presumes that M. Paul is to marry Justine Marie:

Thus it must be. The revelation was indeed come . . . not seeing the true bearing of the oracle, I had thought she muttered of vision when, in truth, her prediction touched reality. (V, 646; chapter 39)

Although Lucy earns a momentary freedom and renewed appreciation of "lowliness and peace" through her attempt to meet jealousy head-on, she wryly finds the next day that "Freedom excused himself, as for the present, impoverished and disabled to assist; and Renovation never spoke; he had died in the night suddenly" (V, 692; chapter 41). Moreover, she soon discovers that the supposed revelation is false, induced by her own cowardly resignation.

When Lucy tries to orchestrate an orderly revelation, natural or supernatural, it eludes her. The fete-night is a glorious feast of impressionistic description, and the crown of the novel for many readers, but Brontë refuses to endorse easeful, fluid, harmonious beauty. Rather, *Villette* is about the difficulty of wrestling with circumstance, warfare in relationships, the storm of bitterness fully felt, and the possibility of trust anyway – although the option of trust, appropriately for this novel, is finally left very much in the reader's hands. Most readers agree that, sunny imagination or not, there is no hope of M. Paul's return. At most, we can expect Lucy to continue as she has, saying "I believe while I tremble; I trust while I weep" (V, 523; chapter 32).

Tempting as it is to end with a glimpse of impending modernity in *Villette*, it is perhaps more interesting and certainly less clichéd to recognize the extent to which Brontë epitomizes Victorian thought. Vargish writes of *Villette*:

It was a step of great importance for Charlotte Brontë to have relinquished the aesthetic felicities and ethical prestige of poetic justice. That she did so without surrendering the authority of a providential intention at work in her text strikes me as necessarily conservative in conviction and as brilliantly radical in form.[40]

"Conservative in conviction" and "radical in form," or at least hyperbolic in metaphorical and narrative style, is a good formula for my view of Brontë's literalization as well. In concluding, however, Vargish succumbs to the pressure to compliment Brontë on her "modernity." Noting the absence of temporal justice in *Villette*, and Lucy's pain in the defeat of her own anticipations of justice, Vargish writes:

This last condition lends *Villette* an irony of peculiar suggestiveness and modernity: that ultimate power will be demonstrated not by the orchestration of harmonies or by the creative drive toward unity, but in the arbitrary, the abrupt, the disconsonant.[41]

But is Brontë's use of the "abrupt" and the "disconsonant" really so modern?

I think we find an excellent summation of the Brontëan world view in Matthew Arnold's concept of Hebraism. In *Culture and Anarchy*, Arnold coins the term "Hebraism" to pair with "Hellenism" as a schematization of the primary intellectual movements in Western culture. Hebraism for Arnold is (to some extent regrettably) the dominant force for Victorian culture, with its concern for Protestant duty, energetic activity, and ethical practice to the neglect of Hellenistic ideals of pure interiority. "The governing idea of Hellenism," writes Arnold, "is *spontaneity of consciousness*; that of Hebraism, *strictness of conscience*."[42] Although he finds Hebraic "strictness" of conduct intellectually constrictive, Arnold acknowledges that Hellenism can err on the side of the "glib" by ignoring the difficulties of actualizing pure thought in a material world. He best captures the Hebraic sense of conflict – not tortured modern interiority, but the conflict of ethical practice – when he writes:

> There is a saying which I have heard attributed to Mr. Carlyle about Socrates, – a very happy saying whether it is really Mr. Carlyle's or not, – which excellently marks the essential point in which Hebraism differs from Hellenism. "Socrates," this saying goes, "is terribly *at ease in Zion*." Hebraism – and here is the source of its wonderful strength – has always been severely preoccupied with an awful sense of the impossibility of being at ease in Zion.[43]

The difficulty, indeed the impossibility of being comfortable in the city of God, or even in the "little city" of *Villette* – this is the condition asserted by both Brontë's Hebraic Christianity and her literalizing feminism. Arnold's famous assessment of Charlotte Brontë, anti-aesthete, indecorous woman, and impatient Christian, was that her mind held nothing but "hunger, rebellion and rage." He might more justly have said, as he said of Victorian Hebraism, that she was "severely preoccupied with the impossibility of being at ease in Zion." Here, I echo, is the source of her wonderful strength.

CHAPTER 6

Charles Darwin and Romantic medicine

At first blush, Charles Darwin may not seem to have much to do with Romantic medicine, or with the narrative and interpretive practices I have been discussing. But in fact, Darwin's thought arises directly out of Romantic medicine, embodying the fullest and, paradoxically, the final expression of Romantic materialism.

Charles Darwin came from a medical family. His grandfather Erasmus Darwin was a renowned physician, as well as a poet. Historian Desmond King-Hele writes,

Patients came to [Erasmus Darwin] from far and wide, and the stories about his almost magical powers became part of Midland folk-lore. King George III wanted Darwin to be his physician, and would no doubt have been better treated during his spells of mental derangement if he had been under Darwin's care: but Darwin would not move south.[1]

Following in his father's footsteps, Erasmus Darwin's son Robert also became a physician of legendary skill, amassing a large fortune from his practice and achieving a high status in the town of Shrewsbury.

Robert's second son Charles – that is, the Charles Darwin who wrote *The Origin of Species* – was from birth destined for medicine as well. He was named after his uncle, who, as a promising young medical student, cut his finger during the dissection of a cadaver and died of the ensuing infection. Young Charles was initially eager to take up the family profession. In his *Autobiography*, Charles recalls that, during the summer before entering medical school,

I began attending some of the poor people, chiefly children and women in Shrewsbury: I wrote down as full an account as I could of the cases with all the symptoms, and read them aloud to my father, who suggested further enquiries, and advised me what medicines to give, which I made up myself. At one time I had at least a dozen patients, and I felt a keen interest in the work. My father, who was by far the best judge of character whom I ever knew, declared that I should make a successful physician, – meaning by this, one who got many patients. (A, 47–48)[2]

Charles joined his brother Erasmus at medical school in Edinburgh, but gave up his medical studies after two years. He was apparently "disgusted" by dissection, and could not tolerate observing surgery:

> I also attended on two occasions the operating theatre in the hospital at Edinburgh, and saw two very bad operations, one on a child, but I rushed away before they were completed. Nor did I ever attend again, for hardly any inducement would have been strong enough to make me do so; this being long before the blessed days of chloroform. The two cases fairly haunted me for many a long year. (A, 48)

Charles's father was apparently sympathetic to his son's sensitivity. The senior Darwin told Charles that "the sight of an operation almost sickened him, and he could scarcely endure to see a person bled" (A, 30). For this reason, Dr. Darwin "at first hated his profession so much that if he had been sure of the smallest pittance, or if his father had given him any choice, nothing should have induced him to follow it" (A, 29). Charles Darwin, who felt increasingly confident of at least a modest inheritance, turned, with his father's blessing, to the prospect of a clergyman's education at Cambridge University.

But the Romantic medicine of Charles's grandfather and father had left its stamp. In his *Autobiography*, Charles devotes at least a third of a chapter on "the development of my mind and character" to recollections of his father in the character of a doctor. The recurrent theme in this section is Dr. Darwin's "powers of observation" and his "sympathy" (A, 29). Charles paints his father as a mystical "Father-Confessor" capable of "reading the characters" of his patients to a degree that was "almost supernatural" (A, 31–32). Although renowned for the "sharpness of his observation" and ready with "a theory for almost everything which occurred," Dr. Darwin did not link his observations to his theory carefully enough in his son's opinion. Thus, writes Charles, his father's contribution was not wholly scientific; rather his example was of "moral service" to his children (A, 42).

Charles Darwin regarded his grandfather's and his father's medicine as a blend of moral sympathy and empirical observation. It is this mixed character of late eighteenth- and early nineteenth-century medicine that nourished extensive discussion of "man's place in nature" from both the moral and the scientific point of view. Of course, the moral and the scientific were not in Charles's grandfather's day so neatly separated. What we would now call science was encompassed within "natural philosophy," and those natural philosophers interested in the human – that is, for the most part, the physicians – frequently contemplated the moral alongside the material. The word "scientist," defining a student of the material world as distinct from a "philosopher," a lover of wisdom, was not coined until 1834, and the men hashing out that distinction still included those whom we would now call humanists, like the poet Samuel Taylor Coleridge and the philosopher of science William Whewell.[3]

Perhaps the most emblematic works of literature to emerge from Erasmus Darwin's blend of science and humanism are his book-length encyclopedic poems, *The Botanic Garden* (comprised of volume I, *The Economy of Vegetation*, and volume II, *The Loves of the Plants*) and his *Temple of Nature*. These poems are best known today for their expression of early evolutionary ideas and for their daring materialism. As literature – although they were tremendously popular in their own time – the poems are now largely dismissed as risible curiosities which incongruously detail the sex lives of the birds and bees in polished formal couplets. As King-Hele points out, however, the humor was quite intentional; Darwin found as much amusement as serious philosophy in his marriage of science and poetry. In the tradition of Alexander Pope, Erasmus Darwin took a delicate interest in the objects of his wit, couching their activities in elaborate epic machinery. Darwin's departure from Pope and the other Augustans, however, was to find plants and animals as worthy of mock-heroic treatment as the card table, coffee house or boudoir.

Erasmus Darwin was a founding member of the Birmingham "Lunar Society," so named because its monthly meetings were held near the full moon, which lit the way for the members riding home at night. The "Lunaticks" were a diverse community, including, among others, the ceramics industrialist Josiah Wedgwood, the steam-engine inventors Matthew Boulton and James Watt, and another doctor, William Small. Even after Darwin had moved away from Birmingham, he and his circle continued to meet, later drawing leading Romantic thinkers. Dr. Thomas Beddoes, also a physician, contributed his substantial knowledge of German Romantic poetry and philosophy. Beddoes founded the Pneumatic Institution, at which he experimented with the therapeutic adminstration of gases. Chemist and poet Humphrey Davy joined Beddoes in this endeavor, thus entering Darwin's circle. Beddoes also, significantly, convinced Samuel Taylor Coleridge to study German Romantic philosophy. Despite all of their common interests, Coleridge met Erasmus Darwin only once and did not feel much personal affection for him, probably because Darwin took religion too lightly. Darwin teased Coleridge that his Unitarian faith was "a feather-bed to catch a falling Christian." Nonetheless, Coleridge recognized Darwin's prominence as "the first literary character in Europe, and the most original-minded Man."[4] The "Lunaticks" and their descendants were among the first to address the problems of relating empiricist and Romantic thought.

The next generation of Darwins blended empiricism and Romanticism in a more subtle way. Robert Darwin married Susannah Wedgwood, one of Josiah's daughters, and the Wedgwoods' Unitarianism came to temper Erasmus Darwin's legacy of worldly humor and skeptical materialism. Thus Charles Darwin grew up with, as he describes it, a good deal of religious and Romantic credulity, as well as a fascination with empirical investigation of the material world.[5] In his *Autobiography*, Darwin comments enthusiastically on his early reading in natural philosophy, which included an eclectic array, from his grandfather's poetic materialism to natural theology and German *Naturphilosophie*. Before the age of thirty, Charles "greatly admired" his grandfather's *Zoonomia*, a medical treatise that sought to establish a natural history of diseases (A, 49). Charles clearly appreciated his grandfather's evolutionism, but equally enjoyed works of natural theology, which by contrast argued for God's design in nature. At Cambridge, Charles not only dutifully "got up" his Paley (i.e., William Paley's *Evidences of Christianity*), he admired it so thoroughly that he could almost recite it by heart (A, 59). He also enjoyed works from the tradition of the clergyman-natural historian, such as the Rev. Gilbert White's *Natural History of Selborne*: "From reading White's *Selborne* I took much pleasure in watching the habits of birds . . . I remember wondering why every gentleman did not become an ornithologist" (A, 45). No wonder that, when medicine no longer seemed a viable career option, Darwin imagined for himself a life as a country clergyman, pursuing the natural history of his parish in his spare time. But next to these comfortable domestic imaginings, Darwin was also inspired by Romantic tales of voyaging, particularly by Alexander von Humboldt's *Personal Narrative*, which he read aloud to friends and professors, in an effort to convince them to set out on a voyage with him (A, 67). In a letter to his sister Caroline, Charles vowed:

I never will be easy till I see the peak of Teneriffe and the great Dragon tree; sandy, dazzling, plains, and gloomy silent forests are alternately uppermost in my mind . . . I have written myself into a Tropical glow.[6]

The dream to retrace Humboldt's travels was displaced by an invitation to join the *Beagle* expedition, which gave Darwin the opportunity to write his own travel narrative. The *Journal of the Voyage of the Beagle* was replete with purple passages of landscape description so indebted to Humboldt that the German wrote to congratulate him on his writing style.

Of course, Humboldt was not Darwin's only Romantic influence. In his *Autobiography*, he writes, "Up to the age of thirty, or beyond it, poetry of many kinds, such as the works of Milton, Gray, Byron, Wordsworth, Coleridge, and Shelley, gave me great pleasure" (A, 138). He even goes so far, perhaps, as to envision himself in the line of epic poets:

About this time I took much delight in Wordsworth's and Coleridge's poetry, and can boast that I read the *Excursion* twice through. Formerly Milton's *Paradise Lost* had been my chief favourite, and in my *excursions* during the voyage of the Beagle, when I could take only a single small volume, I always chose Milton. (A, 85, my emphasis)

Darwin not only reads the *Excursion*, he also makes "excursions"; just as Wordsworth revises Milton, Darwin sallies out as the hero of his own romance. Tropical scenery becomes his land of sublimity. He writes of Rio de Janeiro in *The Voyage of the Beagle*:

Here the woods were ornamented by the Cabbage Palm . . . [I]t waves its elegant head at the height of forty or fifty feet above the ground. If the eye was turned from the world of foliage above, to the ground beneath, it was attracted by the extreme elegance of the leaves of the ferns and mimosae . . . In walking across these thick beds of mimosae, a broad track was marked by the change of shade, produced by the drooping of their sensitive petioles. It is easy to specify the individual objects of admiration in these grand scenes; but it is not possible to give an adequate idea of the higher feelings of wonder, astonishment, and devotion, which fill and elevate the mind. (A, 24)

In this passage, Darwin alternates between the romance of the palm "waving its elegant head" and the language of scientific measurement, estimating the palm's height to be "forty or fifty feet above the ground." He is most comfortable with "specify[ing]" the "individual objects" as a scientific observer, and falters when attempting to express the "higher feelings of wonder, astonishment, and devotion." Sometimes he pokes fun at his inadequacy in the face of wonder:

In England any person fond of natural history enjoys in his walks a great advantage, by always having something to attract his attention; but in these fertile climates, teeming with life, the attractions are so numerous, that he is scarcely able to walk at all. (A, 25)

One imagines a strapping Charles, not so much impeded by the overgrowth as agape at the astonishing variety, so awestruck that he is "scarcely able to walk at all." Recalling something of his grandfather's mocking humor, Charles is both the enthusiastic Romantic and the self-effacing ironist, laughing at the joke the tropics play on the great English Romantic walkers.

But the alliance of Romanticism and empiricism eventually came apart for Darwin. By the end of his life he complained, famously, of a loss of his aesthetic sense:

> [I]n one respect my mind has changed during the last twenty or thirty years. Up to the age of thirty, or beyond it, poetry of many kinds, such as the works of Milton, Gray, Byron, Wordsworth, Coleridge, and Shelley, gave me great pleasure, and even as a schoolboy I took intense delight in Shakespeare, especially in the historical plays. I have also said that formerly pictures gave me considerable, and music very great delight. But now for many years I cannot endure to read a line of poetry: I have tried lately to read Shakespeare, and found it so intolerably dull that it nauseated me. I have also almost lost any taste for pictures or music. I retain some taste for fine scenery, but it does not cause me the exquisite delight which it formerly did. (A, 138)

Darwin clearly regards this decline "of the higher aesthetic tastes" a "curious and lamentable loss," but cannot quite assign a cause (A, 139). Twentieth-century scholars have been eager to supply the explanation. Donald Fleming, in his article "Charles Darwin: The Anaesthetic Man," argues that, because the young Darwin associated the Romantic sublime with religious belief, he lost both when religion began to seem an unnecessary and unreasonable supplement to natural selection:

> In his resolve to be one of the great Truth Bearers, Darwin strove to perfect himself as a fact-and-dust man ... Love of mankind and love of the truth combined with fear of religion to make Darwin suspicious of art, a type of the anaesthetic man, both in the literal sense of "not feeling" and in the derivative sense of taking steps to repress the pain he was capable of feeling.[7]

Yet John Angus Campbell argues, in his turn, that Darwin's affective response was always independent of his theism and always associated with the particularity of nature. For Campbell, Darwin's affective sense remains alive and well (despite the self-deprecating *Autobiography*), but transfers itself almost entirely to his science writing.[8]

George Levine's assessment of Darwin's so-called anesthesia focuses on Darwin's diminished appreciation of literature, which is, after all, the loss of feeling most grievous to Darwin according to his *Autobiography*. In a disarmingly simple phrase, Levine formulates his titular question – of "Why Science Made Shakespeare Nauseating" – and proceeds to answer with a complexity that does justice to Darwin's dialectical mind. Levine first confirms Darwin's early love of the Romantic poets, but thinks that Darwin's scientific observations lead him to part with Romantic anthropomorphism and its comforting interpretation of nature. Then Levine demonstrates Darwin's sensitivity to suffering, and proposes that Darwin cannot tolerate the representation of suffering, particularly in Shakespearean tragedy. Levine summarizes his argument:

I have been making two potentially opposed arguments about Darwin's resistance to poetry in his later years. On the one hand, I have tried to show that his reflections on his voyage led him to reject poetry as being too satisfying to the human, too much determined to make all of nature echo with human associations . . . On the other hand, I have argued that Darwin himself could not endure the pain of suffering, and particularly of suffering without meaning . . . Poetry either lied by giving nature a sympathy his science could not detect in it, or lied by redeeming and consoling for losses that were meaningless and unconsolable.[9]

Levine argues that Darwin preserves even at the end of his life a deep ambivalence toward literature, that he remains too honest to be consoled by comic lies, and too sensitive to tolerate tragic truths. But in Levine's attempt to claim Darwin as both enduring scientist and man of poetic sensibility, he overlooks a telling passage following soon after the one in which Darwin confesses to his Shakespeare-induced nausea:

[N]ovels which are works of the imagination, though not of a very high order, have been for years a wonderful relief and pleasure to me, and I often bless all novelists. A surprising number have been read aloud to me, and I like all if moderately good, and if they do not end unhappily – against which a law ought to be passed. A novel, according to my taste, does not come into the first class unless it contains some person whom one can thoroughly love, and if it be a pretty woman all the better.[10]

Darwin may have begun as a Romantic materialist, as thoroughly schooled in literature as in science, but by the end of his life he has clearly relegated literature to the category of soothing lies. Literature and science, so integrally conjoined in the development of Darwin's thought, come apart for some reason, with science gaining final epistemological authority and literature submitting to handmaidenly service. If this sounds familiar to 21st-century readers, it is because we are Darwin's cultural heirs.

How exactly do Romanticism and materialism fruitfully interact in Darwin's thought, and why do they finally come apart? First, I think we can see the dialectic of Romantic materialism in Darwin's preferred scientific method. Second, Romantic materialism provides Darwin with a convincing rhetoric, intelligible to his Victorian audience because the resultant ethos resembled that of the central figures in Victorian literature. Finally, Romantic materialism accounts for the strange narrative structure of Darwin's self-representation in his autobiography, which in turn heralds a shift in scientific autobiography, in which Romantic elements are confined to childhood experience.

For Darwin, the ideal scientist is a man of inventive genius who loves to collect material facts. For instance, when assessing his scientific colleagues, Darwin weighs them against an ideal proportion of originality and induction. Thus, he insults Spencer's wide theorizing as purely "deductive." At the other end of the spectrum, Darwin considers Robert Brown a "miser" with his "minute observations" in "their perfect accuracy" (A, 103–104). Hooker comes closer to Darwin's ideal, with his "acute" intellect and "great power of generalisation," as untiring in his observation as he is "impulsive" in his temper (A, 105–106). But Darwin's greatest encomium is reserved for Lyell, who combines "clearness, caution, sound judgment and a good deal of originality" (A, 100). Darwin respects inductivism, but only if accompanied by the impulse to imagine; the collection of facts is insufficient without the "power" to synthesize. As often as Darwin derides unsupported speculation, he upholds the Romantic belief in the "great man" who is individually endowed with the power of creative vision.

Did Darwin actually practice this Romantic materialist ideal? He has been accused of promoting himself as a strict inductivist, pretending to gather facts without theory, principally because he claims that in his first notebook he "worked on true Baconian principles, and without any theory collected facts on a wholesale scale" (A, 119). Because his transmutation notebooks demonstrate free speculation early in the process of gathering evidence for *The Origin of Species*, scholars have objected to Darwin's self-representation as a "Baconian" scientist. But Darwin's claims of inductivism, I would argue, have too often been taken out of context, because they are frequently balanced by his claims for his originality in theorizing. Later Darwin writes, "How odd it is that anyone should not see that all observation must be for or against some view if it is to be of any service!"[11] In his final self-assessment, he staunchly defends his own originality:

It has sometimes been said that the success of the Origin proved "that the subject was in the air" or "that men's minds were prepared for it." I do not think that this is strictly true, for I occasionally sounded not a few naturalists, and never happened to come across a single one who seemed to doubt about the permanence of species. Even Lyell and Hooker, though they would listen with interest to me, never seemed to agree . . . What I believe was strictly true is that innumerable well-observed facts were stored in the minds of naturalists ready to take their proper places, as soon as any theory which would receive them was sufficiently explained. (A, 124)

What was "in the air," according to Darwin, was a vast quantity of "well-observed facts." Without his very original theory of natural selection, even Lyell and Hooker – his most powerful models of creative scientific minds – would not have been able to envision the evolution of species.

Romantic genius and empirical method, then, combine in a dialectic in which inventive theory guides industrious fact collection, and in which theory is in turn susceptible to revision by surprising facts. I want to empha-size that this is the dynamic dialectic characteristic of Romantic materialism rather than an inexplicable paradox or a middle-of-the-road compromise. Darwin writes simultaneously of a thorough passion for theory, and of the necessity of giving it up:

I have steadily endeavoured to keep my mind free, so as to give up any hypothesis, however much beloved (and I cannot resist forming one on every subject) as soon as facts are shown to be opposed to it. Indeed I have had no choice but to act in this manner, for with the exception of the Coral Reefs I cannot remember a single first-formed hypothesis which had not after a time to be given up or greatly modified. (A, 141)

Theorizing is an irresistible and much beloved activity in which Darwin freely indulges – but nearly always his facts (equally beloved, given his passion for being surprised out of a favored theory) force him to revise. Darwin's son Francis, his closest scientific collaborator in his later years, confirms this representation of his father's working habits, and in doing so uses the Romantic metaphor of genius as electrical power:

It was as if he were charged with theorizing power ready to flow into any channel on the slightest disturbance, so that no fact, however small, could avoid releasing a stream of theory, and thus the fact became magnified into importance. In this way it naturally happened that many untenable theories occurred to him; but fortunately his richness of imagination was equalled by his power of judging and condemning the thoughts that occurred to him.[12]

Francis's formulation sounds much like his father's: "[r]ichness of imagina-tion" checked by self-critique, which does not hesitate in the end to trim its excesses.

Although a self-effacing autobiography may seem to imply a contradic-tion in terms, I think Darwin gives us plenty of evidence that his alternation between self-effacement and self-assertion is not a zero-sum game – that is, it doesn't result in the cancellation of selfhood, but rather in the creation of a substantial, reliable first-person narrator.[13] Furthermore, this first-person narrator's rhetoric of self-effacement and self-assertion is characteristic of Darwin's scientific writing as well as his autobiography, and may explain the comparatively friendly reception and wide readership of *The Origin of Species* and of the even more controversial *The Descent of Man*. Janet Browne writes that, although the application of evolutionary theory to humankind in *The Descent of Man* created an uproar, the reviewers were "exceedingly polite about Darwin himself":

> A reviewer in the *British Foreign Evangelical Review* praised Darwin's depth of learning. The *Daily Telegraph* referred to his "graceful and conciliatory" prose and "dignified" tone of voice. The *English Independent* suggested that "no loyal servant of the truth will fear the issue of such an appeal." The *New York Express* noted the author's "unassailable integrity and candour" while the *Field* described his "wonderful thoroughness and honest truthfulness."[14]

How is it that Darwin, the author of a theory which still provokes controversy, was so widely respected and protected within his own time? Avon Crismore and Rodney Farnsworth argue that Darwin creates an ethos of trustworthiness through his peculiar rhetoric. They scan two key chapters of *The Origin of Species* for "modality markers," words and phrases that indicate Darwin's level of commitment to the probability of his arguments. They find an abundance of "hedges" (*might, possibly, I doubt that*) and "emphatics" (*must, obviously, I am certain that*). Moreover, at crucial places in the text – at the beginning of chapters, or when opening the argument for natural selection – Darwin uses "hedged emphatics." Examples noted by Crismore and Farnsworth include: *I think we are driven to conclude that, It seems pretty clear, But I am strongly inclined to suspect that*.[15] Darwin smoothly combines hedges and emphatics to produce a metadiscourse which negotiates between certainty and uncertainty, calling attention to both. Darwin's commentary, his very active authorial voice, creates a palpable personality. Crismore and Farnsworth note both the "tentative, cautious . . . non-assertive presenter of ideas" and the "trustworthy expert."[16] Darwin's assertions and hedges do not cancel out his subjectivity; rather they enhance it, becoming one of the most powerful elements of his argument.

The same narrative voice guides even Darwin's famously self-deprecating *Autobiography*. Following Crismore and Farnsworth's model, I have analyzed the *Autobiography*'s final paragraph, and found it laced with hedged emphatics:

Therefore, my underline{success} as a man of science, *whatever this may have amounted to*, has been underline{determined}, *as far as I can judge*, by underline{complex and diversified} mental qualities and conditions. Of these the most underline{important} have been – the love of science – underline{unbounded} patience in long reflecting over any subject – underline{industry} in observing and collecting facts – and underline{a fair share} of underline{invention} as well as of common sense. With such *moderate abilities* as underline{I possess}, it is underline{truly *surprising*} that thus I should have underline{influenced to a considerable extent} the *beliefs* of scientific men on *some* underline{important} points. (A, 145; hedges in italics, emphatics underlined)

As Darwin explains his mental dialectic, he demonstrates it rhetorically. By the time he writes "as far as I can judge," we may think this rather less a hedge than a powerful emphatic. Darwin the speaker, because of his self-conscious assertions and qualifications, appears both sturdy and flexible, at once discriminating and large-minded, a trustworthy narrator.

Victorian autobiographies and autobiographical novels demonstrate one reason why this alternately self-asserting and self-effacing ethos was familiar to Victorians, and also why it constituted a maturation, rather than an erasure, of selfhood. Recurrent patterns in these narratives suggest an inevitable conflict between an innate Romantic aesthetic of creative self-expression and a learned social ethic of self-sacrifice. Especially in the novel, these autobiographical narratives often trace the story of an orphan who defines him- or herself as an isolated individual, struggling defiantly against opposing forces such as unsavory and unsympathetic adults, peers, or conditions. Carlyle's Diogenes Teufelsdrockh is not only an orphan, but a mysterious child from nowhere, arriving at his adoptive parents' cottage, like a modern Moses, in a basket. Orphan Jane Eyre defies the Reed family, withdrawing into the Arctic pleasure of her windowseat and Bewick's *History of Birds*. Dorothea Brooke is raised by her ineffectual uncle, and struggles as an isolated cygnet in the Middlemarch duck pond to express her "passionate ideal Nature." The list of orphans could of course continue, but the point is that these protagonists are almost completely self-created, molded by neither parents nor environment. More often than not, they come to adolescence as selves-against-the world.

These mighty but beset little individuals, guided by a passionate Romantic individualism, fight their way toward adulthood, wielding such creative power that character and reader may both have great expectations – only to encounter social constraints barring the door to maturity. Jane Eyre still experiences an expansive sense of self as she walks the battlements, but she modifies this desire for liberty into a "new servitude." Dorothea Casaubon is entangled in the web of her marriage and of Middlemarch society, just as Lydgate, once a "circumnavigator," is reduced to circling his own little pond.

In her work on Victorian autobiography, Regenia Gagnier sees this pattern, which she calls "literary individualism," as "intense and defensive reflexivity born in opposition to social constraints of Church, family, and school or State."[17] She goes on to exempt Darwin, along with Huxley, Ruskin, Mill, and Beatrice Webb. These writers, because of their scientific or social convictions, find alternatives to antagonistic self-definition and self-absorption through deliberate suppression of their individualism. They are "self-consciously unself-conscious," caught between an awareness of their own subjectivity and their desire to create a dispassionate voice.[18]

While I think there is more individualism in Darwin's *Autobiography* than Gagnier admits, I will grant that it is a problem text, departing in several ways from Victorian literary autobiography. It is so short – scarcely more than a hundred pages in most editions – as to be almost an "anti-autobiography." This, in addition to some of Darwin's self-effacing rhetoric, has led James Olney to conclude that its tone is detached or objective, much like modern scientific writing.[19] It has no conversion or crisis of faith such as those typical to the autobiographies modeled after confessions; rather its losses happen gradually, are unmarked, and are regretted only in retrospect. And finally, the narrative shape of the autobiography is ill proportioned, thick with stories at the beginning and gradually narrowing toward its end into a terse account of dates of publication. At the outset, Darwin writes leisurely anecdotes about his childhood, provides an extended account of his father, sets down a diminishing number of stories about Cambridge life and about the voyage of the *Beagle*, then presents a brief, anecdotal account of professional friendships and finally records a very compressed report of publications. The *Beagle* voyage falls roughly in the middle of the *Autobiography*, with the first twenty years of Darwin's life overbalancing the last fifty, emphasizing his early development. No critic has yet made sense of this odd narrative pattern. For Linda Peterson, Darwin's *Autobiography* is a collection of random facts strung together "without reference to a comprehensive pattern or theory of life, without apparent concern for literary coherence."[20] George Levine seconds Peterson's judgment of the text's incoherence, denominating it, perhaps more affectionately, a "small loose baggy monster."[21]

I want to argue that Darwin's tone throughout much of the *Autobiography* is far from "objective" in Olney's sense of the word, that is, distant or detached. Especially at the beginning of the text, Darwin is a delightful storyteller, extravagant, forgetful, and whimsical. Also the *Autobiography* has an important narrative pattern that Darwin signals through his use of economic language like *profit, loss, cost, compensation, saving*, and *spending*. In brief, the *Autobiography* demonstrates a narrative economy, in which what appears at first to be wasteful turns out in the end to be a good investment. Darwin, as narrator, initially spends time on wayward indirection and narrative whimsicality, but gradually tightens his narrative into an increasingly urgent accounting of things accomplished and time spent accomplishing them. The time-consuming prodigality of his early years seems to have caught up with him by the end of the narrative, as he mourns the loss of every valuable moment; yet he recuperates this time-expenditure in the end as a worthwhile investment – in fact, it is the very secret of his intellectual success. In the end, the dialectic of excess and economy, and the gradual loss of time for wonder or for playful exploration, recapitulate the gradualism of Darwin's theory of natural selection.

A set of notes that Darwin pencilled on the back of a letter in 1838 (Figure 1) serves as an excellent sample of the larger pattern demonstrated in the *Autobiography*, namely the dialectic of wastefulness and economy. Although the columns are jammed closely together, Darwin's notes set out a balance-sheet format. Both the orderly format and the messy execution turn out to be important signals. One notices first that Darwin sets out to perform a cost/benefit analysis – and second that he has a hard time accomplishing this task, failing to confine himself to orderly analysis, joking, confusing his categories, and finishing in a flight of enthusiasm. Figure 1 has two columns, both labeled "Work Finished." Each "list" constitutes not so much an analysis as a dialogue with himself. In the first column, he writes, "If not marry TRAVEL? Europe – Yes? America????" His underscoring and capitalization and multiple question marks suggest an enthusiastic brainstorm rather than a strict accounting. In the second column, he finds the need to refer back to the first column, and so cross-references the final paragraph of the first column as "(B)," and appropriates it into the second column, speculating that he could "do as (B)." He then proceeds to converse with himself, waffling back and forth about living in London: "but could I act thus with children and poor –? No – Then where live in country near London."

Darwin gives up on his first list, beginning anew on a second sheet (figure 2). Here Darwin has realized that he needs not two "Work Finished" columns, but a "Marry" and a "Not Marry" column, announcing with either simple-minded discovery or mock-grandeur that "This is the Question." He takes time out for parenthetical comments and for jokes – in the "Marry" column he writes "Children – (if it please God) – constant

Work Finished

If <u>not</u> marry TRAVEL? Europe – Yes?
America????

If I travel it must be exclusively
geological – United States – Mexico.

Depend upon health and vigour and how
far I become zoological. If I don't travel
– Work at transmission of Species –
microscope – simplest forms of life –
Geology – ? Oldest formations?? Some
experiments – physiological observations
on lower animals.

(B) Live in London – for where else
possible – in small house near Regents
Park – keep horses – take Summer tours
collect specimens some line of Zoolog :
speculations of Geograph : range and
geological general works – systematize
and study affinities.

Work Finished

If marry – means limited – Feel duty to
work for money. London life, nothing
but Society, no country, no tours, no
large Zoolog: collect., no books. –
Cambridge Professorship, either Geolog :
or Zoolog :– comply with all above
requisites – I couldn't systematize
zoologically so well.

But better than hibernating in country –
and where? Better even than near
London country house – I could not
indolently take country house and do
nothing – Could I live in London like a
prisoner? If I were moderately rich I
would live in London, with pretty big
house and do as (B) – but could I act thus
with children and poor – ? No – Then
where live in country near London;
better, but great obstacles to science and
poverty.

Then Cambridge, better, but fish out of
water, not being Professor and poverty.
Then Cambridge Professorship, – and
make best of it – do duty as such and
work at spare times – My destiny will be
Camb. Prof. or poor man; outskirts of
London – some small square etc. – and
work as well as I can.

I have so much more pleasure in direct
observation, that I could not go on as
Lyell does, correcting and adding up new
information to old train, and I do not see
what line can be followed by man tied
down to London. – In country –
experiment and observations on lower
animals, – more space –

Figure 1 Charles Darwin's memorandum on marriage, written in pencil on the back
of a letter dated 7 April 1838, from the Charles Darwin Collections at Cambridge
University Library.

companion, (friend in old age) who will feel interested in one, object to be
beloved and played with – better than a dog anyhow." In the "<u>Not Marry</u>"
column, he forgets which side of the argument he is examining, worrying
about children and a wife who won't like London. Of course, what he
really needs is a cost column and a benefit column for each marital status.

This is the Question

Marry	Not Marry

Marry

Children – (if it please God) – constant
companion, (friend in old age) who will feel
interested in one, object to be beloved and
played with – better than a dog anyhow –
Home, and someone to take care of house –
Charms of music and female chit-chat.
These things good for one's health. Forced
to visit and receive relations but terrible loss
of time.

My God, it is intolerable to think of spending
one's whole life, like a neuter bee, working,
working and nothing after all. – No, no
won't do. – Imagine living all one's day
solitarily in smoky dirty London House. –
Only picture yourself a nice soft wife on a
sofa with good fire, and books and music
perhaps – compare this vision with the dingy
reality of Grt Marlboro' St.
Marry – Marry – Marry Q.E.D.

Not Marry

No children, (no second life) no one to care
for one in old age. – What is the use of
working without sympathy from near and
dear friends – who are near and dear friends
to the old except relatives.

Freedom to go where one liked – Choice of
Society and little of it. Conversation of
clever men at clubs.

Not forced to visit relatives, and to bend in
every trifle – to have the expense and anxiety
of children – perhaps quarrelling.

Loss of time – cannot read in evenings –
fatness and idleness – anxiety and
responsibility – less money for books etc – if
many children forced to gain one's bread. –
(But then it is very bad for one's health to
work too much)

Perhaps my wife won't like London ; then
the sentence is banishment and degradation
with indolent idle fool –

[On the reverse side of the page:]

It being proved necessary to marry – When? Soon or Late. The Governor says soon for
otherwise bad if one has children – one's character is more flexible – one's feelings more lively,
and if one does not marry soon, one misses so much good pure happiness.

But then if I married tomorrow : there would be an infinity of trouble and expense in
getting and furnishing a house, – fighting about no Society – morning calls – awkwardness – loss
of time every day – (without one's wife was an angel and made one keep industrious) – Then how
should I manage all my business if I were obliged to go every day walking with my wife. – Eheu!!
I never should know French, – or see the Continent, – or go to America, or go up in a Balloon, or
take solitary trip in Wales – poor slave, you will be worse than a negro – And then horrid poverty
(without one's wife was better than an angel and had money) – Never mind my boy – Cheer up –
One cannot live this solitary life, with groggy old age, friendless and cold and childless staring
one in one's face, already beginning to wrinkle. Never mind, trust to chance – keep a sharp look
out. – There is many a happy slave –

Figure 2 Charles Darwin's famous "Marry/Not Marry" pencil notes, *circa*. 1838, from the
Charles Darwin Collection at Cambridge University Library.

But despite the sloppy logic, he demonstrates that he thinks in terms of an economy of time. His underscoring betrays his main concern: first the "terrible loss of time" incurred by caring for a wife, visiting relatives, or dealing with a quarrelsome family, and second the likelihood that a wife would wish for a great deal of "Society," whereas he would prefer to have "little of it." His chief fear seems to be the one that he repeats in both columns: "loss of time." Still, having counted the cost, he revolts from his ledger, bursting out with "My God, it is intolerable to think of spending one's whole life, like a neuter bee, working, working and nothing after all." He concludes his "Marry" column by sweeping away the arguments against. "Marry – Marry – Marry," he repeats in his abundant enthusiasm – appending a "Q.E.D." as if he has completed a logical proof. In this balance sheet, then, Darwin is seeking economic structure but has trouble squeezing his extraneous expressions into neat lines of thought.

Although Darwin never claimed to be a political economist himself, he came by his economic language honestly. He was saturated in utilitarian culture; his Whig and mostly Unitarian family circle included several ardent Benthamites. In young adulthood, Darwin developed a friendship with Harriet Martineau, and he was an avid reader of the *Edinburgh Review* and the *Quarterly Review*, both of which featured extensive discussions of political economy.[22] Of course his most celebrated exposure to utilitarianism was through reading Thomas Malthus, the clergyman, population theorist, and professor of political economy. According to Darwin, Malthus's *Essay on Population* was the catalyst for Darwin's own theory of natural selection:

Fifteen months after I had begun my systematic enquiry [into the origin of species] I happened to read for amusement Malthus on Population, and being well prepared to appreciate the struggle for existence which everywhere goes on from long-continued observation of the habits of animals and plants, it at once struck me that under these circumstances favourable variations would tend to be preserved, and unfavourable ones to be destroyed. The result of this would be the formation of new species. Here then, I had at last got a theory by which to work. (A, 120)

Malthus's argument was that, unchecked, the rate of human population growth will always outstrip the rate of food production. It was this model of a population greatly exceeding its food supply that so impressed Darwin that he began to see analogous patterns in all of nature.

Far from being a departure from Darwin's early Romantic materialism, this Malthusian turn confirmed the central tenets of liberal natural theology. Malthus, an ordained clergyman, and, at the time of the publication of his *Essay on the Principle of Population*, a practicing curate, saw his task as a "vindicat[ion] of the ways of God to man."²³ As a clergyman he scanned the Book of Scripture, but as an economist he "turn[ed] [his] eyes to the book of nature."²⁴ But because human knowledge of the Book of Nature is imperfect, Malthus professes the characteristic natural theological humility:

It cannot be considered as an unimproving exercise of the human mind to endeavour to "vindicate the ways of God to man" if we proceed with a proper distrust of our own understanding and a just sense of our insufficiency to comprehend the reason of all we see, if we hail every ray of light with gratitude, and, when no light appears, think that the darkness is from within and not from without, and bow with humble deference to the supreme wisdom of him whose "thoughts are above our thoughts" "as the heavens are high above the earth."²⁵

Because of the limitations of human reason, the natural theologian must think inductively, reasoning "from nature up to nature's God," and not presume to reason teleologically "from God to nature."²⁶ What Malthus reads in the Book of Nature is that the world is out of joint, or that there is a mismatch between the human population and its food supply. Contrary to his reputation as a prophet of doom, Malthus remains faithful to an essentially optimistic interpretation of the Book of Nature. The population/food supply disparity is not a failure of Providence, according to Malthus – such a failure would be contrary to the Book of Scripture – but rather it is an opportunity for humans to exercise "moral restraint." Society may not be perfectible – indeed it is in a "state of probation" – but individuals are thereby allowed to exert themselves toward virtue.²⁷

Malthus's "moral restraint" refers, of course, to abstinence rather than birth control – a prescription that makes him appear absurdly impractical to modern readers. And his notion that evil exists to invite moral exercise can seem self-righteously cruel. But when Malthus tackles the mind-body problem, his Romantic materialism leads him to an intriguingly complex – and modern – proposition. First, like the medical Romantic materialists Abernethy and Lawrence, Malthus enters the debate cautiously:

It could answer no good purpose to enter into the question whether mind be a distinct substance from matter, or only a finer form of it. The question is, perhaps, after all, a question merely of words. Mind is as essentially mind, whether formed from matter or any other substance.²⁸

Still, Malthus in his guise as political economist leans heavily toward mind as matter. Moreover, he notes that mind develops, and concludes, in his role as a clergyman, that there must be as well a developing spirit:

As we shall all be disposed to agree that God is the creator of mind as well as of body, and as they both seem to be forming and unfolding themselves at the same time, it cannot appear inconsistent either with reason or revelation, if it appear to be consistent with phenomena of nature, to suppose that God is constantly occupied in forming mind out of matter and that the various impressions that man receives through life is the process for that purpose.[29]

For Malthus, the vicissitudes of life stimulate mental formation. Like many modern philosophers, Malthus sees mind emerging from matter on a new level of complexity, but retaining all of its materiality.

Darwin leaves no evidence that he specifically absorbed Malthus's conclusions about mental development. We know that he wrote his *Autobiography* in order to chronicle "the development of my mind" (A, 21). And, in the *Autobiography*, Darwin plays out, quite possibly unconsciously, Malthus's economy of superfecundity and limited resources in narrative form. Another way to think of this, if we think of mental superfecundity (as in Blake's concept of the "Prolific") as characteristic of Romanticism, and mental economy as characteristic of utilitarianism, is to see Darwin's dialectic as demonstrating John Stuart Mill's famous claim that the utilitarian Bentham and the Romantic Coleridge were equally influential thinkers for the Victorian period. Darwin's Romantic materialism brings science and literature into contact, but specifically it brings the materialist logic of utilitarianism into contact with the strain of Romanticism that prizes proliferation of imaginative ideas, the credulity we associate with Coleridge's "willing suspension of disbelief," and the state of wonder inspired by the excesses of the sublime.

What does this look like in narrative form? It is as if, in Darwin's *Autobiography*, words proliferate initially, and time gradually devours them. Darwin spends words liberally in narrating his youth, portraying himself as a combination of youthful collector and spendthrift. Young Charles collects, steals, amasses a boyhood wealth of apples, pebbles, bugs, and dogs, but then proceeds to give it away, spend it, or get tricked out of it. There is little forward direction, no guiding commentary, and little obvious connection. The narrative form reflects what I take to be the subtext: that Darwin counts his wasteful, inefficient youth as a significant part of his mental development. For example, Darwin writes,

I had a strong taste for angling, and would sit for any number of hours on the bank of a river or pond watching the float; when at Maer I was told that I could kill the worms with salt and water, and from that day I never spitted a living worm, though at the expense, probably, of some loss of success. (A, 127)

Darwin trades success here for the humane treatment of worms, undoubtedly inefficient for a fisherman, but a wise investment for the naturalist who will later write one of his best-selling volumes from his passion for worms.

According to Darwin, he was in youth "a very simple fellow," cleverer at telling lies than anything else, yet still taken in by other people's stories. He presents himself as mentally slow, but this is not the slowness of a plodder, who just accumulates inert fact-units, rather the slowness of a believer, of one who suspends disbelief, who gets sidetracked by interesting possibilities and fascinating stories – he is one who gets taken in.

Gillian Beer establishes Darwin's early propensity for creating fictions. In an autobiographical fragment, dated 1838, Darwin confesses to being as a youth "a very great story-teller":

I scarcely ever went out walking without saying I had seen a pheasant or some strange bird (natural history taste); these lies, when not detected I presume, excited my attention, as I recollect them vividly, not connected with shame, though some I do, but as something which by having produced a great effect on my mind, gave pleasure like a tragedy. I recollect when I was at Mr. Case's inventing a whole fabric to show how fond I was of speaking the *truth*! My invention is still so vivid in my mind, that I could almost fancy it was true, did not memory of former shame tell me it was false.[30]

Beer notes Darwin's "surviving hope that lies are a form of truth-discovery."[31] Even more remarkable, perhaps, is Darwin's capacity to be taken in by, or to believe in, his own fictions: "I could almost fancy it was true," he writes of the memory, marveling at the strength of his own invention – or perhaps of his own credulity.

This romantic theme of inventiveness and credulity also runs through Darwin's tales of his youth in the complete *Autobiography*, written nearly forty years after the above fragment. As a little boy, Darwin writes, he was "much given to inventing deliberate falsehoods" for the sake of impressing people. Here, too, Darwin links his early inventiveness with his precocious interest in science:

One little event during this year has fixed itself very firmly in my mind, and I hope that it has done so from my conscience having been afterwards sorely troubled by it: it is curious as showing that apparently I was interested at this early age in the variability of plants! I told another little boy (I believe it was Leighton, who afterwards became a well-known Lichenologist and botanist) that I could produce variously coloured Polyanthuses and Primroses by watering them with certain coloured fluids, which was of course a monstrous fable, and had never been tried by me. (A, 23)

In turn, young Charles is repeatedly duped by his acquaintances, fooled by their admiration, and taken in by practical jokes. Darwin also tells how he ran between his home and his boarding school, racing to get back to school before the doors were locked at night: "I well remember that I attributed my success to the prayers and not to my quick running, and marvelled how generally I was aided" (A, 25). Divine intervention, and not quick footwork, prevents his late arrival.

As the *Autobiography* progresses, Charles gains some dignity, but the narrator continues to depict him as overly enthusiastic and gullible. He pokes fun at his zeal for hunting during his college years, and tells how, when shooting with some of his friends, they pretended to shoot at the same time, so that Darwin could not credit the fallen bird as his own – and indeed, Darwin is duped (A, 54). He also shakes his head at his uncritical acceptance of Christianity in his earlier years: "It never struck me how illogical it was to say that I believed in what I could not understand and what is in fact unintelligible" (A, 57). He enjoys the "ludicrous" irony that, as "fiercely" as he had been "attacked by the orthodox," he had once studied to become a clergyman. He provides the following vignette:

If the phrenologists are to be trusted, I was well fitted in one respect to be a clergyman. A few years ago the Secretaries of a German psychological Society asked me earnestly by letter for a photograph of myself; and some time afterwards I received the Proceedings of one of the meetings, in which it seemed that the shape of my head had been the subject of a public discussion, and one of the speakers declared that I had the bump of Reverence developed enough for ten Priests. (A, 57)

Again, under the joke, Darwin seems to be developing a theme of his predisposition to belief. Ridiculous as he finds this tendency, he calls attention to it, signaling perhaps through the phrenologic reference that credulity is a mental trait important to his character development.

Darwin's credulity appears later in conjunction with his scientific work. While studying at the university, Darwin notices pollen tubes "exserting" themselves from pollen grains on a wet surface. Because he was unaware of the phenomenon, he jumps to the conclusion that he has discovered something new, and runs off to tell his mentor Henslow, who gently commends him, but makes him "clearly understand how well it was known" (A, 66). Darwin determines "not to be in such a hurry again to communicate my discoveries," but he is not cured of his impressionable nature. He tells of several, more recent, instances in which he has been taken in by false information. In these stories, he is more cautious in his acceptance, but he does not discredit the account immediately, remaining interested until the error is revealed. Though he "distrust[s] greatly deductive reasoning," he is, "on the other hand . . . not very sceptical" (A, 141). The combination, he feels, is not very efficient – but he offers it as an explanation of the mind that revolutionized biology.

Although Darwin's rhetoric throughout the *Autobiography* is peppered with remarks of "wonder" and "surprise," the narrative itself becomes gradually less and less friendly to the evocation of readerly wonder, and more and more focused on Darwin's drive to complete his professional activity. If at the beginning of the narrative a leisurely, amused, and intimate Darwin seems to be ascendant, by the end of the *Autobiography* his economical approach prevails, with his clipped sentences and his calculations of what each work "cost" him, temporally speaking. He writes, for example:

My *Variation of Animals and Plants under Domestication* was begun, as already stated, in the beginning of 1860, but was not published until the beginning of 1868. It is a big book, and cost me four years and two months' hard labour.

And later,

In 1875 a second and largely corrected edition, which cost me a good deal of labour, was brought out. (A, 130)

One can fairly hear the clock ticking through Darwin's account of his later years. Paragraphs are regularly punctuated by the comments that such and such a project or illness "cost" him time. Time is "consumed" or "lost" in a calculation that seems at once matter of fact and painful. But he splendidly converts a mortal disadvantage into a virtue:

The delay in this case, as with all my other books has been a great advantage to me; for a man after a long interval can criticise his own work, almost as well as if it were that of another person. (A, 132)

Darwin is working toward a closing statement about his mental development that reveals the submerged organizing pattern of the *Autobiography*. He does not formulate his assessment until the last few pages of the memoir, but his summary here makes sense, in retrospect, of the narrative structure of the book. In his concluding comments, Darwin evaluates his "mental powers" as follows:

I have no great quickness of apprehension or wit which is so remarkable in some clever men, for instance Huxley. I am therefore a poor critic: a paper or book, when first read, generally excites my admiration, and it is only after considerable reflection that I perceive the weak points . . . On the favourable side of the balance, I think that I am superior to the common run of men in noticing things which easily escape attention, and in observing them carefully. (A, 140–141)

One wishes Darwin could have announced clearly at the beginning of the narrative: "My mind is slow but selective," or "I am credulous at first, but shrewd later." The claim comes late and is obscured by awkward rhetoric – but it is there. With characteristic modesty, Darwin points out his intellectual slowness, and his credulous "admiration" of even weak arguments, but also "on the favourable side of the balance" he converts the apparent waste of time into an advantage, "noticing things" which quick-witted people miss in the rapid fire of their efficient minds.

In a passage that parallels the last, Darwin applies his economic language to the task of writing:

I have as much difficulty as ever in expressing myself clearly and concisely; and this difficulty has caused me a very great loss of time; but it has had the compensating advantage of forcing me to think long and intently about every sentence, and thus I have been often led to see errors in reasoning and in my own observations or those of others. (A, 136)

The cost/benefit analysis continues to operate for Darwin at the end of his narrative. He has invested large amounts of time in apparent inefficiency – a "very great loss" that has its "compensating advantage," affording him the critical distance to detect errors. As if to illustrate his awkward construction, he writes, "There seems to be a sort of fatality in my mind leading me to put at first my statement and proposition in a wrong or awkward form." Commenting on the strategies he uses to compensate for his disability, he anticipates contemporary composition theory: "Formerly I used to think about my sentences before writing them down; but for several years I have found that it saves time to scribble in a vile hand whole pages as quickly as I possibly can, contracting half the word; and then correct deliberately" (A, 137). In contemporary terms, this model translates to free writing with revision, in which recurrent draft writing precedes a honed revision, and in which revision is intrinsic to the thought process.

I hope it is by now clear that Darwin's narrative economy – that is, the pattern of abundant waste that, when subjected to scrutiny, can yield innovative ideas – recapitulates Darwin's scientific theory, in which fecundity and variety, when subjected to natural selection, can generate new species. Thus, Darwin has, in his narrative pattern, described a sort of mental Darwinism. At one point in the *Autobiography*, Darwin seems to be reaching toward this conclusion:

The success of the *Origin* may, I think, be attributed in large part to my having long before written two condensed sketches, and to my having finally abstracted a much larger manuscript, which was itself an abstract. By this means I was enabled to *select* the more striking facts and conclusions . . . I gained much by my delay in publishing from about 1839, when the theory was clearly conceived, to 1859; and I lost nothing by it, for I cared very little whether men attributed most originality to me or Wallace; and his essay no doubt aided in the reception of the theory. (A, 123–124)

A surplus of writing, an excess of manuscript material, undergoes painstaking selection, consuming time, consuming Darwin himself, but producing, due to this expenditure, a rich harvest of productive theory.

Darwin so involves himself in this dialectic that he applies a startlingly utilitarian attitude toward his own person, regarding even himself as an exhaustible commodity. Darwin opens his *Autobiography* by expressing his desire to write "as if I were a dead man in another world looking back at my own life." He adds, "Nor have I found this difficult, for life is nearly over with me." At the outset, this "deadness" is countered by Darwin's intimate grandfatherly storytelling, but by the end, a dying Darwin predominates. The *Autobiography* is one long exhalation, tapering off at the end, not in the distance or detachment that James Olney complains of, but rather in self-expenditure. There is a deftly played out tension, even at the end, between the passage of time and Darwin's refusal to rush. We are made poignantly aware that this is the memoir of a powerful but aging man. Yet his self-expenditure is very simply captured and casually dramatized in the seemingly off-handed comment, tucked in near the end, that he is ready to exclaim his "*nunc dimittis.*" It is an odd phrase to come out of Darwin's by now agnostic mouth, the Latin name for the canticle of Simeon, who, having waited all his life for the Messiah, holds the baby Jesus in his wizened arms and cries "Now lettest thou thy servant depart in peace." The mix of joy and pain of Simeon's song, the sense of self-giving and imminent expiration, is nowhere explicitly registered in Darwin's narrative, yet the undercurrent is there in the shape of the narrative, the early imaginative dallying and later urgent forward propulsion. In narrative form, Darwin recapitulates his theory of natural selection: those whom nature favors are those who not only survive to reproductive age, but who also expend energy – liberally, often inefficiently – for the purposes of procreation.

But as with the theory of natural selection there is a dark side to Darwin's mental economy, an egoistic cruelty in his blind expenditure of *other* people's time as well as his own. The two most recent biographies of Darwin correct some of the idolatrous tendency, especially in the history of biology community, to lionize Darwin. Michael Ruse, reviewing Desmond and Moore's *Darwin* and Janet Browne's *Voyaging*, phrases his observations, to my delight, in economic terms:

But while Desmond and Moore and Browne are clearly pro-Darwin, their Darwin is becoming more human and less likeable. He is a Darwin who uses people – his family, his teachers, his captain, his wife, his servants, his friends, and everybody else – to his own ends. He is a great scientist, but at a cost – at a moral cost, in a way. Browne writes: "There was a sliver of ice inside enabling him to make the most of all the advantages he possessed and the circumstances in which he found himself."[32]

This aspect of Darwin's personality is abundantly illustrated in the final paragraph of Darwin's 1838 pencil notes:

But then if I married tomorrow: there would be an infinity of trouble and expense in getting and furnishing a house, – fighting about no Society – morning calls – awkwardness – loss of time every day – (without one's wife was an angel and made one keep industrious) – Then how should I manage all my business if I were obliged to go every day walking with my wife. – Eheu!! I never should know French, – or see the Continent, – or go to America, or go up in a Balloon, or take solitary trip in Wales – poor slave, you will be worse than a negro – And then horrid poverty (without one's wife was better than an angel and had money) – Never mind my boy – Cheer up – One cannot live this solitary life, with groggy old age, friendless and cold and childless staring one in one's face, already beginning to wrinkle. Never mind, trust to chance – keep a sharp look out. – There is many a happy slave – [33]

Darwin's wife Emma probably saw these notes, and very likely preserved them herself. She seems to have enjoyed the joke, addressing Darwin in early letters, disturbingly, as "my own dear Nigger."[34] Even a charitable reading of Darwin's balance sheet cannot help remarking Darwin's good-natured willingness to consume all the resources in his path, even his projected children, whom he considers anxiety-provoking and expensive but important as a "second life." Worse is the recasting of his privilege as a comic "enslavement" to a wife who seems either altogether unconscious or altogether accepting of her lot.

If Darwin's role was the big spender of family resources, Emma's was provider particularly of what Darwin saw as the moral fuel. In a brief but superlative encomium to Emma he rates her "infinitely my superior in every single moral quality" (A, 97). Like so many of his compeers, Darwin seems for the most part content to rely on his household angel for moral provisions, yet he seems vaguely worried that his own ethical resources – once robust, as evidenced by his early attachments to friends, as well as his moral outrage at the pain and injustice witnessed on his travels – have gone the way of his aesthetic appreciation. He confesses: "The loss of these [aesthetic] tastes is a loss of happiness, and may possibly be injurious to the intellect, and more probably to the moral character, by enfeebling the emotional part of our nature" (A, 139). Here Darwin links his aesthetic sense not so much to his religious sense, as Donald Fleming would have it, as to his "moral character," recognizing dimly that ethics and aesthetics form an important alliance, and that both have faded in his later years, leaving an "enfeebl[ed] . . . emotional . . . nature" as well as, perhaps, an "injur[ed] . . . intellect."

Puzzling briefly over the causes for the twin losses of his aesthetic and ethical acuities, Darwin again reaches for economic explanations:

My mind seems to have become a kind of machine for grinding general laws out of large collections of facts, but why this should have caused the atrophy of that part of the brain alone, on which the higher tastes depend, I cannot conceive. (A, 139)

Ever since Fleming, commentators have noted the Dickensian language of this passage, as if Darwin, in likening his mind to a "grinding" machine, were comparing himself to Thomas Gradgrind of *Hard Times*. Like Dickens, Darwin by the end of his *Autobiography* has come to expect an opposition between Romantic imagination and utilitarian calculation, seeming to forget the dual heritage to which he gestures in explaining his own genius. In his professed bewilderment, Darwin offers a mechanistic explanation – brain atrophy through lack of use – and proposes an equally mechanistic solution: "If I had to live my life again I would have made a rule to read some poetry and listen to some music at least once every week; for perhaps the parts of my brain now atrophied could thus have been kept active through use" (A, 139). Darwin suggests "a rule" of aesthetic exercise, and even ventures to recommend a frequency, "at least once every week." His solution relies on a prescription of "use," and his argument for aesthetics on its ultimate moral usefulness.

By the late Victorian period, scientific populist John Tyndall was also discussing "The Uses and Limitations of the Imagination for Science" in a lecture by that title. As the status of science rose and that of literature declined, Tyndall sought to recuperate the imagination, not as antithetical to science, but as a useful tool for scientists. Tyndall's effort demonstrates how deeply ingrained was the public perception of an objective science protecting itself from the dangers of the imagination. In scientific autobiography, late nineteenth- and early twentieth-century authors continued to invoke the importance of the imagination in their formative years. Following Darwin, Romantic elements were relegated to accounts of childhood, or to early hunches that were later confirmed more objectively. But of course imaginative elements, particularly those presented in the confessional first person, were increasingly expunged from scientific reporting and from the public presentation of science. The gradual narrowing of Darwin's *Autobiography* anticipates the course of scientific narrative over the next century. To borrow Gilbert Ryles's terms, the kind of thick description that once included stories of the experience of human discovery became increasingly reduced to the thin description of scientific reporting. This lean scientific prose has without a doubt been useful to the practicing scientist, who must quickly review masses of scientific literature, but it has contributed to a mistaken public image of scientific method. Those "thick" accounts of imaginative leaps that save scientists a great deal of thinking time are expunged from the scientific record precisely because, ironically, they "cost" time to write and read.

There is a final irony related to Darwin's attenuated *Autobiography*, specific to the medical community from which he emerged. Although Darwin abandoned his medical heritage, medicine now considers biology its home discipline, and Darwin the father of this larger field of which medicine is but a small part. Romantic medical thought may have fostered Darwin's genius, but medicine later followed Darwin's lead by narrowing and compacting medical narrative. Literature, when considered at all by medical educators, is often regarded as little more than a tool for teaching medical ethics. If we pushed back our knowledge of the history of medicine, however, to the pre-Darwinian period, we would find a fruitful dialectic between the literature and science of Romantic materialism. Perhaps then we could see that, for the art and science of medicine, literary thinking ought to be more than a useful addendum to scientific reasoning. Rather, literary thinking should become an equal half of a process of interpretation that circles between the thick description of narrative and the thin description of scientific report. Literary knowledge would then be, not merely useful, as Darwin would have it, but integral to medical thought.

CHAPTER 7

Middlemarch *and the medical case report: the patient's narrative and the physical exam*

One of the most significant developments of Romantic medicine was the diagnostic practice of weighing two different kinds of evidence: the patient's narrative and the physical exam. Before the nineteenth century, doctors relied for diagnosis primarily on the patient's report of his or her illness – so much so, that it was not uncommon to treat patients via correspondence. Before the clinical era, physical examination was limited to noting the quality of the pulse (not counting it) and occasionally the examination of bodily fluids.[1] Only in the early nineteenth century did doctors begin to practice thorough palpation, auscultation (listening to body sounds), and measuring various bodily signs (pulse, breathing, temperature). With the rise of clinical medicine, as disease was correlated with local pathology through the post-mortem dissection, doctors began to try to elicit evidence of localized disease in the living patient. Physical signs became as telling as the patient's story, but in a completely different way.

Historians of medicine, especially Nicholas Jewson and Roy Porter, have noted this changing balance of power, from a client-dominated doc-tor/patient encounter in the early eighteenth century to the rise of medical power in the nineteenth.[2] Building on their research, Mary Fissell tracks the "disappearance of the patient's narrative" in British hospital medicine in the late eighteenth century. Comparing medical case reports with patients' autobiographical accounts, Fissell finds the patient's experience to be increasingly sidelined by clinical reporting. Fissell writes, "The patient's narrative was replaced by physical diagnosis and post-mortem dissection. The body, the disease, became the focus of the medical gaze, not the patient's version of illness."[3] As this formulation suggests, Fissell relies heavily on Foucault's thesis in *The Birth of the Clinic* for her interpreta-tion of a sample of British case reports. But as I have argued in chapter one, British clinical medicine rose more slowly and with less centralized power than its French counterpart. Patients still had considerable power in early nineteenth-century Britain due to a glut of general practitioners struggling for professional recognition and economic survival. If we arrive too quickly at Fissell's conclusion that by 1800 the patient's narrative was "made utterly redundant," we miss the history of the doctor/patient negotiations during a sustained period of hermeneutic equality – a type of negotiation that seems increasingly desirable today.[4]

My reading of late eighteenth- and early nineteenth-century British case reports from the Wellcome Institute Library, and the published scientific proceedings of the era, supports the postulate of an extended period of dialectical exchange between the patient and doctor. Perhaps the most characteristic feature of the case histories of the period is a dense intermixture of patient's story and doctor's scientific observation. The Romantic doctor-writer often uses the patient's own words, but increasingly notes signs that he has detected from physical examination, often recorded in Latinate medical lingo. For instance, Richard Paxton, a surgeon of Maldon, Essex, records in his casebook[5] the following narrative: "A boy 16 years of age seeking Birds Nests in the Hedges trod upon a Viper, wch fastened on his Leg on the forepart near the Spine of the Tibia midway between the knee and ankle." Paxton includes the patient's own account of his motive for being in the hedges, i.e., "seeking Birds Nests," arguably superfluous from the medical point of view, but certainly the most significant part of the explanation from the boy's standpoint.

In the same sentence Paxton notes the anatomical location of the snakebite "near the Spine of the Tibia," pinpointing the lesion particularly for a medical reader. Paxton also describes the appearance of the snakebite as an "erysipelas redness," erysipelas indicating a red rash with a well-defined, raised border. The addition of "redness" to "erysipelas" is redundant, unnecessary unless Paxton is retelling the story in part from the patient's point of view. Paxton's language is full of such redundant conjunctions that juxtapose something a patient might report with medical shorthand for the professional reader.

Paxton's mixing of the patient's experience with medical observation is particularly evident in his progress notes, which seem as concerned with recording the human drama as with recording prognosis and outcome. In one obstetrical case, a woman "who had formerly bore children, was now and had been three days in Labour," complicated by an intrauterine infection.

[T]he discharge from the uterus was extremely foetid, [which] with other concurring symptoms, gave strong assurances of the death of the Child. Her friends and all the Women present were plainly told, that there did not appear the least Chance of her surviving, and also, that if upon attempting to deliver, much violence should be found necessary, it was to be feared, she would die in the Operation. The poor Woman herself begged to be delivered, and after giving such an Opinion, her entreaties ought not to be resisted.[6]

Paxton then describes the "Operation," which involved easing his fingers into the uterus and delivering the dead child in a breech position. Although this part of Paxton's report is largely focused on procedure and described with anatomical detail, Paxton comments on his own experience at the time of delivery. We are drawn into Paxton's own suspense as he "discovers" the baby's position and makes "gentle" attempts to pull down its legs, first "failing" and then "succeeding" by a different approach. He narrates, again with this strange mixture of medical language and the language of human experience, the delivery of the dead baby's body:

As the child's Face was to the Os Pubis of the Woman, it was to be feared that there would be great difficulty in delivering the Head but here was an agreeable disappointment, for it came down very easily, the reason of wch appeared after- wards, that tho' it was large, the Bones and its composing parts were in such a state of solution, that they freely were moulded to the Passage of the mother's Pelvis.[7]

As he narrates the procedure of delivery, Paxton's point of view remains pri- marily medical – the emotion that he communicates is his own rather than his patient's. His mild anxiety takes the form of polite euphemism: "it was to be feared." And his wry comment that the baby's decaying body was "an agreeable disappointment" registers the ironic collision of the doctor's point of view – his appreciation of an easier delivery – with his "disappointed" awareness of the patient's impending grief.

When Paxton resumes his narrative of the patient's demise, he again attends to the human drama:

After allowing the woman a little respite and giving her some Water with a small quantity of Brandy, the Placenta, [which] was extremely putrid was delivered. She bore the whole with great resolution and expressed great pleasure at being delivered. Such was the disagreeable smell, that one of the Women present fainted away . . . The poor woman herself was revived beyond expectation, but Nature or the Vis Vitae, being too far exhausted, she died in 24 hours.[8]

In Paxton's medical Latin, the "Vis Vitae" is the vital power then thought by many physicians to be the essence of life. He records with scientific precision the 24-hour duration of his patient's survival. But Paxton also records the kind offering of water and brandy, the smell of the room, the response of the bystanders, and finally, the remarkable poise and gratitude of this brave woman. Medical knowledge co-exists, in his account, with the story of human pain and courage.

Such an intermixture of two kinds of evidence seems perhaps more remarkable when we compare it to the bipartite "history and physical" which is the standard of medical case reporting today. The "patient's history" is usually gathered from talking to the patient (or to family members, or sometimes from past charts), whereas the "physical" reports the doctor's findings upon examination of the patient. The history is narrative in form (e.g., this 39-year-old woman was admitted to Whidbey General Hospital with the complaint of "pounding headache and nausea"), and the exam is list-like, with brief, formulaic comments following each body area or organ system examined (e.g., Heart: rate and rhythm regular, with no murmurs, rubs, or gallops, or Abdomen: normal bowel sounds, soft and non-tender). The history and physical are followed by laboratory and radiology reports, an "impression" (or initial diagnosis) and a "plan" (orders for hospitalization, consultation, treatment, and/or follow-up). The first two parts, however, the "history and physical," remain the gold standard of diagnostics, and the doctor must balance the evidence of the two even when they don't seem to match. Laboratory tests may be ordered on the basis of either suspicion aroused by the history or signs detectable on physical examination. Similarly, the diagnosis and plan may rely entirely on the patient's account, with negative physical findings (as in a hospital admission because the patient feels chest pain, in order to rule out myocardial infarction), or entirely on the physical exam, without the patient's awareness of the location or nature of the problem (e.g., the patient reports knee pain, but the exam reveals a hip abnormality). The two different kinds of evidence may support one another; if they do not, the doctor must keep both in mind throughout his or her investigation.

With the exception of the "chief complaint" (a quotable phrase that sums up the patient's main problem: e.g., "a fluttering feeling in my chest"), the patient's history today is not typically recorded in the patient's own words. For this reason, medical sociologists have classed the typical "history" as "medical narrative" in contradistinction to the patient's own story. True, the modern medical "history" looks very little like anything a patient would say. Formulaic and compact, the history is usually driven by a prescribed series of questions the doctor learns in medical school. But even as it is rendered in the twenty-first century, the patient's history is not an entirely medicalized account. Its purpose is to reconstruct, as accurately as possible, an account of the illness that does not rely on the doctor's observation or examination, but rather on the language communicated by the patient. This division between different kinds of evidence is perhaps best illustrated in the progress notes that attempt to perform the medical hermeneutic in an abbreviated fashion. Called SOAP notes (S for "subjective" report of what the patient says he feels; O for the "objective" physical exam; A for the assessment; and P for the plan), these brief notations reveal again the bipartite deep structure of the medical hermeneutic, moving from subjective story to objective exam, and needing to assess these different kinds of evidence before deciding upon a plan of action.

To the present-day medical reader, then, case reporting like Paxton's sounds primitive, or perhaps jumbled – alien, at least, to our way of thinking. A typical 21st-century doctor reading these cases will likely try to sort out the patient's report from the doctor's, particularly when attempting to make a retrospective diagnosis. The 21st-century doctor is also likely to weigh the doctor's observations more heavily, discounting the patient's story if it disagrees with the physical findings. Paxton's closely interwoven accounts at least testify to his consideration of the patient's point of view.

There were efforts in the first half of the nineteenth century to abbreviate and tabulate case reporting in order to gather data "for medical science." Notably, the medical registrar-general issued notebooks for case reporting with printed tabular columns and examples in red ink. The front matter contained the following notice:

Nosology will gain immensely in truth and accuracy whenever, instead of its particular being chronicled by a limited number of authorities, a large number of competent men, spread over a considerable extent of territory, and prolonging their observations throughout a considerable lapse of time, shall unite their labours to generalize the phenomena of disease . . . It [this notebook] has been issued under sanction of the Registrar-General in the earnest hope that its employment will become universal.

The registrar-general's diction reflects the scientific pretensions of the medicine of the period. He urges his doctor-investigators to record "observations" in the service of "nosology," in order to establish the "universal" laws governing "the phenomena of disease." If the doctor were to follow the "Examples as to the mode of filling up" offered in red ink, the patient's history would be reduced to a list including "Name, Residence, Profession, State, and Habits." One elderly woman is even, in these examples, missing a first name or initial. She is simply "North, Widow, Aylesbury, 1, Servant – 2, Married, Nervous, Dark" (Example 3). Example 8 labels another member of the lower class as "C. D., Gloucester, No profession, Idle, Nervous, and Cachetic." The author of these sample cases wastes a few more words on upper-class patients: "E. H., near Gloucester, Magistrate, Very active, intellectual, social, formerly a bon-vivant, latterly abstemious and depressed" (Example 4). But for the most part patients are reduced to type – e.g. "Irregular, unmanageable," or "Temperate, Delicate" – with two or three adjectives. The recommended mode of case reporting does indeed exclude the patient's story, condensing it to fit the stereotypes recognized by the medical community.

But this project of tabular recording seems to have failed at that time; nearly all of the surviving case reports from this period are narratives rather than tabular charts. One well-meaning young practitioner, Buxton Shillitoe, purchased two of the printed registers early in his career. The first few pages are filled out with dutiful imitations of the samples provided. But before long Shillitoe started to write sentences across the columns; by the end of the notebook, he had reverted completely to narrative form. Significantly, the second register remains empty, although Shillitoe continued practicing and recording cases long after.[9]

It is telling that even the most scientifically influential published and widely distributed case reports of the period preserve narrative form, including significant fragments of history derived from the patient's own story. Edward Jenner, in his *Inquiry into the Causes and Effects of the Variolae Vaccinae . . . The Cow Pox*, gives a remarkably full sense of the patient's life circumstances as he purports to chronicle primarily the "causes" and "effects" of a disease. Jenner gives occupational detail that brings into view the daily circumstance of the patient as a person outside of the medical encounter.

Joseph Merret, now an Under Gardener to the Earl of Berkeley, lived as a Servant with a Farmer near this place in the year 1770, and occasionally assisted in milking his master's cows. Several horses belonging to the farm began to have sore heels, which Merret frequently attended. The cows soon became affected with the Cow Pox, and soon after several sores appeared on his hands. Swellings and stiffness in each axilla followed, and he was so much indisposed for several days as to be incapable of pursuing his ordinary employment.[10]

Jenner's brief narrative somewhat superfluously acknowledges Merret's current position as "Under Gardener to the Earl of Berkeley," which gives the reader a thickened sense of what has happened to him after his case of cow pox. Further, we get an inkling of the cost to Merret of this disease: he became "incapable of pursuing his ordinary employment." In part, Jenner's style arises from the fact that he was investigating a disease that frequently presented as an occupational hazard. But it is remarkable that the narrative focuses so much on the patient's personal circumstance and less on the facts, figures, and dates characteristic of public health reports of the later nineteenth and twentieth centuries.

Even after the addition of the post-mortem examination to case reporting, the narrative form persisted. With Richard Bright's morbid anatomy cases, published in 1827, we see the beginnings of the bipartite "history and physical" format. In the following case, Bright recounts the patient's experience prior to launching his physical exam.

Case LVII
William Midwinter, age 34, was admitted into Guy's Hospital under my care, October 27th, 1826. He had been suffering from a cough for about four months, in consequence of a neglected cold; during the last month he had been under medical treatment, without deriving any relief. His cough had gone on increasing, but was chiefly troublesome when lying in bed; and there was a remarkable hoarseness in his voice. He found some difficulty of deglutition, and experienced a pain from his throat toward his ears when he swallowed. His expectoration, though considerable, had never been tinged with blood. On examination, it was found that the posterior fauces and the right tonsil were slightly ulcerated. Pulse 140. Respiration about 30. Countenance sallow; tongue red at the point; frequent night perspirations.

SECTIO CADAVERIS
By no means emaciated. Larynx affected with two very confirmed ulcers just below the rima glottidis on each side ... The upper lobe of each lung was thickly filled with miliary tubercles collected into large clusters, with hard, semi-transparent central masses. A few tubercular abscesses were formed in each superior lobe, about the size of small nutmegs. The greater part of the lungs, more particularly the lower lobes, although they contained some miliary deposits, were freely pervious to the air. [11]

The first seven lines of this case report constitute the patient's history. Although Bright resorts to medical shorthand such as "deglutition" and "expectoration," every piece of the narrative attends to the patient's experience, recording details that Bright could not know without Midwinter's own narration. Bright may have questioned Midwinter formally with a doctorly catechism designed to elicit responses of medical relevance, but nonetheless he includes superfluous and possibly misleading details, such as Midwinter's suspicion that his illness arose "in consequence of a neglected cold." The phrase "on examination" signals the beginning of the physical exam, even though it is not yet occupying, as it will by the twentieth century, its own paragraph, announced by its own title. But note that Bright's style shifts from narrative sentences to bullet-like observations: "Pulse 140. Respiration about 30." Even the descriptive moments of the exam, such as "countenance sallow," dispense with pronouns and verbs. References to Midwinter's identity and being (such as "his" and "is") disappear entirely.

The evidence gathered from the dead and dissected body is formally cordoned off from the story and examination of the living patient by the heading: "SECTIO CADAVERIS." As implied by the title of the book, "Morbid Anatomy" is clearly Bright's important contribution to "Illustrating the Symptoms and Cure of Diseases" – not even the case title, assigned the roman numerals "LVII," receives such impressive and serious treatment as the Latin heading in full capital letters. Interestingly, despite the near separation of history and physical and the clear demarcation of living patient and dead cadaver, Bright does not include a discussion attempting to interpret or mediate between these disparate types of evidence. Certainly there are points of disagreement. Midwinter attributed his cough to a "neglected cold," and was more concerned, apparently, about hoarseness and throat pain than about the chest complaints typical of a tuberculosis sufferer. The exam reveals a rapid pulse and elevated respirations, signaling a lung infection rather than a routine upper-respiratory "cold." The post-mortem examination reveals tuberculosis, but in an unusual combination. The miliary lesions indicate a first infection with tuberculosis; but they are combined with the tubercles of an advanced case of the disease. This combination, which suggests a first infection with TB that has advanced with unusual rapidity, helps to explain Midwinter's atypical experience. He does not have a long, wasting illness, nor does he produce the bloody sputum characteristic of a tuberculosis patient. The throat lesions match his upper-respiratory symptoms of hoarseness and exquisite throat pain. Presumably, one of the lessons of Bright's clinical-pathological comparison is that the doctor should be alert to individual exceptions to the general rule. The SECTIO confirms both the patient's story and the physical examination.

By at least the early 1840s, the history and physical format was taught to medical students and reproduced in their case reports.[12] Charles John Hare, who won the Fellowe's Clinical Prize at University College, London, for his book of case reports, divides his reports into "Previous History," "Present State" (equivalent to today's "history of present illness"), and "Physical Signs." In his preface, he marvels at "the value of this Plan" of recording. Although the symptoms as narrated by the patient may appear "at first entirely anomalous, yet on looking over the description of them, when their true cause was known, we can trace throughout the Progress" of the disease. Hare's case reports are uncharacteristically long and detailed in comparison to those of experienced practitioners of the period – he was, after all, a medical student entering them in a contest – but the fact that he won the prize demonstrates that his method of reporting was sanctioned by the University of London. And, interestingly, Hare records the history as much as possible in the patient's own words, not infrequently putting words and phrases in quotation marks.[13]

Experienced clinicians have always touted the importance of listening to the patient's story for its diagnostic value. Even today, medical educators routinely warn students of the dangers of relying on physical evidence alone. But the therapeutic value of attending to the patient's story has yet to receive adequate attention in medical education and practice. Some theorists are preparing fertile ground for the reconsideration of the importance of patient narratives. Kathryn Montgomery Hunter, in *Doctors' Stories*, argues that medicine is not a science, but an exercise of hermeneutic skill:

The practice of medicine is an interpretive activity. It is the art of adjusting scientific abstractions to the individual case . . . The details of individual maladies are made sense of and treatment is undertaken in light of the principles of biological science. Yet medicine's focus on the individual patient, fitting general principles to the particular case, means that the knowledge possessed by clinicians is narratively constructed and transmitted. How else can the individual be known?[14]

Because, as philosophers and psychologists increasingly agree, individual identity is narratively constructed, only narrative communicates the lived experience of the person as patient. Hunter also remarks that hermeneutic models tackle the difficulty of a basic incommensurability between the patient's story of the course of his or her illness and the doctor's story of the disease process. Although both the patient's and the doctor's stories refer to the same illness, the patient's lived experience of being ill cannot be reduced to or replaced by medical description. A hermeneutic circling between two kinds of evidence is necessary for both diagnosis and treatment.

Theorists of the doctor/patient relationship over the past two centuries have recognized, at least implicitly, the duality of the doctor's ideal stance toward the patient. Because of the difference between the doctor's and the patient's story, the doctor must be able to shuttle back and forth between narratives, must be able both to identify and to distance himself or herself from the patient's perspective. John Gregory's Baconian "two books" model, discussed in chapter two, yoked "sympathy" with "composure," arguing that a gentle temper could easily co-exist with vigorous scientific intelligence.[15] By the late nineteenth century, one can still detect this double ideal, although composure receives a good deal more attention than sensibility. Sir William Osler, in his influential valedictory address of 1889, sends his graduating medical students off with "the watchword of the good old Roman – *Aequanimitas*." Osler acknowledges, almost in passing, the place of sympathy, but prizes equanimity above all:

Keen sensibility is doubtless a virtue of high order, when it does not interfere with steadiness of hand or coolness of nerve; but for the practitioner in his working-day world, a callousness which thinks only of the good to be effected, and goes ahead regardless of smaller considerations, is the preferable quality.[16]

For Osler, imperturbability is susceptible of cultivation. "Education," he writes, "will do much" to promote equanimity, and "with practice and experience the majority of you may expect to attain to a fair measure." Although he doesn't wish to harden "'the human heart by which we live,'" Osler apparently thinks the "heart" need not be trained. Rather, he advises the pursuit of equanimity: "Cultivate, then, gentlemen, such a judicious measure of obtuseness as will enable you to meet the exigencies of practice with firmness and courage."[17]

The cultivation of any kind of "obtuseness" may seem a strange prescription for newly minted doctors, but it has persisted in twentieth-century theory of doctor/patient relationships. In the 1960s, Renée Fox developed the notion of "detached concern" which was widely embraced over the next few decades as a medical ideal. In Fox's definition, the physician with "detached concern" was "sufficiently detached or objective in his attitude toward the patient to exercise sound medical judgment and keep his equanimity, yet he also has enough concern for the patient to give him sensitive, understanding care."[18] In 1963, Fox collaborated with Harold Lief on a study that tracked medical students' attitudes throughout the course of their training. They concluded that medical education was well designed to promote detached concern in its graduates. During the first two years of medical school, which then (as is often the case now) included coursework in gross anatomy as well as limited exposure to hospital wards, students demonstrated considerable anxiety about cadaver dissection and about their first confrontations with medical uncertainty and patients' deaths. Fortunately, however, according to Fox and Lief, during the last two "clinical" years, spent largely in the management of hospital patients, students acquired a "professional" detachment which balanced their earlier sensitivity:

During the first two years the primary problem for students is that of acquiring greater detachment in the face of some of the cardinal professional experiences of the physician. These emotion-laden experiences include: exploring, examining, and cutting into the human body; dealing with the fears, anger, sense of helplessness, and despair of patients' meeting emergency situations; accepting the limitations of medical science in dealing with chronic or incurable disease; being confronted with death itself. During their clinical apprenticeship, in the last two years of medical school, chiefly through their experiences and responsibility in caring for patients, students gradually approach the balance of attitudes termed detached concern.[19]

Fox positions sensitivity to "emotion-laden" experience as the inevitable "primary problem" to be overcome; medical students learn detachment only through the rigors and responsibilities of patient care. Although Fox seems to redress Osler's lopsided emphasis on equanimity, restoring the place of empathy in doctor/patient theory, she in fact reinscribes Osler's assumption that affective sensitivity is natural, and that equanimity must be fostered during the course of medical education.

From my own professional experience and from observation of medical students, I would grant that most students experience a degree of anxiety stemming from identification (the most elementary and reflexive of emotional responses) with their cadavers and first patients. That is, they think, "That could be me (or my mother, or brother)" or "How would I feel if that were me?" And I would agree that most acquire a crude detachment during the "clinical years." In fact, amongst 21st-century residents, I have observed a good deal of what Fox in the 1960s called "pathologic overdetachment":

Beginning with the anatomy laboratory, for some students a pathologic process of overdetachment begins, which may eventually lead them, as mature physicians, to perceive and treat patients mechanistically. The process of overdetachment may not stop at the failure to see the patient as a person but may go on to the unconscious fantasy that the best patient is one who is completely passive and submissive and that the most cooperative patient is inert, anesthetized, or even dead. The ramifications of this are beyond the scope of this chapter, and, fortunately, very few medical students become that detached.[20]

Whether "overdetachment" went undetected in the 1960s or whether we have experienced an epidemic of late, I will not attempt to consider. But the "fantasy" of the patient as a passive object has entered the realm of resident consciousness and language games, at worst as the accepted parlance of the culture of residency, or at best as self-critiquing irony.

I mean to argue in this chapter for a more dynamic model for doctor/patient relationships than that of balance between (natural) emotion and (cultivated) detachment. First, I think that physicians need emotional education and practice – that, while identification may be natural, the most sophisticated compassion, attuned to the differences of another person, requires a great deal of skill. Second, I think that detachment comes rather easily through exposure to the experiences common in medical school. As medical practitioners, we quickly cease to identify once we realize that there is no necessary communication between our nerves and another's – that is, once our experience disproves the old myths about physiological sympathy (see chapter two). So, while we may expect a certain kind of detachment to arise without much cultivation, we should be working harder at practical education in sympathetic concern. Those who teach courses in "literature and medicine" or "narrative ethics" are aiming at fostering skills in applying general rules of emotional competence to particular cases of individual need, whether real or fictional, as articulated by the best writers on these topics.

As Kathryn Montgomery Hunter has argued, hermeneutics provides not only a description of the structure of medical knowledge, but also a model for doctor/patient relationships. Like the traditional theories of doctor/patient relationships, hermeneutics posits that understanding arises from a species of double vision, a complex combination of proximity and distance between interpreter and interpreted. But beyond the theories of doctor/patient relationships, hermeneutic theory insists on the dynamic interplay, the movement back and forth between such positions, rather than a static or ideal "balance" between them. So, for instance, one could imagine a physician's practice of circling between empathy and respectful distance from a patient. Just as a medical student might move from identification to detachment, we might encourage physicians to take a few more turns – or, better, to make a life-long commitment to turning – on the hermeneutic circle. One might alternate between such questions as "What is it like to be that patient?" and such questions as "How could I possibly assume what someone from another race, class, or gender (or any body other than mine) is feeling?" In this model, emotion is neither automatic nor dangerous. True, some kinds of emotion (especially a rudimentary identification, which arouses fight-or-flight physiology) interfere with clear medical thinking. But mature compassion will surely assist medical decision-making, particularly in ethical quandaries, but also, one might argue, in exercising the capacity of medical judgment.[21]

Hunter cautions against nostalgia for a "pretechnological time when social and personal detail were entered into the medical record," urging that "special, reconstructive attention" be focused on the doctor/patient relationships "of a mobile, urban, fragile society that lacks a binding communal religious belief."[22] Indeed, the history of medicine and literature, if it is to be useful, must avoid idealizing the past. But revival of interest in hermeneutics makes it vital that we know the history of this interpretive practice both in medicine and in literature, so that we can better assess past experiments and plan new approaches for the future.

In literature, George Eliot's *Middlemarch* gives us the most clear-sighted study of Romantic hermeneutics. Published in 1874, but set in and fundamentally about the crosscurrents of the early 1830s, *Middlemarch* is a historical novel focusing on the twin births of clinical medicine and hermeneutic philosophy in Britain. J. Hillis Miller has long maintained that *Middlemarch* is "about" interpretation, representing the "contradictory struggle of individual human energies, each seen as a center of interpretation, which means misinterpretation of the whole."[23] But, as Suzy Anger argues, deconstructive critics like Miller are too eager to claim Eliot as a precursor:

These critics ascribe to her a radical hermeneutics in which interpretation is an endless and unconstrained activity. They take her as a proto-deconstructionist, apprehending the metaphorical nature of all language and the completely perspectival quality of all knowledge, demonstrating, wittingly or not, a fundamental relativism and skepticism. On this view signs refer only to other signs; there is no transcendental signifier to ground meaning, thus there is no such thing as correct interpretation.[24]

Anger argues that Eliot's hermeneutics are more closely related to the Romantic hermeneutics of Friedrich Schleiermacher. Like Schleiermacher, Eliot acknowledges at once the endless process of interpretation and the goal of comprehending meaning. Interpretations may be "illimitable," as Eliot's narrator famously intones in *Middlemarch*, but the narrator nonetheless distinguishes between less and more appropriate interpretations, affirming the possibility of intelligible dialogue and shared understanding.

David Carroll considers *Middlemarch* to be a product of nineteenth-century hermeneutics, particularly the hermeneutics of empiricism.[25] In what Carroll calls "the empiricist fable," the empiricist is unsettled by innumerable imaginative hypotheses, and yet comforted by a commonsensical affirmation of an ordinary, real-world course of action. Moving back and forth between hypothesis and testing, or credulity and skepticism, the empiricist describes one form of the hermeneutic circle. Although Carroll is not primarily concerned with the specifically medical forms of empiricism developing in the nineteenth century, he does note one of the narrator's peculiarly medical instances of interpretation. In examining Casaubon's character, Eliot's narrator proposes a thought experiment: "Suppose we turn from outside estimates of a man, to wonder, with keener interest,

what is the report of his own consciousness about his doings or capacity."
Carroll explains this passage via medical analogy:

There is a medical quality to this kind of shift: after the diagnosis of symptoms the doctor asks the patient how he feels. The two, of course, never coincide fully. The discrepancy, the tension between the outside and inside estimate, is what character consists of and makes the future possible.[26]

I would argue, of course, that Carroll has the order reversed. The doctor, in taking the history, first asks how the patient feels, and then collects physical evidence for the diagnosis. But, of course, the medical hermeneutic circle continues as the doctor later inquires into the patient's progress. I quite agree that the "tension between the outside and inside estimate" constitutes the medical dilemma, as well as Eliot's narrative technique.

Although Carroll doesn't explore the history of Romantic medicine, his insight about the novel's hermeneutic character takes us in a more promising direction than the more specifically *Middlemarch*-and-medicine studies recently produced by Jeremy Tambling and Peter Logan. Tambling's article is a Foucauldian reading of the novelist as a pathologist:

[Eliot] asks for a single vision – one that comes from the Foucauldian "eye of research", which in its anatomizing gaze, "pierces the obscurity" to detect process and growth . . . The study [of this process] may believe in relations, but they are relationships gathered round a knowable center or body, under the dominant gaze of the novelist.[27]

George Eliot's realist narrator, according to Tambling, participates in the systematic, totalizing knowledge of the pathologist. Peter Logan, by contrast, differentiates the narrator's point of view from Lydgate's, and in the process concludes the opposite: that the Eliot narrator thinks it's representation all the way down. He claims that, while Lydgate is a naïve realist, incapable of acknowledging the fictional status of medicine, the narrator continually returns us to representation: "This looking beyond the surface, so paradigmatic in Lydgate's medicine, is itself the act of representation. And so, in a perfect circularity, realism comes to hinge on the representation of representation."[28] Tambling and Logan, both examining *Middlemarch* through the lens of medicine, recapitulate a familiar disagreement about *Middlemarch* over whether the narrator is nearer naïve realism or skeptical constructivism.

In *Vital Signs*, Lawrence Rothfield navigates between these two extremes. Like Logan, he distinguishes between the narrator and Lydgate, but he views the narrator as a pluralist who embraces both the clinical and other competing perspectives:

Eliot's major innovation is to contextualize and historicize, for the first time in the realist novel, the clinical epistemology to which she – as a realist – must remain committed . . . Eliot delimits this scientific "point of view," not only by ascribing it to a character – Lydgate – whose fate can then be thought of as an allegory of the fate of clinical medicine as a human science, but also by supplementing her own formal use of the clinical notion of the body with others that are valid without being medical. Although the clinical perspective remains central, the novel makes room for entire sets of characters and plots imagined according to rules that do not match those of the clinic but that nevertheless have the ring of truth.[29]

Rothfield's seems a more balanced assessment of the narrator's complex position, but in order to account for what he perceives as Eliot's departure from a strictly clinical perspective (which, according to his thesis, she must maintain in order to qualify as a realist) Rothfield posits a decline in the cultural authority of medicine – precisely when, according to most medical historians, the authority of the profession is steadily rising.

If we leave the Foucauldian paradigm long enough to search for influential cultural formations other than disciplinary power, Romantic hermeneutics provides an excellent explanatory matrix for the interpretive practices of Eliot's narrator. George Eliot herself described her writing process as "the severe effort of trying to make certain ideas thoroughly incarnate, as if they had revealed themselves to me first in the flesh and not in the spirit."[30] That is, Eliot's ideas originate in the spirit; she strives to make them incarnate, "as if" she had first experienced them as real. The fictional incarnation is of course distinct both from the real-world encounter with flesh and blood and from Eliot's "spiritual" or creative apprehension of it. As Catherine Gallagher puts it, Eliot gives a "special turn" to "empiricist logic"

by invoking both an understanding that types are induced from persons in the world and a further awareness that its characters are deduced from types. It requires two sorts of individuals; those given in and those twice removed from an inferred world . . . Eliot here explicitly carries the reader through the arc of induction and deduction, deduction and induction that give generalities weight and substance.[31]

Although Gallagher does not specifically name Romantic hermeneutics as the source of her model, her recurrence to an "arc" circling between the general and the particular suggests the hermeneutic circle practiced by both literary interpreters and empirical investigators.

Perhaps the most impressive example of this arc that Gallagher discusses is the "Prelude" to *Middlemarch*. Here we are first introduced to the historical

Saint Theresa, and then to the category of latter-day "Theresas," meaning the passionate women who, unlike the original saint, "found for themselves no epic life." The "Theresas" of Eliot's new category differ significantly from the original by finding no opportunity for expressing their idealism. We are curious, then, to meet Dorothea, an instantiation of this already destabilized category, who will further challenge our notions of "the limits of variation" of female kind that the narrator discusses in the Prelude. As Gallagher puts it,

To learn about the unknown through fictional particulars is to resolve the mysteries of daily life: mysteries such as how could a Theresa, in the very act of aspiring toward her type, become a drudging wife-scribe to a provincial pedant? In the "Prelude" to *Middlemarch*, Eliot rouses our desire for fiction by promising to show us just exactly how it is that one does not conform to type.[32]

Gallagher points out that this circle between typifying and particularizing continues, driven by the desire to experience incarnation more fully. By the close of the novel, the narrator creates a new category of, in Eliot's words, "Dorotheas, some of which may present a far sadder sacrifice than that of the Dorothea whose story we know" (M, 825).[33] Gallagher describes the process:

[E]ven as she presents the departure of the latter-day Theresas from their heroic type as a pity, and even as she gathers up her instances of failure into new categories, Eliot uses the gap between type and instance to create a momentum, an impulse toward the prosaic that is indistinguishable from the desire to read a fiction.[34]

Gallagher's position – that George Eliot is not merely a moralist, but rather a master of fictional desire – is an important corrective to the persistent misconception that Eliot is the stern monitor of Victorian morals. Eliot's ethic becomes, in Gallagher's reading, "indistinguishable" from the pleasure of reading fiction.[35]

Without explicitly invoking Romantic hermeneutics, Gallagher places this movement at the center of Eliot's realism. She argues, for instance, that the gap between type and instance creates the sense of a realist character: "[T]he extravagance of characters, their wastefulness as referential vehicles, is precisely what makes them seem real."[36] This sounds like a sophisticated reformulation of E. M. Forster's definition of that central realist concept, the "round character": that he or she should "surprise convincingly." Both Forster and Gallagher agree that the thickness of the realist character arises from the combination of referential familiarity with a type, and enough material outside of the reader's inductive experience to stimulate a disruption and reformulation of knowledge about that which is given as "real." Furthermore, Gallagher calls George Eliot "the greatest English realist" because she inspires her readers to seek this disruption and reformulation of categories; narrator and reader alike practice the circling between type and instance.[37]

Not only does the *Middlemarch* narrator practice hermeneutic circling, her two main characters also embrace a hermeneutic dialectic, as if Eliot wished to place the roots of her own philosophy in the Romantic hermeneutics of the 1830s. Dorothea is an idealist with a desire to build cottages to meet the basic physical needs of her neighbors. And Lydgate works back and forth between anatomical theory and medical practice. Lydgate's assertion that "there must be a systole and diastole in all inquiry," is a beautifully physiologic analogy for the method of Romantic hermeneutics, in which the interpreter's point of view is, as Lydgate puts it, "continually expanding and shrinking between the whole human horizon and the horizon of an object-glass" (M, 628). Indeed, his research interest is a larger anatomical analogy for Romantic hermeneutic technique. Lydgate seeks the "primary tissue," the Ur-tissue giving rise to variant anatomical structures: skin, muscle, nerve, bone, viscera, and so on. Like Xavier Bichat and his fellow transcendental anatomists, Lydgate believes that investigation of anatomical parts will reveal the wholes, or overarching ideas in the "mind" of Nature.

Furthermore, Lydgate's transcendental anatomy supplies the reigning metaphors of *Middlemarch*: Lydgate trains the *light* of his microscope on various *tissues*. Eliot's narrator deliberately adopts these light and web metaphors to describe his[38] own process, concentrating "all the light I can command" on "this particular web," the tissue of *Middlemarch* society (M, 91). In his landmark paper, J. Hillis Miller has called these two groups of metaphors "optic" and "semiotic." Miller groups together the metaphors of light, vision, and lenses, and points out that, although these optical metaphors hint at the uncertainties of perception, they at the same time reinstate the traditional association of light with reason, or, in this instance, with scientific knowledge. Even the pier glass parable, which is often read as an affirmation of perspectivalism, is derived from a scientific experiment which demonstrates that the shifting arrangement of reflections is no more than an illusion. Miller's "semiotic" category, on the other hand, encompasses the tissue or "web" metaphors that suggest human connection, particularly via language. Miller rehearses the by now familiar relationship of "tissue" to "text," from the Latin *textus*, meaning both "literary composition" and "woven thing."[39] The full breadth of the semiotic metaphor in

Middlemarch is perhaps best explicated by Gillian Beer, who points out how its connotations range from possibilities of kinship to those of entanglement or entrapment.[40]

Noting the complexity or "contamination" within these categories of metaphors, as well as the way in which the two categories seem to contradict one another, Miller argues that the metaphors deconstruct one another, thereby undermining the narrator's pretensions to totalizing knowledge. While I quite agree with his observation that the light metaphors suggest a complicated epistemology, and the web metaphors the complications of human relationship, I think that Miller misconstrues the narrator's stance. Miller sees the narrator as a synecdochic thinker who relates the "part to [the] whole" just as one might "a sample to the whole cloth," assuming "a strict homogeneity between the large-scale and small-scale grain or texture of things."[41] Although Miller recognizes the hermeneutic activity of comparing part to whole, he misses the narrator's acute awareness that these two ways of thinking are often in conflict, demanding dialectical adjustment. As the narrator explicitly concludes in the "Finale," "[T]he fragment of a life, however typical, is *not* the sample of an even web" (M, 818, my emphasis). Miller's deconstructive reading assumes a blindness on the part of the narrator, and a cleverness in the deconstructive critic who alone notices the latent contradictions. In contrast, approaching the text from the standpoint of Romantic hermeneutics reveals a consistency in Eliot's narration, her choice of metaphors, and her historical setting. Eliot's narrator self-consciously circles between the two metaphors in an interpretive (rather than a deconstructive) process, in search of partial and provisional, rather than absolute or positive, knowledge. Furthermore, the application of light to webs, and the frustration of light by webs, applies equally to the narrator's technique, to Lydgate's Romantic science, and to Dorothea's developing religion. Romantic hermeneutics runs like a glimmering thread through them all.

Although both Dorothea and Lydgate, as I have said, aspire to a hermeneutic ideal, neither on his or her own is able to achieve full hermeneutic circling. Each fumbles where the other is deft. As William Deresiewicz writes,

It is part of the novel's tragic irony that its two leading figures possess all the elements necessary for heroism, only divided between them. Lydgate has the potential and the opportunity but lacks the moral courage; Dorothea has the potential and the courage but lacks the opportunity. It is for this reason that their failures cannot be taken as a blanket statement of heroism's impossibility. In this respect, as in so many others, *Middlemarch* seeks not to discourage, but to instruct.[42]

One might easily substitute "empirical knowledge" and "devotion to human relationship" for Deresiewicz's terms "opportunity" and "moral courage." Dorothea longs to be useful to her neighbors, but she lacks the knowledge to actualize her ideals. Lydgate has the medical knowledge to make a difference in his community, but he lacks wisdom about social relationship. Or, to cast this in George Eliot's metaphors, Dorothea has faith enough to bring healing to the social web, but fumbles myopically with her schemes for practical change. "What can I do?" she is always quite practically asking, but for lack of answers is labeled "theoretic" and "short-sighted." Lydgate, on the other hand, sees acutely when professionally engaged, but mismanages his social relationships. He gets entangled with Rosamond, and later with Bulstrode; in neither case has he the aptitude to foresee the difficulties, or to explain himself – i.e., to narrate his own story – once entrapped. While Lydgate wields the acute power of cutting-edge scientific knowledge, Dorothea is the expert at understanding the tissue of human connection, and eliciting those narratives that heal the social fabric.

Why, then, does Eliot keep the two characters at arm's length from one another? Of course the two yield multiple parallels that emphasize the affinities, in the late Romantic era, between a would-be saint and a reforming physician. Yet the plots remain strangely separated, the two protagonists barely realizing their potential to assist one another. We know, from work on the genesis of the novel, that Dorothea's story was conceived apart from Lydgate's. But the separation of the two plots is more than an artifact of composition. From the beginning of the novel, the narrator prepares us for the irony of these two plots remaining largely separate from, though necessary to, one another. Dorothea and Lydgate first meet at Dorothea's engagement party, and we already know, from the "animated conversation" she addresses to Lydgate, that when speaking of reform she craves his practical knowledge (M, 90). Lydgate enjoys the exchange much less, concluding that "It is troublesome to talk to such women. They are always wanting reasons, yet they are too ignorant to understand the merits of any question, and usually fall back on their moral sense to settle things after their own taste" (M, 92). Dorothea may have an excess of "moral sense," but she is found wanting in the category of "adornment," which Lydgate rates as holding "first place among wifely functions." He complains that Dorothea "did not look at things from the proper feminine angle. The society of such women was about as relaxing as going from your work to teach the second form, instead of reclining in a paradise with sweet laughs for bird-notes, and blue eyes for a heaven." Lydgate expects relaxation from the company of women, and release from the rigors of scientific inquiry. He does not expect to have to work at human relationships – at least not with the fair sex.

From this first encounter, the narrator prepares us – misleadingly, perhaps – for an eventual intersection of the two plots. He comments dryly that Lydgate "might possibly have experience before him which would modify his opinion as to the most excellent things in woman" (M, 92). And this first meeting between Dorothea and Lydgate is the context for the oft-quoted passage asserting "the stealthy convergence of human lots":

But any one watching keenly the stealthy convergence of human lots, sees a slow preparation of effects from one life on another, which tells like a calculated irony on the indifference or the frozen stare with which we look at our unintroduced neighbour. Destiny stands by sarcastic with our *dramatis personae* folded in her hand. (M, 93)

If "destiny" exercises her sarcasm by joining people once indifferent to one another, the narrator, throughout the course of the novel, develops his own more complicated irony: that two people so suited to assist one another should so briefly encounter one another and part. It is as if Eliot were acknowledging the increasing difficulty of joining the two ways of knowing championed by Lydgate and Dorothea.

Nonetheless Lydgate and Dorothea succeed in offering crucial assistance to one another at the most severe crises in their lives. In this book about missed opportunities and failures of interpretation, each administers deft and expert help precisely when it is needed. Their subsequent encounters are brief, but, interestingly, quite symmetrical, as if to indicate the reciprocal importance of their proffered assistance. First, Lydgate consults with the Casaubons about Edward's illness. Next, Dorothea offers Lydgate financial assistance with the failing fever hospital. Then Lydgate treats Dorothea in her delirium after Edward's death. Finally Dorothea demonstrates the belief in Lydgate that prompts his confession and public restitution.

In his professional visits to the Casaubons, Lydgate demonstrates extraordinary clinical prowess. By "clinical," however, I do not mean to imply that Lydgate wields Foucauldian disciplinary power. Eliot's portrayal of Lydgate supports instead my earlier characterization, in chapter one, of the British clinical scene. Lydgate's status as a general practitioner, struggling to make a living, necessitates deference toward his patients and humility in his medical opinions. A strong believer himself in scientific advances, Lydgate adjusts his rigorous French medical training to his British practice, gradually introducing his patients to the stethoscope and the research hospital, and, ever so gently, to the idea of the autopsy. When we see him with patients in the actual practice of medicine, he behaves with the canny personal perception of his eighteenth-century predecessors who relied almost entirely on narrative skills for their healing power. "Clinical" in this British sense has no better illustrator than George Eliot: she shows the general practitioner at the intersection not only of interpersonal and scientific medicine, but also of patient-centered and doctor-centered medicine.

When Lydgate examines Edward Casaubon, for instance, he combines scientific advances with techniques developed long before such technology. The narrator tells us that Lydgate "used his stethoscope (which had not become a matter of course in practice at that time)" (M, 279). The stethoscope, invented by the French physician Laennec in 1819, was still an innovation, especially in British rural areas. Medical historians have considered its invention and use a landmark in diagnosis. Laennec developed the instrument to assist in correlating the lesions found on post-mortem dissection to evidence of similar lesions in the living patient. Thus the stethoscope has become symbolic of the clinical era, and of breakthroughs in clinical-pathological correlation. For historian Stanley Joel Reiser, the stethoscope also signifies the ways in which clinical medicine has distanced itself from patients. Initially, auscultation (listening to the sounds emitted by the body) was performed with the physician's ear to the patient's body. Then a wooden tube was developed, and finally a much longer rubber tube, largely for the convenience of the doctor. More important than this literal distance, however, was the realization that expert auscultation was more reliable than the patient's story, which might be distorted by beliefs, emotions, or outright deception. Reiser writes:

[A]uscultation helped to create the objective physician, who could move away from involvement with the patient's experiences and sensations, to a more detached relation, less with the patient but more with the sounds from within the body. Undistracted by the motives and beliefs of the patient, the auscultator could make a diagnosis from sounds that he alone heard emanating from body organs, sounds that he believed to be objective, bias-free representations of the disease process.[43]

Interestingly, however, George Eliot regards the stethoscope less as a distancing technology than as evidence of careful attention. "Lydgate seemed to think the case worth a great deal of attention. He not only used his stethoscope (which had not become a matter of course in practice at that time), but sat quietly by his patient and watched him" (M, 279). Here she emphasizes the receptive capacity of the auscultator: he is literally listening to the body, patiently attending to its language. Lydgate watches his patient, but the implication is less that of the disciplinary gaze than the receptive listener.

In his advice to both of the Casaubons, Lydgate also shows deference for his patients, as if they, rather than he, were the masters of the situation. He advises rest for Casaubon, and when Casaubon objects he acknowledges the difficulty of complying with such advice. "'I confess,' said Lydgate, smiling, 'amusement is rather an unsatisfactory prescription. It is something like telling people to keep up their spirits'" (M, 280). Similarly, in dealing with Dorothea, he tells her what he can while avoiding grim prognostication. He acknowledges the uncertainty of the Casaubons' future:

[Lydgate] said to himself that he was only doing right in telling her the truth about her husband's probable future, but he certainly thought also that it would be interesting to talk confidentially with her. A medical man likes to make psychological observations, and sometimes in the pursuit of such studies is too easily tempted into momentous prophecy which life and death easily set at nought. Lydgate had often been satirical on this gratuitous prediction, and he meant now to be guarded. (M, 281)

Lydgate is interested in Dorothea's psychological life, but "guarded" lest he assume too much authority in this consultation. Dorothea, in her characteristic quest for knowledge, pleads for help, "'Oh you are a wise man, are you not? You know all about life and death. Advise me. Think what I can do'" (M, 283). Even now, Lydgate resists the temptation to pronounce, supplying sympathy instead of medical knowledge: "'I wish that I could have spared you this pain,' said Lydgate, deeply touched" (M, 283).

Though ostensibly the authority figure in this encounter, Lydgate considers himself the recipient of something important from Dorothea:

For years after Lydgate remembered the impression produced in him by this involuntary appeal – this cry from soul to soul, without other consciousness than their moving with kindred natures in the same embroiled medium, the same troublous fitfully-illuminated life. (M, 283)

This is Lydgate's first lesson in Dorothea's wisdom about human relationships – that despite the "fitfully-illuminated" uncertainty of life, perhaps particularly in the medico-personal encounter, doctor and patient can become "kindred natures," swirling in the same "embroiled medium." The piercing "cry from soul to soul" provides the clarity in this case, not the light of scientific knowledge.

The next time Dorothea and Lydgate meet, Lydgate is more clearly the beneficiary of Dorothea's goodwill. Recalling their first meeting at Tipton, when Dorothea revealed her social conscience, he hopes to enlist her in rescuing the New Hospital. He presents his case with "abrupt energy" and full knowledge of the practical complications. Dorothea in her turn offers "naïve" and "fascinated" trust, as well as a generous monetary subscription. Of course, Dorothea is grateful for the opportunity to help, as we know from her oft-repeated refrain: "I have some money, and don't know what to do with it – that is often an uncomfortable thought to me" (M, 432). Dorothea converts her beneficence into a reciprocal exchange – her excess for Lydgate's knowledge in "the good use" of her funds.

In the two subsequent encounters, Dorothea and Lydgate rise to a new level of intimacy, each eliciting and reconstructing the other's narrative identity. First, Lydgate attends Dorothea in her shock following Edmund's death. Though delirious, Dorothea "knew him [Lydgate] and called him by his name, but appeared to think it right that she should explain everything to him" (M, 473). Lydgate's treatment consists of gathering the fragments of her delirium into a coherent narrative:

His attendance on Dorothea while her brain was excited, had enabled him to form some true conclusions concerning the trials of her life. He felt sure that she had been suffering from the strain and conflict of self-repression; and that she was likely now to feel herself only in another sort of pinfold than that from which she had been released. (M, 482)

Reweaving Dorothea's narrative, Lydgate feels nearly "sure" of his diagnosis, and of what Dorothea is "likely" to feel now. Yet when Celia urges him to prohibit Dorothea's return to her responsibilities at Lowick, Lydgate hesitates.

"She wants to go to Lowick, to look over papers," said Celia. "She ought not, ought she?"

Lydgate did not speak for a few moments. Then he said, looking at Dorothea, "I hardly know. In my opinion Mrs. Casaubon should do what would give her the most repose of mind. That repose will not always come from being forbidden to act." (M, 482)

Lydgate's approach is again delicately nuanced, at first admitting his partial knowledge: "I hardly know." Celia's assumptions, after all, reflect the popular wisdom later to become medical orthodoxy as Silas Weir Mitchell's "rest cure." Lydgate ventures an "opinion" contrary to Celia's, all the while "looking at Dorothea" for her response. Apparently, he sees enough to confirm his interpretation of Dorothea's story, because his "opinion" strengthens into a "prescription" by the time he leaves the house. "Let Mrs. Casaubon do as she likes," Lydgate instructs Sir James, whom he summons just prior to his departure. "She wants perfect freedom, I think, more than any other prescription" (M, 482). At this point, Lydgate's role has become more clearly that of an advocate for his patient in the presence of a dissenting family.

Reciprocating this advocacy, Dorothea later offers Lydgate the trust necessary for the reweaving of his narrative identity. David Carroll has already remarked the healing nature of this hermeneutic encounter.

Lydgate undergoes no miraculous cure but the healing begins as he makes his confession . . . narrating his version of events without equivocation, and "recovering his old self in the consciousness that he was with one who believed in it" (752). Within this illuminated space, as in the account of his research, the hypothesis and the reality it explains become inseparable as each creates the other; or, in religious terms, Dorothea imputes righteousness to Lydgate and so imparts it.[44]

Carroll moves from Lydgate's scientific terms (hypothesis and reality) to religious terms (the imputing and imparting of righteousness), recognizing that both science and religion, at least in George Eliot's reconstruction of the late Romantic era, perform a version of hermeneutic circling. In this case, it is Dorothea's belief in Lydgate's coherent self or "character" that permits the realignment of Lydgate's fragmented thoughts. In some ways, Carroll's religious language is appropriate, given Dorothea's status as a would-be saint, and the frequency with which the words "trust" and "belief" are repeated by both partners in this dialogue. The narrator tells us that Dorothea's "was the first assurance of *belief* in him that had fallen on Lydgate's ears . . . [I]t was something very new and strange in his life that these few words of *trust* from a woman should be so much to him" (M, 751, my emphases). Dorothea pleads with Lydgate, "Do *trust* me," reassuring him that "Mr. Farebrother will *believe* – others will *believe*" (M, 752, 758, my emphases). Lydgate responds in kind, "It will be a comfort to me to speak where *belief* has gone beforehand," and "[Y]ou have made a great difference in my courage by *believing* in me" (M, 752, 758, my emphases). The healing element in this exchange is Dorothea's saintly capacity to imagine for Lydgate what he has not been able to imagine for himself, to anticipate the substance of his narrative and to summon that vision "beforehand." Of course, by this point in the novel, Dorothea's religion is quite vague. She explains to Will that her belief is "[t]hat by desiring what is perfectly good, even when we don't quite know what it is and cannot do what we would, we are part of the divine power against evil" (M, 382). Her faith seems active particularly when "we don't quite know" what to do. When Will tries to identify her "mysticism," Dorothea entreats him "Please not to call it by any name," as if a fuller definition of her religion would rob it of its potential. "You will say it is Persian, or something else geographical," she teases, then returning more seriously with "It is my life. I have found it out, and cannot part with it. I have always been finding out my religion since I was a little girl" (M, 382). Dorothea treasures, not knowledge itself, but the process of living through uncertainty, guided by imaginative impulse, "desiring" "beforehand" the good and "finding [it] out" by moving through the mixed and middling conditions of lived experience.

Because Dorothea's vision grows out of her uncertain condition, George Eliot declines to give it a name, instead narrating her life story so that we feel this "religion" as a desire that instantiates itself in her actions. As Dorothea tells Celia, "[Y]ou would have to *feel* with me, else you would never *know*" (M, 810, my emphases). We feel the fullest weight of Dorothea's religion in her life story, particularly in her final redemption of Lydgate. Vague as her system of belief seems, there are some qualities that set it apart from either traditional Christianity or a positivist religion of humanity. As Dorothea waits for Lydgate, the narrator tells us,

The idea of some active good within her reach "haunted her like a passion," and another's need having once come to her as a distinct image, preoccupied her desire with the yearning to give relief, and made her own ease tasteless. She was full of confident hope about this interview with Lydgate, never heeding what was said of his personal reserve; never heeding that she was a very young woman. Nothing could have seemed more irrelevant to Dorothea than insistence on her youth and sex when she was moved to show her human fellowship. (M, 750)

First, we see that Dorothea's faith is not so much typically Christian as it is typically Romantic. The narrator reaches for Wordsworthian language to describe her desire for active good. In contrast to Wordsworth's recollected youth, Dorothea's is a moral rather than an animal passion – but it is remarkable for being classed as a "desire" and a "yearning" rather than as an obedience to stereotypically Victorian duty. Second, Dorothea's "confident hope" refuses obstacles, much more successfully than does Farebrother's otherwise exemplary compassion, which has stooped to doubting Lydgate. This is one instance in which Dorothea overleaps the muddles of *Middlemarch*, when her short-sightedness becomes an asset precisely because it overlooks that which she deems "irrelevant" – "youth" and "sex" – that very lack of knowledge that the narrator has bemoaned since the "Prelude."

Perhaps because her passion is for ethical action, Dorothea's Romantic faith has a distinctly narrative quality. The narrator refers to the Romantic poets (Byron and Shelley, especially) when speaking of Will, but it is easy to lose sight of Dorothea's Romanticism because she does not seem particularly poetic. Her mode is dramatic narrative, as we see when she prepares herself to meet Lydgate by recalling their prior conversations:

As she sat waiting in the library, she could do nothing but live through again all the past scenes which had wrought Lydgate into her memories . . . These thoughts were like a drama to her, and made her eyes bright, and gave an attitude of suspense to her whole frame. (M, 750)

In this passage, the "scenes" Dorothea recalls and her "suspense" are so vivid that the narrator describes them as a "drama" that she "live[s] through again." This preliminary exercise of dramatic sympathy is followed, however, by the much more difficult task of eliciting Lydgate's own narrative.

Although Dorothea's faith has overleapt the obstacles of her youth and sex, she must still contend with Lydgate's skepticism about the efficacy of his own narrative. Lydgate has already considered – and rejected – the possibility of offering up a full narrative explanation of Raffles's demise:

[H]e had so often gone over in his mind the possibility of explaining everything without aggravating appearances that would tell, perhaps unfairly, against Bulstrode, and had so often decided against it – he had so often said to himself that his assertions would not change people's impressions – that Dorothea's words sounded like a temptation to do something which in his soberness he had pronounced to be unreasonable. (M, 751)

To this rational scientist, the invitation to narrate sounds like a "temptation" to dabble in the "unreasonable." Despite the fact that Lydgate has successfully exercised his own readerly acuity in eliciting and interpreting Dorothea's shock-induced and fragmentary narrative, Lydgate, the "emotional elephant," fears his own technique. Dorothea deftly reframes her plea in Lydgate's own medical language: "'Tell me, pray,' said Dorothea, with simple earnestness; 'then we can consult together'" (M, 751). Dorothea uses the common medical verb for doctor/patient negotiation, inviting the doctor into consultation on his own problem. Wisely, she levels the playing field: "we can consult together." Lydgate's confession, first in fragments, and finally more fully, becomes a surrender to Dorothea's sympathy:

[Lydgate] gave himself up, for the first time in his life, to the exquisite sense of leaning entirely on a generous sympathy, without any check of proud reserve. And he told her everything, from the time when, under the pressure of his difficulties, he unwillingly made his first application to Bulstrode; gradually, in the relief of speaking, getting into a more thorough utterance of what had gone on in his mind – entering fully into the fact that his treatment of the patient was opposed to the dominant practice, into his doubts at the last, his ideal of medical duty, and his uneasy consciousness that the acceptance of the money had made some difference in his private inclination and professional behaviour, though not in his fulfilment of any publicly recognized obligation. (M, 752–753)

Lydgate's confession is thorough, building toward the complication of his own self-doubt and his qualified evaluation of his public responsibility. Yet still he requires Dorothea's interpretation of it. When Dorothea articulates Lydgate's chief difficulty, her diagnosis itself brings relief:

"There is no sorrow I have thought more about than that – to love what is great, and try to reach it, and yet to fail."

"Yes," said Lydgate, feeling that here he had found room for the full meaning of his grief. (M, 753–754)

Dorothea at once diagnoses and sympathizes – she recognizes this common misery in which she herself has participated. She also, however, in a turn of the hermeneutic circle, moves from sympathetic identification to a delicate respect for her patient's dignity. "Dorothea refrained from saying what was in her mind – how well she knew that there might be invisible barriers to speech between husband and wife. This was a point on which even sympathy might make a wound." From believing to knowing, listening to interpreting, sympathy to respect, Dorothea proves herself a deft practitioner of various kinds of hermeneutic circling.

In this final encounter between Dorothea and Lydgate, the narrator seems to be making a place for Dorothea's narrative knowledge as an alternative, and equally important, epistemology parallel to Lydgate's medical knowledge. Rather than sustaining the light-as-knowledge metaphor in contradistinction to the web-as-relationship metaphor, at this point in the novel the narrator intermixes his metaphors:

The presence of a noble nature, generous in its wishes, ardent in its charity, changes the lights for us: we begin to see things again in their larger, quieter masses, and to believe that we too can be seen and judged in the wholeness of our character . . . He . . . felt that he was recovering his old self in the consciousness that he was with one who believed in it. (M, 751–752)

In Lydgate's medical model, light penetrates tissue, splitting it through analysis, until imagination reconnects the fragments in the form of a theory. In Dorothea's model, human relationship "changes the lights" – it is itself a distinct kind of knowledge – by which we re-see the "larger, quieter masses" of social connections, as well as the "wholeness" of our individual character. The splitting light of scientific knowledge becomes, in Dorothea's hands, the changing "lights" of "belief" that can draw things together.

To some degree, we are familiar with the idea that narrative knowledge is akin to faith, via Coleridge's oft-repeated Romantic assertion that readers practice a "willing suspension of disbelief." George Eliot gives us a story, a fictional incarnation, which limns her idea of what such a faith may have looked like to late Romantics, especially to medical Romantics and their larger cohort of Romantic materialists. We begin, at the engagement party, with the contrast between Dorothea's "animated" identification with Lydgate, and his cold detachment from her. This warm proximity and cold detachment are then, over the course of four encounters, made to mix within each character, until each learns the art of approaching the other with narrative sympathy, and receding with a delicate respect for his/her otherness. Although this narrative knowledge combines proximity and distance, it is a more complicated interweaving than the reflex identification and natural detachment that Renée Fox describes as "detached concern" in medical students. In brief, Dorothea and Lydgate learn to imagine the other, crucially, as different from the self. George Eliot emphasizes the precarious difficulty of such an art, and the medical and literary prowess required to practice it.

And practice we must. George Eliot reminds us of an alternate meaning of "clinical," one lost, largely, to literary critics under the influence of Foucault. Today, "clinical" in one register implies the detachment we have been critiquing. In another register it refers to daily practice, the hands-on work of doctor/patient consultations carried on in an outpatient "clinic" rather than a teaching hospital. Today's family practice resident might sign out her hospital service to the covering resident, announcing "I'm going to my clinic" – and she usually means she's leaving the hospital (often quite happily) to go to the place where she meets her own patients, where she "practices" the kind of real-world doctor/patient negotiation that makes the more critical hospital encounters endurable for both doctor and patient. This sort of "clinic" is one where doctors and patients might truly encounter one another, building the relationships of trust and mutual understanding so important to the quest for health and healing. George Eliot returns to us this early nineteenth-century British sense of the "clinic" in *Middlemarch*, her consummate vision of Romantic materialism. Through her twin-plotted medical novel, she provokes the desire for narrative knowledge that drives us to cultivate emotion, to train it into wisdom, rather than to restrain it in a misguided effort to achieve a distancing objectivity.

Notes

I. INTRODUCTION

1. Gillian Beer, *Darwin's Plots: Evolutionary Narrative in Darwin, George Eliot and Nineteenth-Century Fiction* (1983; Cambridge: Cambridge University Press, 2000), 37.
2. George Levine, *Darwin and the Novelists: Patterns of Science in Victorian Fiction* (Chicago: University of Chicago Press, 1988), 36.
3. George Levine, *The Realistic Imagination: English Fiction from Frankenstein to Lady Chatterley* (Chicago: University of Chicago Press, 1981). Levine writes, "The epistemology that lay behind realism was empiricist, with its tendency to value immediate experience over continuities or systems of order, and it was obviously related to the developments in empirical science as they ran through the century" (18).
4. Nancy Armstrong, "Emily Brontë In and Out of Her Time," *Genre: Forms of Discourse and Culture* 15.3 (Fall 1982): 243–264.
5. M. H. Abrams, *Natural Supernaturalism: Tradition and Revolution in Romantic Literature* (New York: Norton, 1971).
6. Alan Richardson also emphasizes the materialism of the romantic "Science of the Mind." See his *British Romanticism and the Science of the Mind* (Cambridge: Cambridge University Press, 2001).
7. For other works on the paradox of natural supernaturalism in the nineteenth century, see Kathryn Bond Stockton, *God between Their Lips: Desire between Women in Irigaray, Brontë, and Eliot* (Stanford: Stanford University Press, 1994) and Deborah Harter, *Bodies in Pieces: Fantastic Narrative and the Poetics of the Fragment* (Stanford: Stanford University Press, 1996). Stockton finds a "spiritual materialism" particularly in the discourse between women. Harter links fantastic narratives with the violated or dismembered body.
8. Anne K. Mellor, *English Romantic Irony* (Cambridge, Massachusetts: Harvard University Press, 1980) and Clyde de L. Ryals, *A World of Possibilities: Romantic Irony in Victorian Literature* (Columbus: Ohio State University Press, 1990).
9. Anne K. Mellor, review of *A World of Possibilities: Romantic Irony in Victorian Literature*, by Clyde de L. Ryals, *Victorian Studies* 35.4 (1992): 435.
10. Gary J. Handwerk, *Irony and Ethics in Narrative: From Schlegel to Lacan* (New Haven: Yale University Press, 1985).

11. G. S. Rousseau, "On Romanticism, Science and Medicine," *History of European Ideas* 17.5 (1993): 659.

12. Ibid., 663.

13. Andrew Cunningham and Nicholas Jardine, eds., *Romanticism and the Sciences* (Cambridge: Cambridge University Press, 1990). See also *The Third Culture: Literature and Science*, ed. Elinor S. Shaffer (Berlin and New York: Walter de Gruyter, 1998), which has a section devoted to Romanticism. Ludmilla Jordanova, in her excellent *Nature Displayed: Gender, Science and Medicine, 1760–1820* (London: Longman, 1999), presents a series of related essays on representations of women in Romantic medicine.

14. Michel Foucault, *The Birth of the Clinic: An Archaeology of Medical Perception*, trans. A. M. Sheridan Smith (New York: Vintage, 1975), 195.

15. Ibid., 147.

16. Ibid., 198.

17. Important exceptions include Miriam Bailin, *The Sickroom in Victorian Fiction: The Art of Being Ill* (Cambridge: Cambridge University Press, 1994) and Lilian Furst, *Between Doctors and Patients: The Changing Balance of Power* (Charlottesville: University Press of Virginia, 1998). Bailin focuses on "the personal and collective meanings" of nursing narratives rather than the "institutional constructions and deployments of sickness" (2). Furst contextualizes the interpersonal in a larger historical narrative, tracing the "changing balance of power" from more to less patient control in the doctor/patient encounter. Although Furst attends to issues of disciplinary power, she is not typically Foucauldian in her focus on small-scale ethics of the interactions between doctors and patients.

18. Lawrence Rothfield, *Vital Signs: Medical Realism in Nineteenth-Century Fiction* (Princeton: Princeton University Press, 1992). See also Peter Logan, *Nerves and Narratives: A Cultural History of Hysteria in Nineteenth-Century British Prose* (Berkeley: University of California Press, 1997) and Alan Bewell, *Romanticism and Colonial Disease* (Baltimore: Johns Hopkins University Press, 1999). Logan adds a new twist to the cultural history of hysteria: one falls ill from indulgence in luxury consumerism. Bewell describes a "medical geography" in which disease is associated with place – particularly with foreign or colonial landscapes. Both books critique important aspects of nineteenth-century medical ideology, particularly with respect to the meanings of pathology. My work, in contrast, emphasizes interpretive techniques used for reading the healthy body as well as the ill.

19. Athena Vrettos, in her *Somatic Fictions: Imagining Illness in Victorian Culture* (Stanford: Stanford University Press, 1995), also applies a Foucauldian approach to texts from later in the century. Vrettos nuances her argument with a recognition of the multiplicities of response to disciplinary dynamics, but she so qualifies Foucault as to leave us asking whether the theory has much explanatory power.

20. Roger French and Andrew Wear, eds., *British Medicine in an Age of Reform* (London: Routledge, 1991), 3.

21. See Stanley Joel Reiser, *Medicine and the Reign of Technology* (Cambridge: Cambridge University Press, 1985).
22. Edward Shorter, "The Doctor-Patient Relationship," in *Companion Encyclopedia of the History of Medicine*, ed. W. F. Bynum and Roy Porter (London: Routledge, 1993), vol. II, 789.
23. Steven Shapin, *The Scientific Revolution* (Chicago: University of Chicago Press, 1996), 135–136.
24. Ibid., 78.
25. Ibid., 78.
26. Sir Francis Bacon, *The Advancement of Learning* (1605), quoted in James R. Moore, "Geologists and Interpreters of Genesis in the Nineteenth Century," in *God and Nature: Historical Essays on the Encounter between Christianity and Science*, ed. David C. Lindberg and Ronald L. Numbers (Berkeley: University of California Press, 1986), 153.
27. Edward Young, *Night Thoughts*, Night IV, lines 703–705, quoted by Susan Faye Cannon, *Science in Culture: The Early Victorian Period* (Folkestone: Dawson, and New York: Science History Publications, 1978), 263.
28. John Keble, *The Christian Year*, 2nd American edn. (Philadelphia, 1840), 71, quoted in Cannon, *Science in Culture*, 10.
29. Cannon, *Science in Culture*, 1.
30. John Hedley Brooke, *Science and Religion: Some Historical Perspectives* (Cambridge: Cambridge University Press, 1991), 194.
31. Moore, "Geologists and Interpreters of Genesis," 323, 344.
32. John Milton, *Paradise Lost*, book VIII, lines 66–69, quoted by Roland Mushat Frye, "The Two Books of God," *Theology Today* 39 (Oct. 1982): 260–266. See page 264.
33. Elaine Scarry, "Donne: 'But Yet the Body is His Booke,'" in *Literature and the Body: Essays on Populations and Persons*, ed. Elaine Scarry (Baltimore: Johns Hopkins University Press, 1988), 70–105. See pages 70–71.
34. See Edmund Gosse, *Father and Son: A Study of Two Temperaments*, ed. James Hepburn (London: Oxford University Press, 1974).
35. Levine, *Darwin and the Novelists*, 31.
36. Mark Francis, "Naturalism and William Paley," *History of European Ideas* 10.2 (1989): 203–220. See page 214.
37. Dov Ospovat, *The Development of Darwin's Theory: Natural History, Natural Theology, and Natural Selection, 1838–1859* (Cambridge: Cambridge University Press, 1981). Ospovat sees continuity between natural theology and Darwin via perfect adaptation. He shows that late natural theologians mixed teleology (in Ospovat's usage, referring to function as a final cause) with acceptance of form (transcendental anatomy) as a cause.
38. William Paley, *Natural Theology, or Evidences of the Existence and Attributes of the Deity* (London, 1830), 27.
39. William Whewell, *Astronomy and General Physics Considered with Reference to Natural Theology* (London: H. G. Bohn, 1852), 305, quoted in Levine, *Darwin and the Novelists*, 28.

40. John Durant, "Darwinism and Divinity: A Century of Debate," in *Darwinism and Divinity: Essays on Evolution and Religious Belief*, ed. John Durant (Oxford: Basil Blackwell, 1985), 17.
41. Philip F. Rehbock, "Transcendental Anatomy," in *Romanticism and the Sciences*, ed. Andrew Cunningham and Nicholas Jardine (Cambridge: Cambridge University Press, 1990), 144.
42. Ibid., 145.
43. Adrian Desmond, *The Politics of Evolution: Morphology, Medicine and Reform in Radical London* (Chicago: University of Chicago Press, 1989).
44. Peter Mark Roget, *An Introductory Lecture on Human and Comparative Physiology* (London: Longman, 1826), quoted in Desmond, *Politics of Evolution*, 227.
45. Durant, "Darwinism and Divinity," 16.
46. Charles Darwin, *The Life and Letters of Charles Darwin*, ed. Francis Darwin (London: John Murray, 1887), vol. II, 219, quoted in Levine, *Darwin and the Novelists*, 29.
47. Peter Galison and Lorraine Daston, "The Image of Objectivity," *Representations* 40 (1992): 81–128.
48. George P. Landow, *Victorian Types, Victorian Shadows: Biblical Typology in Victorian Literature, Art and Thought* (Boston and London: Routledge and Kegan Paul, 1980), 4.
49. Herbert L. Sussman, *Fact in Figure: Typology in Carlyle, Ruskin, and the Pre-Raphaelite Brotherhood* (Columbus: Ohio State University Press, 1979), xvii.
50. Ibid., 4.
51. Cannon, *Science in Culture*, 17.
52. Martin J. S. Rudwick, *The Great Devonian Controversy: The Shaping of Scientific Knowledge among Gentlemanly Specialists* (Chicago: University of Chicago Press, 1985), 44.
53. Basil Willey, *Nineteenth-Century Studies: Coleridge to Matthew Arnold* (New York: Columbia University Press, 1949), 210–211.
54. Cannon, *Science in Culture*, 48.
55. Friedrich Ast, *Basic Elements of Grammar, Hermeneutics, and Criticism*, trans. Dora Van Vranken (1808), 75, quoted in Ronald Bontekoe, *Dimensions of the Hermeneutic Circle* (Atlantic Highlands, New Jersey: Humanities Press, 1996), 15.
56. Friedrich D. E. Schleiermacher, *Hermeneutics: The Handwritten Manuscripts*, ed. Heinz Kimmerle, trans. James Duke and Jack Forstman (Missoula: Scholars' Press, 1977), 100, quoted in Bontekoe, *Dimensions of the Hermeneutic Circle*, 30.
57. Clifford Geertz, "From the Native's Point of View: On the Nature of Anthropological Understanding," in *Interpretive Social Science: A Reader*, ed. Paul Rabinow and William M. Sullivan (Berkeley: University of California Press, 1979), 239, quoted in Richard J. Bernstein, *Beyond Objectivism and Relativism: Science, Hermeneutics and Praxis* (Philadelphia: University of Pennsylvania Press, 1983), 95. Geertz, in his practical anthropological hermeneutics, contrasts "local" and "global" interpretations. He defines the hermeneutic circle as a

"dialectical tacking between the most local of local detail and the most global of global structure in such a way as to bring both into view simultaneously."

58. Robert Baker, Introduction to Part 3, "The Formalization of Medical Ethics," in *The Codification of Medical Morality: Historical and Philosophical Studies of the Formalization of Western Medical Morality in the Eighteenth and Nineteenth Centuries*, ed. Robert Baker, Dorothy Porter, and Roy Porter (Dordrecht: Kluwer, 1993–1995), vol. I, 144.

59. Robert Baker, "The History of Medical Ethics," in *Companion Encyclopedia of the History of Medicine*, ed. W. F. Bynum and Roy Porter (London: Routledge, 1993), vol. II, 852, 853.

2. SCIENCE AND SYMPATHY IN *FRANKENSTEIN*

This chapter is a revised version of my "Science and Sympathy in *Frankenstein*," in *The Ethics in Literature*, ed. Andrew Hadfield, Dominic Rainsford, and Tim Woods (Basingstoke: Macmillan, 1998), 262–274.

1. Mary Shelley, "Introduction to the Third Edition (1831)," reprinted in *Frankenstein, or the Modern Prometheus: The 1818 Text*, ed. James Rieger (Chicago: University of Chicago Press, 1982), 227 (italics added).

2. John Abernethy, *An Enquiry into the Probability and Rationality of Mr. Hunter's "Theory of Life"* (London: Longman, 1814), 39.

3. Ibid., 42.

4. William Lawrence, *Two Introductory Lectures . . . at the Royal College of Surgeons* (London, 1816), 120. Lawrence's definition closely resembles Bichat's more famous pronouncement: "Life is the sum of all the functions by which death is resisted" (quoted in O. Temkin, "Basic Science, Medicine and the Romantic Era," in his *The Double Face of Janus* [Baltimore: Johns Hopkins University Press, 1977], 106).

5. See the *Quarterly Review* (London, 1819).

6. Susan C. Lawrence, *Charitable Knowledge: Hospital Pupils and Practitioners in Eighteenth-Century London* (Cambridge: Cambridge University Press, 1996), 330–331.

7. William Lawrence, *Lectures on Physiology, Zoology and the Natural History of Man* (London: Callow, 1819), 7.

8. Marilyn Butler, Introduction to *Frankenstein, or The Modern Prometheus: The 1818 Text*, by Mary Shelley (Oxford: Oxford University Press, 1993), xix–xx. Butler draws on Maurice Hindle's earlier work in his "Vital Matters: Mary Shelley's *Frankenstein* and Romantic Science," *Critical Survey* 2.1 (1990): 29–35.

9. Ibid., xlviii.

10. Quotations from Mary Shelley's *Frankenstein, or The Modern Prometheus: The 1818 Text*, ed. Marilyn Butler (Oxford: Oxford University Press, 1993) are cited in this chapter by the abbreviation "F [page number]."

11. Butler, Introduction, xlvii.

12. For a more extended discussion of the problem of sympathy and its relationship to theatricality, see David Marshall, *The Surprising Effects of Sympathy:*

Marivaux, Diderot, Rousseau, and Mary Shelley (Chicago: University of Chicago Press, 1988).

13. Ibid., 3.
14. *Oxford English Dictionary*, 2nd edn. (Oxford: Clarendon Press, 1989), s.v. "sympathy."
15. David Hartley, *Observations on Man, His Frame, His Duty, and His Expectations* (1749; facsimile reprint, Gainesville, Florida: Scholars' Facsimiles and Reprints, 1966), 13.
16. George Cheyne, *The Natural Method of Cureing the Diseases of the Body, and the Disorders of the Mind Depending on the Body* (London, 1742), 82–83.
17. David Hume, *A Treatise of Human Nature* (1739; ed. L. A. Selby-Bigge, Oxford: Clarendon Press, 1951), 576.
18. Quoted in John Mullan, *Sentiment and Sociability: The Language of Feeling in the Eighteenth Century* (Oxford: Clarendon Press, 1988), 26.
19. Robert Whytt, *Observations on the Nature, Causes, and Cure of those Disorders Which Have Been Called Nervous, Hypochondriac, or Hysteric* (Edinburgh, 1765), 213–214.
20. Michel Foucault, *Madness and Civilization: A History of Insanity in the Age of Reason*, trans. Richard Howard (New York: Pantheon Books, 1965), 157.
21. See Peter Melville Logan, *Nerves and Narratives: A Cultural History of Hysteria in Nineteenth-Century British Prose* (Berkeley: University of California Press, 1997).
22. Adam Smith. *The Theory of Moral Sentiments* (Oxford: Clarendon Press, 1976), 9.
23. John Gregory, "Lectures on the Duties and Qualifications of a Physician," (1772) in *John Gregory's Writings on Medical Ethics and Philosophy of Medicine*, ed. Laurence McCullough (Dordrecht: Kluwer, 1998), 189–190.
24. Ibid., 219–220.
25. Ibid., 171.
26. Ibid., 216.
27. Ibid., 217.
28. Francis Bacon, *Essays, Advancement of Learning, New Atlantis, and Other Pieces*, selected and edited by Richard Foster Jones (New York: Odyssey Press, 1937), 179.
29. Ibid., 179.
30. Quoted in Laurence B. McCullough, Introduction to *John Gregory's Writings*, ed. McCullough, 25.
31. I am indebted to Caroline Levine for defining and drawing attention to this kind of suspense in Victorian literature, and I differ from her only in finding earlier instances. See her *The Serious Pleasures of Suspense: Victorian Realism and Narrative Doubt* (Charlottesville: University of Virginia Press, 2003).
32. Quoted in Trevor Harvey Levere, *Poetry Realized in Nature: Samuel Taylor Coleridge and Early Nineteenth-Century Science* (Cambridge: Cambridge University Press, 1981), 52.
33. Ibid., 40.

34. Ibid., 40.
35. John Keats, *Letters of John Keats*, ed. Robert Gittings (Oxford: Oxford University Press, 1970), 43.
36. Beth Newman, "Narratives of Seduction and the Seductions of Narrative: The Frame Structure of *Frankenstein*," *ELH* 53.1 (1986): 146.
37. Anne K. Mellor, "*Frankenstein*: A Feminist Critique of Science," in *One Culture: Essays in Science and Literature*, ed. George Levine (Madison: University of Wisconsin Press, 1987), 59.
38. David M. Knight, "The Physical Sciences and the Romantic Movement," *History of Sciences* 9 (1970): 59.
39. Thomas Frosch, "The New Body of English Romanticism," *Soundings* 54.4 (1971): 380.
40. G. J. Barker-Benfield, *The Culture of Sensibility: Sex and Society in Eighteenth-Century Britain* (Chicago: University of Chicago Press, 1992), 21–23.
41. Peter Brooks, *Body Work: Objects of Desire in Modern Narrative* (Cambridge, Massachusetts: Harvard University Press, 1993), 201.

3. NATURAL SUPERNATURALISM IN THOMAS CARLYLE AND
RICHARD OWEN

1. M. H. Abrams, *Natural Supernaturalism: Tradition and Revolution in Romantic Literature* (New York: Norton, 1971), 13.
2. Anne K. Mellor, *English Romantic Irony* (Cambridge, Massachusetts: Harvard University Press, 1980), 4.
3. Quotations from Thomas Carlyle's *Sartor Resartus* (edited with an introduction and notes by Kerry McSweeney and Peter Sabor [Oxford: Oxford University Press, 1987]) are cited in this chapter by the abbreviation "SR [page number]."
4. Anne K. Mellor, review of *A World of Possibilities*, by Clyde de L. Ryals, *Victorian Studies* 35-4 (Summer 1992): 435.
5. Janice L. Haney, "'Shadow Hunting': Romantic Irony, *Sartor Resartus*, and Victorian Romanticism," *Studies in Romanticism* 17 (Summer 1978): 319.
6. Wolfgang Iser, "The Emergence of a Cross-Cultural Discourse: Thomas Carlyle's *Sartor Resartus*," in *The Translatability of Cultures: Figurations of the Space Between*, edited by Sanford Budick and Wolfgang Iser (Stanford: Stanford University Press, 1996), 245.
7. Ibid., 262.
8. Thomas Henry Huxley, quoted by Frank Turner, "Victorian Scientific Naturalism and Thomas Carlyle," *Victorian Studies* 18 (1975), 330.
9. John Tyndall, quoted by Turner, "Victorian Scientific Naturalism," 330.
10. Turner, "Victorian Scientific Naturalism," 330.
11. Ibid., 330. See also James Paradis, "Satire and Science in Victorian Culture," in *Victorian Science in Context*, ed. Bernard Lightman (Chicago: University of Chicago Press, 1997), 143–175. Here, Paradis proposes a more convincing commonality between *Sartor* and the scientists: the deployment of similar strategies of irony. Paradis argues that Huxley uses Carlyle's tools, but not his philosophy,

thereby recruiting irony to the service of a progressive new scientific culture. Paradis's emphasis on the ironic technique the scientific naturalists shared with Carlyle relieves him of the problem of accounting for any affinity between their projects, and therefore, I think, falls short of providing a satisfying explanation. I quite agree that Huxley shares Carlyle's brand of irony, but will contend that the dualism in *Sartor* and in pre-Darwinian science runs deeper than style.

12. Quoted in Turner, "Victorian Scientific Naturalism," 334.

13. Carlyle to John Sterling, 29 Aug. 1842, in Clyde de L. Ryals and Kenneth J. Fielding (eds.), *Collected Letters of Thomas and Jane Welsh Carlyle* (Durham: Duke University Press, 1987), vol. xv, 55.

14. Pym, Horace N., ed., *Memories of Old Friends, Being Abstracts from the Journals and Letters of Caroline Fox of Penjerrick, Cornwall from 1835 to 1871*, vol. i, 264. Quoted in Nicolaas A. Rupke, *Richard Owen: Victorian Naturalist* (New Haven: Yale University Press, 1994), 66.

15. Rupke, *Richard Owen*, 341.

16. Ibid., 342.

17. Ibid., 220.

18. Adrian Desmond, *Archetypes and Ancestors: Palaeontology in Victorian London 1850–1875* (London: Blond and Briggs, 1982), 43.

19. Richard Owen, *On the Nature of Limbs: A Discourse Delivered on Friday, February 9, at an Evening Meeting of the Royal Institution of Great Britain* (London: J. Van Voorst, 1849), 1.

20. Richard Owen, quoted in Jacob W. Gruber and John C. Thackray, *Richard Owen Commemoration: Three Studies* (London: Natural History Museum Publications, 1992), 75.

21. Richard Owen, closing passage of *On the Nature of Limbs*, quoted in Desmond, *Archetypes*, 47.

22. Charles Darwin, quoted in Desmond, *Archetypes*, 50.

23. Adrian Desmond, *The Politics of Evolution: Morphology, Medicine, and Reform in Radical London* (Chicago: University of Chicago Press, 1989), 372.

24. Desmond, *Archetypes*, 43.

25. Quoted in Rupke, *Richard Owen*, 210.

26. Ibid., 210.

27. Ibid., 68.

28. Ibid., 69.

29. In his *The Politics of Evolution*, Adrian Desmond arrays his various transcendental anatomists along a left-to-right spectrum, and narrates his history as a tale of the silencing of the more radical by the more conservative MDs. Whether or not this engaging narrative makes good history, it does illustrate the extent to which transcendental anatomy attracted and accommodated doctors from a range of political perspectives.

30. George Douglas Campbell, 8th Duke of Argyll, in *The Edinburgh Review* 116 (1862): 378–397.

31. Suzy Anger, "Carlyle: Between Biblical Exegesis and Romantic Hermeneutics," *Texas Studies in Literature and Language* 40.1 (1998): 80.
32. George Levine, "Carlyle, Descartes, and Objectivity," *Raritan* 17.1 (1997): 48.
33. Elaine Scarry, "Donne: 'But Yet the Body is His Booke,'" in *Literature and the Body: Essays on Populations and Persons*, ed. Elaine Scarry (Baltimore: Johns Hopkins University Press, 1988), 71.
34. "This is the way to the stars." *Aeneid*, book 11, l. 641.
35. T. H. Huxley, *Evolution & Ethics: T. H. Huxley's* Evolution and Ethics *with New Essays on Its Victorian and Sociobiological Context*, by James Paradis and George C. Williams (Princeton: Princeton University Press, 1989), 107.
36. James Paradis, "*Evolution & Ethics* in Its Victorian Context," in T. H. Huxley, *Evolution & Ethics: T. H. Huxley's* Evolution and Ethics *with New Essays*, by Paradis and Williams, 42, 44.

4. WUTHERING HEIGHTS AND DOMESTIC MEDICINE: THE CHILD'S BODY AND THE BOOK

1. Charlotte Brontë, in a letter to Mr. Williams, quoted in Winifred Gérin, *Emily Brontë: A Biography* (Oxford: Oxford University Press, 1971; 1978), 251.
2. Quotations from Emily Brontë, *"Wuthering Heights": Authoritative Text, Backgrounds, Criticism*, 3rd edn., ed. William M. Sale, Jr. and Richard J. Dunn (New York: Norton, 1990), are cited in this chapter by the abbreviation "WH [page number]."
3. Paul Starr, *The Social Transformation of American Medicine* (New York: Basic Books, 1982), 32.
4. Thomas John Graham, *Modern Domestic Medicine; or, a Popular Treatise, Illustrating the Character, Symptoms, Causes, Distinction, and Correct Treatment, of All Diseases Incident to the Human Frame; . . . the Whole Intended as a Medical Guide for the Use of Clergymen, Families, and Students in Medicine* (London: Simpkin and Marshall, 1826). Patrick Brontë's note on the title page of Graham's *Domestic Medicine* reveals his medical source when the children were younger: he has read a work by Dr. "R," [probably Richard Reece] and "proved it was greatly inferior to this – & tended only to puzzle &c. I therefore parted with it – & will retain only this work of Dr. Gr.am, & Buchan . . . 1831 – B."
5. Graham, *Modern Domestic Medicine*, 187–190.
6. Juliet Mitchell, *Women, the Longest Revolution: Essays on Feminism, Literature and Psychoanalysis* (London: Virago, 1984), 143–144, quoted in Patsy Stoneman, ed., *Emily Brontë:* Wuthering Heights (New York: Columbia University Press, 1998), 90.
7. Terry Eagleton, *Myths of Power: A Marxist Study of the Brontës*, 2nd edn. (London and New York: Macmillan, 1988), 109.
8. Juliet Barker, *The Brontës*, 111.
9. Gérin, *Emily Brontë*, 8.
10. Ibid., 172.

11. Ibid., 179.
12. Stevie Davies, *Emily Brontë: Heretic* (London: Women's Press, 1994), 38–39.
13. Emily Jane Brontë, "Stanzas" (manuscript lost), reprinted in *"Wuthering Heights": Authoritative Text*, ed. Sale and Dunn, 287.
14. William Buchan, *Domestic Medicine: A Treatise on the Prevention and Cure of Diseases, by Regimen and Simple Medicines; with an Appendix Containing a Dispensatory for the Use of Private Practitioners* (London: T. Kinnersley, 1821), 212–213.
15. Ibid., 268–269.
16. Ibid., 269.
17. Quoted in Hugh Cunningham, *Children and Childhood in Western Society since 1500* (London: Longman, 1995), 66–67.
18. Edward John Tilt, *On the Preservation of the Health of Women at the Critical Periods of Life* (London: Churchill, 1851), 31.
19. E. H. Ruddock, *The Common Diseases of Women*, 6th edn. (1888), 23–24, quoted in *Women from Birth to Death: The Female Life Cycle in Britain, 1830–1914*, ed. Pat Jalland and John Hooper (Atlantic Highlands, New Jersey: Humanities Press International, 1986).
20. Graham, *Modern Domestic Medicine*, title page.
21. See Barbara Munson Goff, "Between Natural Theology and Natural Selection: Breeding the Human Animal in *Wuthering Heights*," *Victorian Studies* 27.4 (Summer 1984): 482.
22. John Lock and W. T. Dixon, *A Man of Sorrows: The Life, Letters and Times of the Rev. Patrick Brontë 1777–1861*, 2nd edn. (Westport, Connecticut: Meckler Books, 1979), 249–252.
23. Elizabeth Gaskell, *The Life of Charlotte Brontë* (1857), ed. Alan Shelston (London: Penguin Books, 1975; reprinted in Penguin Classics, 1985), quoted in Gérin, *Emily Brontë*, 5.
24. Miriam Francis Allott, *The Brontës: The Critical Heritage* (London: Routledge and Kegan Paul, 1974), 367, quoted in Stoneman, ed., *Emily Brontë*: Wuthering Heights, 23.
25. Goff, "Between Natural Theology and Natural Selection," 489.
26. Ibid., 495. Heather Glen and Stevie Davies have both suggested that *Wuthering Heights* is proto-Darwinian in its depiction of the struggle for existence (Stoneman, ed., *Emily Brontë*: Wuthering Heights, 27, 125).
27. Goff, "Between Natural Theology and Natural Selection," 488.
28. Davies, *Heretic*, 248.
29. Emily Brontë, "The Butterfly," trans. Davies, in *Heretic*, 250.
30. Brontë, "The Butterfly," trans. Davies, in *Heretic*, 251.
31. Cunningham, *Children and Childhood*, 70.
32. Charlotte Brontë, *Jane Eyre*, ed. Jane Jack and Margaret Smith (Oxford: Clarendon Press, 1969), 34.
33. David Wilson, "Emily Brontë: First of the Moderns," *Modern Quarterly Miscellany* 1 (1947): 94, quoted in Stoneman, ed., *Emily Brontë*: Wuthering Heights, 135.

34. Arnold Kettle, *An Introduction to the English Novel*, 2 vols. (London and New York: Hutchinson's University Library, 1951–1953), vol. 1, 139, quoted in Stoneman, ed., *Emily Brontë: Wuthering Heights*, 138.
35. Nancy Armstrong, "Emily Brontë in and out of Her Time," *Genre* 15.3 (Fall 1982): 243–264.
36. J. Hillis Miller, *Fiction and Repetition: Seven English Novels* (Cambridge, Massachusetts: Harvard University Press, 1982), 42–72.
37. Beth Newman, "Narratives of Seduction and the Seductions of Narrative: The Frame Structure of *Frankenstein*," *ELH* 53.1 (1986): 141–163, quotation on 144.
38. Tilt, *On the Preservation of the Health of Women*, 20, 31 [this excerpt], 70.
39. Carol Jacobs, "*Wuthering Heights*: At the Threshold of Interpretation," in *Gendered Agents: Women and Institutional Knowledge*, ed. Silvestra Mariniello and Paul A. Bove (Durham: Duke University Press, 1998), 371–395, see especially p. 386. Jacobs's sophisticated reading does not, of course, miss Lockwood's irony – but her perpetuation of Lockwood's irony with mention of Catherine's "interpretation of the religious books of her library" has eluded some readers.
40. Ibid., 371.
41. In her deconstructive reading of the subsequent parable in Matthew, Carol Jacobs argues that the Matthew text, like Branderham's dream sermon, deconstructs itself. This, I think skates over the dream-Branderham's ridiculously overt misinterpretation of Scripture (and Emily Brontë's hilarious satire on all Branderhamish misinterpretation), in reaching for a more subtle, and I think more arguable point.
42. Ibid., 389.
43. Ibid., 382.
44. U. C. Knoepflmacher, *Wuthering Heights: A Study* (Athens: Ohio University Press, 1994), 18.

5. LITERALIZATION IN THE NOVELS OF CHARLOTTE BRONTË

This chapter is a revised version of my "Conflict and Revelation in the Novels of Charlotte Brontë," *Victorian Literature and Culture* 31.2 (2003): 483–499.
1. Quotations from Charlotte Brontë's works are cited using the following abbreviations:
   JE: *Jane Eyre*, ed. Jane Jack and Margaret Smith (Oxford: Clarendon Press, 1969)
   S: *Shirley*, ed. Herbert Rosengarten and Margaret Smith (Oxford: Clarendon Press, 1979)
   P: *The Professor*, ed. Margaret Smith and Herbert Rosengarten (Oxford: Clarendon Press, 1987)
   V: *Villette*, ed. Herbert Rosengarten and Margaret Smith (Oxford: Clarendon Press, 1984)
The reader should note that Clarendon edition chapter numbers differ from those of modern editions. The page numbers given here for all Brontë novels

will refer to the Clarendon edition page numbers. Chapter numbers are provided for readers of modern editions.

2. Matthew Arnold, *The Letters of Matthew Arnold to Arthur Hugh Clough*, ed. Howard Foster Lowry (London: Oxford University Press, 1932), 132.

3. Virginia Woolf, "*Jane Eyre* and *Wuthering Heights*," in her *The Common Reader* (New York: Harcourt Brace, 1925), 222–23.

4. Terry Eagleton, *Myths of Power: A Marxist Study of the Brontës* (New York: Barnes and Noble, 1975; London: Macmillan, 1988), xix; Eagleton's emphasis.

5. Sandra M. Gilbert and Susan Gubar, *The Madwoman in the Attic: The Woman Writer and the Nineteenth-Century Literary Imagination* (1979; New Haven: Yale University Press, 1984), 440. Gilbert and Gubar consider Brontë's opus, especially *Villette*, "a literature of consciousness," and claim that Brontë is "in some ways, a phenomenologist – attacking the discrepancy between reason and imagination, insisting on the subjectivity of the objective work of art, choosing as the subject of her fiction the victims of objectification, inviting her readers to experience with her the interiority of the Other" (440).

6. Janet Gezari, *Charlotte Brontë and Defensive Conduct: The Author and the Body at Risk* (Philadelphia: University of Pennsylvania Press, 1992).

7. Margaret Homans, *Bearing the Word: Language and Female Experience in Nineteenth-Century Women's Writing* (Chicago: University of Chicago Press, 1986), 26.

8. Ibid., 99.

9. Two recent books explore Brontë's interest in materiality, especially the body. Kathryn Bond Stockton (*God between Their Lips: Desire between Women in Irigaray, Brontë, and Eliot*. Stanford: Stanford University Press, 1994) reads Brontë through the post-structuralist feminism of Luce Irigaray, finding desire between women the source of Brontëan spirituality; Janet Gezari (*Charlotte Brontë and Defensive Conduct*) links Brontë's corporeal images to her concerns with self-defense. Both authors' explanations offer bracingly specific frameworks for interpretation, but arguably define Brontë's concerns too narrowly. My philosophical approach in turn risks abstraction – a serious problem when discussing the body – hence my recourse to multiple textual examples ranging across linguistic, religious, ethical, and social registers.

10. Homans, *Bearing the Word*, 6. Homans writes of Lacan's myth, "I am aware that I am myself taking this myth literally, in connecting those psychoanalytic or linguistic positions, 'masculine' and 'feminine,' with the experiences of real women who wrote. But 'taking it literally' is what these writers have learned women might happily do, or are supposed to do, and it is only by our taking literally the myth of women's literality that we can find out what is at stake in the very process of taking it literally."

11. Paul Ricoeur, *Interpretation Theory: Discourse and the Surplus of Meaning* (Fort Worth: Texas Christian University, 1976), 36–37.

12. Mario J. Valdés, introduction to *A Ricoeur Reader: Reflection and Imagination* (New York: Harvester, 1991), 8.

13. Ricoeur, *Interpretation Theory*, 92.

14. Ibid., 43.
15. Ibid., 52.
16. Ibid., 55.
17. See Juliet Barker, *The Brontës* (New York: St. Martin's Press, 1994), 631.
18. Anne Mozley, in *The Christian Remembrancer*, April 1853, quoted in Christina Crosby, *The Ends of History: Victorians and the "Woman Question"* (New York: Routledge, 1991), 133.
19. Luke 11.11, Authorized (King James) Version.
20. Arguments for secularization include those of Peter Allan Dale, "Varieties of Blasphemy: Feminism and the Brontës," *Review* (Charlottesville, Virginia) 14 (1992): 281–304; Barry Qualls, *The Secular Pilgrims of Victorian Fiction: The Novel as Book of Life* (Cambridge: Cambridge University Press, 1982); and Carolyn Williams, "Closing the Book: The Intertextual End of *Jane Eyre*," in *Victorian Connections*, ed. Jerome McGann (Charlottesville: University Press of Virginia, 1989), 60–87.
21. Thomas Vargish, *The Providential Aesthetic in Victorian Fiction* (Charlottesville: University Press of Virginia, 1985), 72–73.
22. Ibid., 84.
23. Ibid., 85.
24. Winifred Gérin, *Charlotte Brontë: The Evolution of Genius* (Oxford: Oxford University Press, 1969), 589.
25. George Landow, *Victorian Types, Victorian Shadows: Biblical Typology in Victorian Literature, Art, and Thought* (Boston: Routledge and Kegan Paul, 1980), 54.
26. Lyndall Gordon, *Charlotte Brontë: A Passionate Life* (New York and London: Norton, 1996), 193.
27. Janet Larson identifies this trope as "lady-wrestling," also finding it in the work of Elizabeth Barrett Browning and Virginia Woolf. "Lady-Wrestling for Victorian Soul: Discourse, Gender, and Spirituality in Women's Texts," *Religion and Literature* 23.3 (1991): 43–64.
28. Genesis 32.24–32.
29. See footnote, lines 1–2, Clarendon *Shirley*, 498.
30. See Luke 22.44.
31. Sally Shuttleworth, "Psychological Definition and Social Power: Phrenology in the Novels of Charlotte Brontë," in *Nature Transfigured*, ed. John Christie and Sally Shuttleworth (Manchester: Manchester University Press, 1989), 126.
32. See Nicholas Dames, "The Clinical Novel: Phrenology and *Villette*," *Novel* 29.3 (1996): 367–390. Dames notes the contest of phrenologic reading in *Villette*. Whereas Dames emphasizes the frustration and resentment aroused in such contests, I find evidence for revelation arising from the contests in all of Brontë's novels, including *Villette*.
33. Heather Glen, introduction to *The Professor*, by Charlotte Brontë (London: Penguin Books, 1989), 18–19. For a similar argument about the Foucauldian gaze in *Villette*, see Sally Shuttleworth, "'The Surveillance of a Sleepless Eye': The Constitution of Neurosis in *Villette*," in *One Culture: Essays in Science and*

Literature, ed. George Levine (Madison: University of Wisconsin Press, 1987), 313–335.

34. Charlotte Brontë, preface to *The Professor* (1857; reprint, ed. Heather Glen, London: Penguin Books, 1989), 38.

35. Francesca Kazan, "Heresy, the Image and Description; or, Picturing the Invisible: Charlotte Brontë's *Villette*," *Texas Studies in Literature and Language* 32.4 (1990): 557. Kazan's page references are to the Penguin English Library edition of *Villette* (London, 1979). Mine will continue to be to the Clarendon edition.

36. Kazan, "Heresy," 559.

37. Henri Bergson, *Laughter: An Essay on the Meaning of the Comic*, trans. Cloudesley Brereton and Fred Rothwell (New York: Macmillan, 1912), 37.

38. Shuttleworth, "Surveillance of a Sleepless Eye," 330.

39. Lucy alludes to I Corinthians 13.12.

40. Vargish, *Providential Aesthetic*, 74.

41. Ibid., 88.

42. Matthew Arnold, *Culture and Anarchy: An Essay in Political and Social Criticism*, ed. and with introduction and notes by Ian Gregor (New York: Bobbs-Merrill, 1971), 109.

43. Ibid., 112.

6. CHARLES DARWIN AND ROMANTIC MEDICINE

1. Desmond King-Hele, *Erasmus Darwin and the Romantic Poets* (New York: St. Martin's Press, 1986), 21.

2. Quotations from *The Autobiography of Charles Darwin, 1809–1882: With Original Omissions Restored*, ed. Nora Barlow (New York: Norton, 1993) are cited in this chapter by the abbreviation "A [page number]."

3. William Whewell, review of *On the Connexion of the Physical Sciences* by Mary Sommerville, *Quarterly Review* 51 (1834): 59–60. Trevor Levere identifies this anonymous review as Whewell's in his *Poetry Realized in Nature: Samuel Taylor Coleridge and Early Nineteenth-Century Science* (Cambridge: Cambridge University Press, 1981), 73.

4. King-Hele, *Erasmus Darwin*, 23–5.

5. See chapter one for a discussion of "Romantic materialism," a term introduced by Gillian Beer in *Darwin's Plots: Evolutionary Narrative in Darwin, George Eliot and Nineteenth-Century Fiction* (1983; Cambridge: Cambridge University Press, 2000) and echoed by George Levine in *Darwin and the Novelists: Patterns of Science in Victorian Fiction* (Chicago: University of Chicago Press, 1988).

6. Quoted in George Levine, "Darwin and Pain: Why Science Made Shakespeare Nauseating," *Raritan* 15.2 (Fall 1995): 99.

7. Donald Fleming, "Charles Darwin: The Anaesthetic Man," *Victorian Studies* 4 (1961): 233–234.

8. John Angus Campbell, "Nature, Religion and Emotional Response: A Reconsideration of Darwin's Affective Decline," *Victorian Studies* 18 (1974): 159–174.

9. Levine, "Darwin and Pain," III–II2.
10. A, 138–139.
11. Charles Darwin, *More Letters of Charles Darwin: A Record of His Work in a Series of Hitherto Unpublished Letters*, ed. Francis Darwin (New York: Appleton, 1903), vol. I, 195; quoted in Janet Browne, *Charles Darwin: The Power of Place* (Princeton: Princeton University Press, 2003), 56.
12. Charles Darwin, *The Life and Letters of Charles Darwin*, ed. Francis Darwin (London: John Murray, 1887), vol. I, 129, 130, quoted in Browne, *Charles Darwin: The Power of Place*, 169.
13. See George Levine, *Dying to Know: Scientific Epistemology and Narrative in Victorian England* (Chicago: University of Chicago Press, 2002). Throughout *Dying to Know*, Levine emphasizes the self-sacrificial or even suicidal language of nineteenth-century scientific inquiry, but even so he acknowledges, in his chapter on autobiography, what he sees as the "paradox" that self-effacement is often a form of self-assertion:

    [O]ne moral of the story is that the self can't do without self-denial; and self-denial can't do without the self. So self-deprecation lapses over into arrogance; the plain style becomes rhetorical after all. The implicit hubris of scientific intellectual imperialism shyly reasserts itself. The complications of the passion to know, dying to know, are inextricably entangled in the life it must renounce. (103)

    If we understand the oscillation between self-assertive Romantic imagining and self-critical empirical testing as a dialectical process that does conceptual work for Darwin, then it need not be so mysteriously contradictory.
14. Browne, *Charles Darwin: The Power of Place*, 351.
15. Avon Crismore and Rodney Farnsworth, "Mr. Darwin and His Readers: Exploring Interpersonal Metadiscourse as a Dimension of *Ethos*," *Rhetoric Review* 8.1 (1989): 104.
16. Ibid., 101.
17. Regenia Gagnier, *Subjectivities: A History of Self-Representation in Britain, 1832–1920* (New York: Oxford University Press, 1991), 239.
18. Ibid., 223.
19. James Olney, *Metaphors of Self: The Meaning of Autobiography* (Princeton: Princeton University Press, 1972), 184.
20. Linda Peterson, *Victorian Autobiography: The Tradition of Self-Interpretation* (New Haven: Yale University Press, 1986), 159.
21. George Levine, "Objectivity and Death in Victorian Autobiography," *Victorian Literature and Culture* 20 (1992): 286.
22. For further discussion of Darwin and utilitarianism, see Silvan Schweber, "Darwin and the Political Economists: Divergence of Character," *Journal of the History of Biology* 13.2 (1980): 195–289.
23. Thomas Robert Malthus, *An Essay on the Principle of Population*, ed. Antony Flew (London: Penguin, 1985), 200.
24. Ibid., 20.
25. Ibid., 200.

26. Ibid., 201.
27. Ibid., 272.
28. Ibid., 202.
29. Ibid., 202.
30. Quoted in Gillian Beer, *Darwin's Plots: Evolutionary Narrative in Darwin, George Eliot and Nineteenth-Century Fiction* (1983; Cambridge: Cambridge University Press, 2000), 25.
31. Ibid., 25.
32. Michael Ruse, "The Darwin Industry: A Guide," *Victorian Studies* 39.2 (1996): 220.
33. Quoted in *The Autobiography of Charles Darwin*, ed. Barlow, 234.
34. The "Nigger" joke raises the question of Darwin's view on slavery. Though not a political activist, his writings demonstrate him to be firmly and consistently against slavery. Darwin remains a target for post-colonial criticism, however, especially in the *Voyage of the Beagle*, which demonstrates attitudes toward "savages" quite typical of British imperialism.

7. MIDDLEMARCH AND THE MEDICAL CASE REPORT: THE PATIENT'S NARRATIVE AND THE PHYSICAL EXAM

1. See Stanley Joel Reiser, *Medicine and the Reign of Technology* (Cambridge: Cambridge University Press, 1985), chapter 1.
2. See Nicholas Jewson, "Medical Knowledge and the Patronage System in Eighteenth-Century England," *Sociology* 8 (1974): 369–385, and Roy Porter, "Lay Medical Knowledge in the Eighteenth Century: The Evidence of the *Gentleman's Magazine*," *Medical History* 29 (April 1985): 138–168.
3. Mary E. Fissell, "The Disappearance of the Patient's Narrative and the Invention of Hospital Medicine," in *British Medicine in an Age of Reform*, ed. Roger French and Andrew Wear (London: Routledge, 1991), 100.
4. At one juncture, Fissell concedes that "the patient's narrative did not disappear quickly or completely, even in the hospital" (Fissell, "The Disappearance of the Patient's Narrative," 93). Nonetheless, she focuses on the disappearance of the patient's narrative, rather than on the interactions between the patient's and the doctor's story during this period.
5. Richard Paxton, doctor and surgeon of Maldon, Essex, case-book, 1799, MS 3820, Western Manuscripts Collection, Wellcome Institute for the History and Understanding of Medicine Library.
6. Ibid., 49–50.
7. Ibid., 51.
8. Ibid., 51–52.
9. Buxton Shillitoe, clinical notes of cases in a "Register of Cases Professionally Attended." Notebooks containing clinical notes, MS 4523, Western Manuscript Collection, Wellcome Institute Library.
10. Edward Jenner, *An Inquiry into the Causes and Effects of the Variolae Vaccinae, a Disease Discovered in Some of the Western Counties of England, Particularly*

Gloucestershire, and Known by the Name of "The Cow Pox," 2nd edn. (London: Sampson Low, 1800), 9.

11. Richard Bright, *Reports of Medical Cases, Selected with a View to Illustrating the Symptoms and Cure of Diseases by a Reference to Morbid Anatomy* (London: Longman, Rees, Orme, Brown and Green, 1827), 161.

12. This pushes the date of the teaching of the "history and physical" in medical schools to an earlier period than that noted by Julia Epstein, who places it around 1890. See her "Historiography, Diagnosis, and Poetics," *Literature and Medicine* 2.1 (1992): 23–44, 32.

13. Charles John Hare, "Fellowe's Clinical Prize Reports" (London, 1842), 135 (MS 2778, Western Manuscripts Collection, Wellcome Institute Library).

14. Kathryn Montgomery Hunter, *Doctors' Stories: The Narrative Structure of Medical Knowledge* (Princeton: Princeton University Press, 1991), xvii.

15. John Gregory, "Lectures on the Duties and Qualifications of a Physician" (1772), in *John Gregory's Writings on Medical Ethics and Philosophy of Medicine*, ed. Laurence McCullough (Dordrecht: Kluwer, 1998), 170–171.

16. William Osler, *Aequanimitas: With Other Addresses to Medical Students, Nurses and Practitioners of Medicine* (Philadelphia: P. Blakiston's Son & Co., 1904), 5.

17. Ibid.

18. Harold I. Lief and Renée C. Fox, "Training for 'Detached Concern' in Medical Students," in *The Psychological Basis of Medical Practice*, ed. Harold I. Lief, Victor F. Lief, and Nina R. Lief (New York: Harper and Row, 1963), 12.

19. Ibid., 13.

20. Ibid., 21.

21. In his *Descartes' Error: Emotion, Reason, and the Human Brain* (New York: Avon Books, 1994), Antonio R. Damasio argues that emotion is integral to clear reasoning.

22. Hunter, *Doctors' Stories*, 172.

23. J. Hillis Miller, "Narrative and History," *ELH* 41.3 (Autumn 1974): 467.

24. Suzy Anger, "George Eliot and Philosophy," in *Cambridge Companion to George Eliot*, ed. George Levine (Cambridge: Cambridge University Press, 2001), 91.

25. David Carroll, *George Eliot and the Conflict of Interpretations: A Reading of the Novels* (Cambridge: Cambridge University Press, 1992). Carroll writes "George Eliot's career and fiction can best be understood in the context of nineteenth century hermeneutics. It was during her lifetime that hermeneutics developed from a body of rules for the translation and understanding of ancient texts, biblical and classical, to the recognition that interpretation was a foundational activity in which everyone was inescapably involved" (3). Carroll also recognizes the hermeneutic nature of early nineteenth-century medicine. He writes "The representation of Lydgate's career provides George Eliot with the opportunity to exploit the fictional possibilities of two other hermeneutic disciplines – diagnostic medicine and anatomical research" (265).

26. Ibid., 8.

188   *Notes to pages 156–166*

27. Jeremy Tambling, *"Middlemarch,* Realism and the Birth of the Clinic," *ELH* 57 (1990): 953.
28. Peter M. Logan, "Conceiving the Body: Realism and Medicine in *Middlemarch," History of the Human Sciences* 4.2 (1991): 217.
29. Lawrence Rothfield, *Vital Signs: Medical Realism in Nineteenth-Century Fiction* (Princeton: Princeton University Press, 1992), 88.
30. Quoted in Carroll, *George Eliot and the Conflict of Interpretations,* 26.
31. Catherine Gallagher, "George Eliot: Immanent Victorian," in *Proceedings of the British Academy: 1996 Lectures and Memoirs,* ed. Marjorie Chibnall (Oxford: Oxford University Press, 1997), 159–160.
32. Ibid., 166.
33. Quotations from George Eliot's *Middlemarch: Authoritative Text, Backgrounds, Criticism,* 2nd edn., ed. Bert Hornback (New York: Norton, 2000) are cited in this chapter by the abbreviation "M [page number]."
34. Gallagher, "George Eliot," 166.
35. Caroline Levine, in her book *The Serious Pleasures of Suspense: Victorian Realism and Narrative Doubt* (Charlottesville: University of Virginia Press, 2003) establishes the important connection between pleasure and ethics across a broad spectrum of Victorian narrative.
36. Gallagher, "George Eliot," 163.
37. Ibid., 172.
38. Although I think there are good reasons for reading the narrator as female at this point in George Eliot's career, I have opted to refer to the narrator as male, in part to make sure that we distinguish "him" from the author.
39. J. Hillis Miller, "Optic and Semiotic in *Middlemarch,"* in *The Worlds of Victorian Fiction,* ed. Jerome H. Buckley (Cambridge, Massachusetts: Harvard University Press, 1975), 128.
40. Gillian Beer, *Darwin's Plots: Evolutionary Narrative in Darwin, George Eliot and Nineteenth-Century Fiction* (1983; Cambridge: Cambridge University Press, 2000), 156–168.
41. Miller, "Optic and Semiotic," 126; 129.
42. William Deresiewicz, "Heroism and Organicism in the Case of Lydgate," *SEL: Studies in Literature* 38.4 (Autumn 1998): 737.
43. Stanley Joel Reiser, *Medicine and the Reign of Technology* (Cambridge: Cambridge University Press, 1978), 38.
44. Carroll, *George Eliot and the Conflict of Interpretations,* 271.

Bibliography

Abernethy, John. *An Enquiry into the Probability and Rationality of Mr. Hunter's "Theory of Life."* London: Longman, 1814.

Abrams, M. H. *Natural Supernaturalism: Tradition and Revolution in Romantic Literature.* New York: Norton, 1971.

Allott, Miriam Francis. *The Brontës: The Critical Heritage.* London: Routledge and Kegan Paul, 1974.

Anger, Suzy. "Carlyle: Between Biblical Exegesis and Romantic Hermeneutics." *Texas Studies in Literature and Language* 40.1 (1998): 78–96.

"George Eliot and Philosophy." In *Cambridge Companion to George Eliot.* Edited by George Levine. Cambridge: Cambridge University Press, 2001. 76–97.

Armstrong, Nancy. "Emily Brontë in and out of Her Time." *Genre: Forms of Discourse and Culture* 15.3 (Fall 1982): 243–264.

Arnold, Matthew. *The Letters of Matthew Arnold to Arthur Hugh Clough.* Edited with an introductory study by Howard Foster Lowry. London: Oxford University Press, 1932.

Culture and Anarchy: An Essay in Political and Social Criticism. Edited and with an introduction and notes by Ian Gregor. New York: Bobbs-Merrill, 1971.

Bacon, Francis. *Essays, Advancement of Learning, New Atlantis, and Other Pieces.* Selected and edited by Richard Foster Jones. New York: Odyssey Press, 1937.

Bailin, Miriam. *The Sickroom in Victorian Fiction: The Art of Being Ill.* Cambridge: Cambridge University Press, 1994.

Baker, Robert. "The History of Medical Ethics." In *Companion Encyclopedia of the History of Medicine.* Edited by W. F. Bynum and Roy Porter. 2 vols. London: Routledge, 1993. Vol. II, 852–887.

Baker, Robert, Dorothy Porter, and Roy Porter, eds. *The Codification of Medical Morality: Historical and Philosophical Studies of the Formalization of Western Medical Morality in the Eighteenth and Nineteenth Centuries.* 2 vols. Dordrecht: Kluwer, 1993–1995.

Barker, Juliet. *The Brontës.* New York: St. Martin's Press, 1994.

Barker-Benfield, G. J. *The Culture of Sensibility: Sex and Society in Eighteenth-Century Britain.* Chicago: University of Chicago Press, 1992.

Beer, Gillian. *Darwin's Plots: Evolutionary Narrative in Darwin, George Eliot and Nineteenth-Century Fiction.* 1983. Cambridge: Cambridge University Press, 2000.

Bergson, Henri. *Laughter: An Essay on the Meaning of the Comic.* Translated by Cloudesley Brereton and Fred Rothwell. New York: Macmillan, 1912.

Bernstein, Richard J. *Beyond Objectivism and Relativism: Science, Hermeneutics and Praxis.* Philadelphia: University of Pennsylvania Press, 1983.

Bewell, Alan. *Romanticism and Colonial Disease.* Baltimore: Johns Hopkins University Press, 1999.

Bontekoe, Ronald. *Dimensions of the Hermeneutic Circle.* Atlantic Highlands, New Jersey: Humanities Press, 1996.

Bright, Richard. *Reports of Medical Cases, Selected with a View to Illustrating the Symptoms and Cure of Diseases by a Reference to Morbid Anatomy.* London: Longman, Rees, Orme, Brown and Green, 1827.

Brontë, Charlotte. *Jane Eyre.* Edited by Jane Jack and Margaret Smith. Oxford: Clarendon Press, 1969.

Shirley. Edited by Herbert Rosengarten and Margaret Smith. Oxford: Clarendon Press, 1979.

Villette. Edited by Herbert Rosengarten and Margaret Smith. Oxford: Clarendon Press, 1984.

The Professor. Edited by Margaret Smith and Herbert Rosengarten. Oxford: Clarendon Press, 1987.

Brontë, Emily. *"Wuthering Heights": Authoritative Text, Backgrounds, Criticism.* 3rd Edition. Edited by William M. Sale, Jr. and Richard J. Dunn. New York: Norton, 1990.

Brooke, John Hedley. *Science and Religion: Some Historical Perspectives.* Cambridge: Cambridge University Press, 1991.

Brooks, Peter. *Body Work: Objects of Desire in Modern Narrative.* Cambridge, Massachusetts: Harvard University Press, 1993.

Browne, Janet. *Charles Darwin: The Power of Place.* Princeton: Princeton University Press, 2003.

Buchan, William. *Domestic Medicine: A Treatise on the Prevention and Cure of Diseases, by Regimen and Simple Medicines; With an Appendix Containing a Dispensatory for the Use of Private Practitioners.* London: T. Kinnersley, 1821. [Many editions of this text exist.]

Butler, Marilyn. Introduction to *Frankenstein, or The Modern Prometheus: The 1818 Text,* by Mary Shelley. Edited by Butler. Oxford: Oxford University Press, 1993. ix–li.

Campbell, John Angus. "Nature, Religion and Emotional Response: A Reconsideration of Darwin's Affective Decline." *Victorian Studies* 18 (1974): 159–174.

Cannon, Susan Faye. *Science in Culture: The Early Victorian Period.* Folkestone: Dawson, and New York: Science History Publications, 1978.

Carlyle, Thomas. *Sartor Resartus.* Edited with an introduction and notes by Kerry McSweeney and Peter Sabor. Oxford: Oxford University Press, 1987.

Carroll, David. *George Eliot and the Conflict of Interpretations: A Reading of the Novels.* Cambridge: Cambridge University Press, 1992.

Cheyne, George. *The Natural Method of Cureing the Diseases of the Body, and the Disorders of the Mind Depending on the Body.* London, 1742.

Crismore, Avon and Rodney Farnsworth. "Mr. Darwin and His Readers: Exploring Interpersonal Metadiscourse as a Dimension of *Ethos*." *Rhetoric Review* 8.1 (1989): 91–112.

Crosby, Christina. *The Ends of History: Victorians and the "Woman Question".* New York: Routledge, 1991.

Cunningham, Andrew and Nicholas Jardine, eds. *Romanticism and the Sciences.* Cambridge: Cambridge University Press, 1990.

Cunningham, Hugh. *Children and Childhood in Western Society since 1500.* London: Longman, 1995.

Dale, Peter Allan. "Varieties of Blasphemy: Feminism and the Brontës." *Review* (Charlottesville, Virginia) 14 (1992): 281–304.

Damasio, Antonio R. *Descartes' Error: Emotion, Reason, and the Human Brain.* New York: Avon Books, 1994.

Dames, Nicholas. "The Clinical Novel: Phrenology and *Villette*." *Novel* 29.3 (1996): 367–390.

Darwin, Charles. *The Life and Letters of Charles Darwin.* Edited by Francis Darwin. 3 vols. London: John Murray, 1887.

More Letters of Charles Darwin: A Record of His Work in a Series of Hitherto Unpublished Letters. Edited by Francis Darwin. 2 vols. New York: Appleton, 1903.

The Autobiography of Charles Darwin, 1809–1882: With Original Omissions Restored. Edited by Nora Barlow. New York: Norton, 1993.

Davies, Stevie. *Emily Brontë: Heretic.* London: Women's Press, 1994.

De Almeida, Hermione. *Romantic Medicine and John Keats.* New York: Oxford University Press, 1991.

Deresiewicz, William. "Heroism and Organicism in the Case of Lydgate." *SEL: Studies in English Literature* 38.4 (Autumn 1998): 723–740.

Desmond, Adrian. *Archetypes and Ancestors: Palaeontology in Victorian London 1850–1875.* London: Blond and Briggs, 1982.

The Politics of Evolution: Morphology, Medicine and Reform in Radical London. Chicago: University of Chicago Press, 1989.

Durant, John. "Darwinism and Divinity: A Century of Debate." In *Darwinism and Divinity: Essays on Evolution and Religious Belief.* Edited by John Durant. Oxford: Basil Blackwell, 1985. 9–39.

Eagleton, Terry. *Myths of Power: A Marxist Study of the Brontës.* New York: Barnes and Noble, 1975. 2nd edn., London and New York: Macmillan, 1988.

Eliot, George. *Middlemarch: Authoritative Text, Backgrounds, Criticism.* 2nd Edition. Edited by Bert Hornback. New York: Norton, 2000.

Epstein, Julia. "History, Diagnosis, and Poetics." *Literature and Medicine* 2.1 (1992): 23–44.

Fish, Stanley. *Self-Consuming Artifacts: The Experience of Seventeenth-Century Literature.* Berkeley: University of California Press, 1972.

Fissell, Mary E. "The Disappearance of the Patient's Narrative and the Invention of Hospital Medicine." In *British Medicine in an Age of Reform.* Edited by Roger French and Andrew Wear. London: Routledge, 1991. 42–109.

Fleming, Donald. "Charles Darwin: The Anaesthetic Man." *Victorian Studies* 4 (1961): 119–236.

Foucault, Michel. *Madness and Civilization: A History of Insanity in the Age of Reason.* Translated from the French by Richard Howard. New York: Pantheon, 1965.

The *Birth of the Clinic: An Archaeology of Medical Perception.* Translated from the French by A. M. Sheridan Smith. New York: Vintage, 1975.

Francis, Mark. "Naturalism and William Paley." *History of European Ideas* 10.2 (1989): 203–220.

French, Roger and Andrew Wear, eds. *British Medicine in an Age of Reform.* London: Routledge, 1991.

Frosch, Thomas. "The New Body of English Romanticism." *Soundings* 54.4 (1971): 372–387.

Frye, Roland Mushat. "The Two Books of God." *Theology Today* 39 (Oct. 1982): 260–266.

Furst, Lilian. *Between Doctors and Patients: The Changing Balance of Power.* Charlottesville: University Press of Virginia, 1998.

Gagnier, Regenia. *Subjectivities: A History of Self-Representation in Britain, 1832–1920.* New York: Oxford University Press, 1991.

Galison, Peter and Lorraine Daston. "The Image of Objectivity." *Representations* 40 (1992): 81–128.

Gallagher, Catherine. "George Eliot: Immanent Victorian." In *Proceedings of the British Academy: 1996 Lectures and Memoirs.* Edited by Marjorie Chibnall. Oxford: Oxford University Press, 1997. 157–172.

Gaskell, Elizabeth. *The Life of Charlotte Brontë.* 1857. Edited by Alan Shelston. London: Penguin Books, 1975. Reprinted in Penguin Classics, 1985.

Geertz, Clifford. "From the Native's Point of View: On the Nature of Anthropological Understanding." In *Interpretive Social Science: A Reader.* Edited by Paul Rabinow and William M. Sullivan. Berkeley: University of California Press, 1979. 225–241.

Gérin, Winifred. *Charlotte Brontë: The Evolution of Genius.* Oxford: Oxford University Press, 1969.

Emily *Brontë: A Biography.* Oxford: Oxford University Press, 1971. Paperback 1978.

Gezari, Janet. *Charlotte Brontë and Defensive Conduct: The Author and the Body at Risk.* Philadelphia: University of Pennsylvania Press, 1992.

Gilbert, Sandra M. and Susan Gubar. *The Madwoman in the Attic: The Woman Writer and the Nineteenth-Century Literary Imagination.* 1979. New Haven: Yale University Press, 1984.

Glen, Heather. Introduction to *The Professor,* by Charlotte Brontë. London: Penguin Books, 1989. 7–31.

Goff, Barbara Munson. "Between Natural Theology and Natural Selection: Breeding the Human Animal in *Wuthering Heights.*" *Victorian Studies* 27.4 (Summer 1984): 477–508.

Gordon, Lyndall. *Charlotte Brontë: A Passionate Life.* New York and London: Norton, 1996.

Gosse, Edmund. *Father and Son: A Study of Two Temperaments.* Edited by James Hepburn. London: Oxford University Press, 1974.

Graham, Thomas John. *Modern Domestic Medicine; or, a Popular Treatise, Illustrating the Character, Symptoms, Causes, Distinction, and Correct Treatment, of All Diseases Incident to the Human Frame; . . . the Whole Intended as a Medical Guide for the Use of Clergymen, Families, and Students in Medicine.* London: Simpkin and Marshall, 1826.

Gregory, John. "Lectures on the Duties and Qualifications of a Physician." In *John Gregory's Writings on Medical Ethics and Philosophy of Medicine.* Edited by Laurence B. McCullough. Dordrecht: Kluwer, 1998. 161–245.

Gruber, Jacob W. and John C. Thackray. *Richard Owen Commemoration: Three Studies.* London: Natural History Museum Publications, 1992.

Handwerk, Gary J. *Irony and Ethics in Narrative: From Schlegel to Lacan.* New Haven: Yale University Press, 1985.

Haney, Janice L. "'Shadow Hunting': Romantic Irony, *Sartor Resartus,* and Victorian Romanticism." *Studies in Romanticism* 17 (Summer 1978): 307–333.

Hare, Charles John. "Fellowe's Clinical Prize Reports." Awarded Gold Medal at University College, London, 1842. MS 2778, Western Manuscripts Collection, Wellcome Institute Library.

Harter, Deborah. *Bodies in Pieces: Fantastic Narrative and the Poetics of the Fragment.* Stanford: Stanford University Press, 1996.

Hartley, David. *Observations on Man, His Frame, His Duty, and His Expectations.* 1749. Facsimile reproduction with an introduction by Theodore L. Huguelet. Gainesville, Florida: Scholars' Facsimiles and Reprints, 1966.

Hindle, Maurice. "Vital Matters: Mary Shelley's *Frankenstein* and Romantic Science." *Critical Survey* 2.1 (1990): 29–35.

Homans, Margaret. *Bearing the Word: Language and Female Experience in Nineteenth-Century Women's Writing.* Chicago: University of Chicago Press, 1986.

Hume, David. *A Treatise of Human Nature.* 1739. Edited by L. A. Selby-Bigge. Oxford: Clarendon Press, 1951.

Hunter, Kathryn Montgomery. *Doctors' Stories: The Narrative Structure of Medical Knowledge.* Princeton: Princeton University Press, 1991.

Huxley, T[homas] H[enry]. *Evolution & Ethics: T. H. Huxley's Evolution and Ethics with New Essays on Its Victorian and Sociobiological Context,* by James Paradis and George C. Williams. Princeton: Princeton University Press, 1989.

Iser, Wolfgang. "The Emergence of a Cross-Cultural Discourse: Thomas Carlyle's *Sartor Resartus.*" In *The Translatability of Cultures: Figurations of the Space Between.* Edited by Sanford Budick and Wolfgang Iser. Stanford: Stanford University Press, 1996. 245–264.

Jacobs, Carol. "*Wuthering Heights*: At the Threshold of Interpretation." In *Gendered Agents: Women and Institutional Knowledge.* Edited by Silvestra Mariniello and Paul A. Bove. Durham: Duke University Press, 1998. 371–395.

Jalland, Pat and John Hooper, eds. *Women from Birth to Death: The Female Life Cycle in Britain, 1830–1914*. Atlantic Highlands, New Jersey: Humanities Press International, 1986.

Jenner, Edward. *An Inquiry into the Causes and Effects of the Variolae Vaccinae, a Disease Discovered in Some of the Western Counties of England, Particularly Gloucestershire, and Known by the Name of "The Cow Pox."* 2nd Edition. London: Sampson Low, 1800.

Jewson, Nicholas. "Medical Knowledge and the Patronage System in Eighteenth-Century England." *Sociology* 8 (1974): 369–385.

Jordanova, Ludmilla. *Nature Displayed: Gender, Science and Medicine, 1760–1820*. London: Longman, 1999.

Kazan, Francesca. "Heresy, the Image and Description, or, Picturing the Invisible: Charlotte Brontë's *Villette*." *Texas Studies in Literature and Language* 32.4 (1990): 543–566.

Keats, John. *Letters of John Keats*. Edited by Robert Gittings. Oxford: Oxford University Press, 1970.

Kettle, Arnold. *An Introduction to the English Novel*. 2 vols. London and New York: Hutchinson's University Library, 1951–1953.

King-Hele, Desmond. *Erasmus Darwin and the Romantic Poets*. New York: St. Martin's Press, 1986.

Knight, David M. "The Physical Sciences and the Romantic Movement." *History of Science* 9 (1970): 54–75.

Knoepflmacher, U. C. *Wuthering Heights: A Study*. Athens: Ohio University Press, 1994.

Landow, George P. *Victorian Types, Victorian Shadows: Biblical Typology in Victorian Literature, Art, and Thought*. London and Boston: Routledge and Kegan Paul, 1980.

Larson, Janet. "Lady-Wrestling for Victorian Soul: Discourse, Gender, and Spirituality in Women's Texts." *Religion and Literature* 23.3 (1991): 43–64.

Lawrence, Susan C. *Charitable Knowledge: Hospital Pupils and Practitioners in Eighteenth-Century London*. Cambridge: Cambridge University Press, 1996.

Lawrence, William. *Two Introductory Lectures . . . at the Royal College of Surgeons*. London, 1816.

Lectures on Physiology, Zoology and the Natural History of Man. London: Callow, 1819.

Levere, Trevor. *Poetry Realized in Nature: Samuel Taylor Coleridge and Early Nineteenth-Century Science*. Cambridge: Cambridge University Press, 1981.

Levine, Caroline. *The Serious Pleasures of Suspense: Victorian Realism and Narrative Doubt*. Charlottesville: University of Virginia Press, 2003.

Levine, George. *The Realistic Imagination: English Fiction from Frankenstein to Lady Chatterley*. Chicago: University of Chicago Press, 1981.

Darwin and the Novelists: Patterns of Science in Victorian Fiction. Chicago: University of Chicago Press, 1988.

"Objectivity and Death in Victorian Autobiography." *Victorian Literature and Culture* 20 (1992): 273–291.

"Darwin and Pain: Why Science Made Shakespeare Nauseating." *Raritan* 15.2 (Fall 1995): 97–114.

"Carlyle, Descartes, and Objectivity." *Raritan* 17.1 (1997): 45–58.

Dying to Know: Scientific Epistemology and Narrative in Victorian England. Chicago: University of Chicago Press, 2002.

Lief, Harold I. and Renée C. Fox. "Training for 'Detached Concern' in Medical Students." In *The Psychological Basis of Medical Practice.* Edited by Harold I. Lief, Victor F. Lief, and Nina R. Lief. New York: Harper and Row, 1963. 12–35.

Lightman, Bernard, ed. *Victorian Science in Context.* Chicago: University of Chicago Press, 1997.

Lock, John and W. T. Dixon. *A Man of Sorrows: The Life, Letters and Times of the Rev. Patrick Brontë 1777–1861.* 2nd Edition. Westport, Connecticut: Meckler Books, 1979.

Logan, Peter Melville. "Conceiving the Body: Realism and Medicine in *Middlemarch.*" *History of the Human Sciences* 4.2 (1991): 197–222.

Nerves and Narratives: A Cultural History of Hysteria in Nineteenth-Century British Prose. Berkeley: University of California Press, 1997.

Malthus, Thomas Robert. *An Essay on the Principle of Population.* Edited by Antony Flew. London: Penguin, 1985.

Marshall, David. *The Surprising Effects of Sympathy: Marivaux, Diderot, Rousseau, and Mary Shelley.* Chicago: University of Chicago Press, 1988.

McCullough, Laurence B. Introduction to *John Gregory's Writings on Medical Ethics and Philosophy of Medicine*, by John Gregory. Edited by Laurence B. McCullough. Dordrecht: Kluwer, 1998. 1–51.

Mellor, Anne K. *English Romantic Irony.* Cambridge, Massachusetts: Harvard University Press, 1980.

"*Frankenstein*: A Feminist Critique of Science." In *One Culture: Essays in Science and Literature.* Edited by George Levine. Madison: University of Wisconsin Press, 1987. 287–312.

Review of *A World of Possibilities: Romantic Irony in Victorian Literature*, by Clyde de L. Ryals. *Victorian Studies* 35.4 (Summer 1992): 434–435.

Miller, J. Hillis. "Narrative and History." *ELH* 41.3 (Autumn 1974): 455–473.

"Optic and Semiotic in *Middlemarch.*" In *The Worlds of Victorian Fiction.* Edited by Jerome H. Buckley. Cambridge, Massachusetts: Harvard University Press, 1975. 125–145.

Fiction and Repetition: Seven English Novels. Cambridge, Massachusetts: Harvard University Press, 1982.

Mitchell, Juliet. *Women, the Longest Revolution: Essays on Feminism, Literature and Psychoanalysis.* London: Virago, 1984.

Moore, James R. "Geologists and Interpreters of Genesis in the Nineteenth Century." In *God and Nature: Historical Essays on the Encounter between Christianity and Science.* Edited by David C. Lindberg and Ronald L. Numbers. Berkeley: University of California Press, 1986. 322–350.

Mullan, John. *Sentiment and Sociability: The Language of Feeling in the Eighteenth Century.* Oxford: Clarendon Press, 1988.

Newman, Beth. "Narratives of Seduction and the Seductions of Narrative: The Frame Structure of *Frankenstein*." *ELH* 53. (1986): 141–163.

Olney, James. *Metaphors of Self: The Meaning of Autobiography.* Princeton: Princeton University Press, 1972.

Osler, William. *Aequanimitas: With Other Addresses to Medical Students, Nurses and Practitioners of Medicine.* Philadelphia: P. Blakiston's Son & Co., 1904.

Ospovat, Dov. *The Development of Darwin's Theory: Natural History, Natural Theology, and Natural Selection, 1838–1859.* Cambridge: Cambridge University Press, 1981.

Owen, Richard. *On the Nature of Limbs: A Discourse Delivered on Friday, February 9, at an Evening Meeting of the Royal Institution of Great Britain.* London: J. Van Voorst, 1849.

Oxford English Dictionary. 2nd Edition. Oxford: Clarendon Press, 1989.

Paley, William. *Natural Theology, or Evidences of the Existence and Attributes of the Deity.* London, 1830.

Paradis, James. "*Evolution and Ethics* in Its Victorian Context." In T. H. Huxley, *Evolution & Ethics: T. H. Huxley's* Evolution and Ethics *with New Essays on Its Victorian and Sociobiological Context.* By James Paradis and George C. Williams. Princeton: Princeton University Press, 1989. 3–55.

"Satire and Science in Victorian Culture." In *Victorian Science in Context.* Edited by Bernard Lightman. Chicago: University of Chicago Press, 1997. 143–175.

Peterson, Linda. *Victorian Autobiography: The Tradition of Self-Interpretation.* New Haven: Yale University Press, 1986.

Porter, Roy. "Lay Medical Knowledge in the Eighteenth Century: The Evidence of the *Gentleman's Magazine*." *Medical History* 29 (April 1985): 138–168.

Qualls, Barry. *The Secular Pilgrims of Victorian Fiction: The Novel as Book of Life.* Cambridge: Cambridge University Press, 1982.

Rehbock, Philip F. "Transcendental Anatomy." In *Romanticism and the Sciences.* Edited by Andrew Cunningham and Nicholas Jardine. Cambridge: Cambridge University Press, 1990. 144–160.

Reiser, Stanley Joel. *Medicine and the Reign of Technology.* Cambridge: Cambridge University Press, 1985.

Richardson, Alan. *British Romanticism and the Science of the Mind.* Cambridge: Cambridge University Press, 2001.

Ricoeur, Paul. *Interpretation Theory: Discourse and the Surplus of Meaning.* Fort Worth: Texas Christian University, 1976.

Rothfield, Lawrence. *Vital Signs: Medical Realism in Nineteenth-Century Fiction.* Princeton: Princeton University Press, 1992.

Rousseau, G. S. "On Romanticism, Science and Medicine." *History of European Ideas* 17.5 (1993): 659–663.

Rudwick, Martin J. S. *The Great Devonian Controversy: The Shaping of Scientific Knowledge among Gentlemanly Specialists.* Chicago: University of Chicago Press, 1985.

Rupke, Nicolaas A. *Richard Owen: Victorian Naturalist.* New Haven: Yale University Press, 1994.

Ruse, Michael. "The Darwin Industry: A Guide." *Victorian Studies* 39.2 (1996): 217–235.

Ryals, Clyde de L. *A World of Possibilities: Romantic Irony in Victorian Literature.* Columbus: Ohio State University Press, 1990.

Ryals, Clyde de L. and Kenneth J. Fielding, eds. *Collected Letters of Thomas and Jane Welsh Carlyle.* Vol. xv. Durham, North Carolina: Duke University Press, 1987.

Scarry, Elaine, ed. *Literature and the Body: Essays on Populations and Persons.* Baltimore: Johns Hopkins University Press, 1988.

Schleiermacher, Friedrich D. E. *Hermeneutics: The Handwritten Manuscripts.* Edited by Heinz Kimmerle and translated from the German by James Duke and Jack Forstman. Missoula: Scholars' Press, 1977.

Schweber, Silvan. "Darwin and the Political Economists: Divergence of Character." *Journal of the History of Biology* 13.2 (1980): 195–289.

Shaffer, Elinor S., ed. *The Third Culture: Literature and Science.* Berlin and New York: Walter de Gruyter, 1998.

Shapin, Steven. *The Scientific Revolution.* Chicago: University of Chicago Press, 1996.

Shelley, Mary Wollstonecraft. *Frankenstein, or the Modern Prometheus: The 1818 Text.* Edited by James Rieger. Chicago: University of Chicago Press, 1982.

Shorter, Edward. "The Doctor-Patient Relationship." In *Companion Encyclopedia of the History of Medicine.* Edited by W. F. Bynum and Roy Porter. 2 vols. London: Routledge, 1993. Vol. ii, 783–800.

Shuttleworth, Sally. "'The Surveillance of a Sleepless Eye': The Constitution of Neurosis in *Villette*." In *One Culture: Essays in Science and Literature.* Edited by George Levine. Madison: University of Wisconsin Press, 1987. 313–335.

"Psychological Definition and Social Power: Phrenology in the Novels of Charlotte Brontë." In *Nature Transfigured.* Edited by John Christie and Sally Shuttleworth. Manchester: Manchester University Press, 1989. 121–151.

Smith, Adam. *The Theory of Moral Sentiments.* Oxford: Clarendon Press, 1976.

Starr, Paul. *The Social Transformation of American Medicine.* New York: Basic Books, 1982.

Stockton, Kathryn Bond. *God between Their Lips: Desire between Women in Irigaray, Brontë, and Eliot.* Stanford: Stanford University Press, 1994.

Stoneman, Patsy, ed. *Emily Brontë: Wuthering Heights.* New York: Columbia University Press, 1998.

Sussman, Herbert L. *Fact in Figure: Typology in Carlyle, Ruskin, and the Pre-Raphaelite Brotherhood.* Columbus: Ohio State University Press, 1979.

Tambling, Jeremy. "*Middlemarch*, Realism and the Birth of the Clinic." *ELH* 57 (1990): 939–960.

Temkin, O. "Basic Science, Medicine and the Romantic Era." In his *The Double Face of Janus.* Baltimore: Johns Hopkins University Press, 1977. 345–372.

Tilt, Edward John. *On the Preservation of the Health of Women at the Critical Periods of Life.* London: Churchill, 1851.

Turner, Frank. "Victorian Scientific Naturalism and Thomas Carlyle." *Victorian Studies* 18 (1975): 325–343.

Valdés, Mario J. Introduction to *A Ricoeur Reader: Reflection and Imagination*. New York: Harvester, 1991. 3–40.

Vargish, Thomas. *The Providential Aesthetic in Victorian Fiction*. Charlottesville: University Press of Virginia, 1985.

Vrettos, Athena. *Somatic Fictions: Imagining Illness in Victorian Culture*. Stanford: Stanford University Press, 1995.

Whewell, William. Review of *On the Connexion of the Physical Sciences*, by Mary Sommerville. *Quarterly Review* 51 (1834): 54–67.

Astronomy and General Physics Considered with Reference to Natural Theology. London: H. G. Bohn, 1852.

Whytt, Robert. *Observations on the Nature, Causes, and Cure of those Disorders Which Have Been Called Nervous, Hypochondriac, or Hysteric*. Edinburgh, 1765.

Willey, Basil. *Nineteenth-Century Studies: Coleridge to Matthew Arnold*. New York: Columbia University Press, 1949.

Williams, Carolyn. "Closing the Book: The Intertextual End of *Jane Eyre*." In *Victorian Connections*. Edited by Jerome McGann. Charlottesville: University Press of Virginia, 1989. 60–87.

Wilson, David. "Emily Brontë: First of the Moderns." *Modern Quarterly Miscellany* 1 (1947): 94–115.

Woolf, Virginia. "*Jane Eyre* and *Wuthering Heights*." In her *The Common Reader*. New York: Harcourt, Brace and Co., 1925. 219–227.

Index

CAMBRIDGE STUDIES IN NINETEENTH-CENTURY
LITERATURE AND CULTURE

General editor
Gillian Beer, *University of Cambridge*

Titles published

1. The Sickroom in Victorian Fiction: The Art of Being Ill
by Miriam Bailin, *Washington University*

2. Muscular Christianity: Embodying the Victorian Age
edited by Donald E. Hall, *California State University, Northridge*

3. Victorian Masculinities: Manhood and Masculine Poetics in Early Victorian
Literature and Art
by Herbert Sussman, *Northeastern University, Boston*

4. Byron and the Victorians
by Andrew Elfenbein, *University of Minnesota*

5. Literature in the Marketplace: Nineteenth-Century British Publishing
and the Circulation of Books
edited by John O. Jordan, *University of California, Santa Cruz*
and Robert L. Patten, *Rice University, Houston*

6. Victorian Photography, Painting and Poetry
by Lindsay Smith, *University of Sussex*

7. Charlotte Brontë and Victorian Psychology
by Sally Shuttleworth, *University of Sheffield*

8. The Gothic Body:
Sexuality, Materialism, and Degeneration at the *Fin de Siècle*
by Kelly Hurley, *University of Colorado at Boulder*

9. Rereading Walter Pater
by William F. Shuter, *Eastern Michigan University*

10. Remaking Queen Victoria
edited by Margaret Homans, *Yale University*
and Adrienne Munich, *State University of New York, Stony Brook*

11. Disease, Desire, and the Body in Victorian Women's Popular Novels
by Pamela K. Gilbert, *University of Florida*

12. Realism, Representation, and the Arts in Nineteenth-Century Literature
by Alison Byerly, *Middlebury College, Vermont*

13. Literary Culture and the Pacific
by Vanessa Smith, *University of Sydney*

Graeme Gooday, *University of Leeds*
Richard Noakes, *Cambridge University*
Sally Shuttleworth, *University of Sheffield*
and Jonathan R. Topham, *University of Leeds*

46. Literature and Medicine in Nineteenth-Century Britain:
From Mary Shelley to George Eliot
Janis McLarren Caldwell, *Wake Forest University*